THE ROLE OF THE ARAB DEVELOPMENT FUNDS IN THE WORLD ECONOMY

The Role of the Arab Development Funds in the World Economy

Edited by
MICHELE ACHILLI and MOHAMED KHALDI

CROOM HELM
London & Sydney
in association with
ICEI

Croom Helm Ltd, Provident House, Burrell Row,
Beckenham, Kent BR3 1AT
Croom Helm Australia Pty Ltd, First Floor, 139 King Street,
Sydney, NSW 2001, Australia

British Library Cataloguing in Publication Data

Achilli, Michele

The role of the Arab development funds in the world economy.

1. Europe——Foreign economic relations——Arab countries 2. Arab countries——Foreign economic relations——Europe

I. Title

337.1'174927 HF1532.5.A7

ISBN 0-7099-0535-1

Printed and bound in Great Britain
by Billing & Sons Limited, Worcester.

CONTENTS

ACKNOWLEDGEMENTS

This volume groups together the proceedings of a conference organised in Milan from 11–13 February 1983, on 'The Role of the Arab Development Funds in the World Economy'. ICEI (the (Italian) Institute for International Economic Co-operation, together with the Milan Chamber of Commerce, Industry and Agriculture, and in collaboration with the League of Arab States, the Foreign Department of the Lombardy Chamber of Commerce, the EEC, the Department for Development of the Italian Ministry for Foreign Affairs, and the Regional Administration of Lombardy, organised it.

There were other important speeches given at the conference in addition to those reproduced as chapters here. Unfortunately, for reasons of space, the following could not be included: that of Camillo Ferrari, President of FINAFRICA, Milan; Luigi Tranfo, Deputy General Director of the ICE (Institute for Foreign Commerce), Rome; and Luciano de Pascalis, Deputy President of IPALMO, Rome.

Michele Achilli

INTRODUCTION
Michele Achilli

The necessity to work constructively towards a closer integration of European political and financial institutions and those of the Arab world has long been felt in those economic fields most sensitive and open to the problems of developmental aid.

For a number of years, in fact, many European countries have been applying a policy of active co-operation with the newly independent countries of the Third and Fourth Worlds, both availing themselves of their own funds and turning to such super-national financial and political institutions as the World Bank, the European Bank for Investment and the European Community.

Some of those who have a greater knowledge of the economic and political workings of the Middle East and Africa have initiated a relationship of fertile collaboration with the Arab Development Funds and the Arab Development Banks. In fact, the Common Market has itself established extremely good relationships with them, as is documented in, and testified by, the reports presented at the conference that is the basis of this book. Italy has been late in confronting this matter and, like many other countries, was for a long time unaware of the tasks which it had undertaken at the United Nations. Aid to developing countries was for years limited to a few programmes aimed primarily at African countries which had gained independence after the Second World War. Both a global strategy and adequate funds were lacking: however, thanks to parliamentary pressure put on the government, the tendency has been reversed and we are slowly making up for lost time.

During the course of the discussion on the Balance of the State in 1982, the Italian Parliament attended to the problems connected with co-operation with the developing countries and approved an order of the day which states, among other things:

> At the beginning of the third decade for development of the United Nations, no appreciable progress has been made, either on the structural level or in the struggle against hunger and poverty. The principle blame for this must be placed on the development policy pursued for the past twenty years, based on the

naive export of the development models of the rich countries, and on the growth of the GNP through a process which has concentrated too much on forced industrialisation. The result of this process has been the isolating of the ruling class from its own social context and the excluding of the poorest strata of the population.

The Chamber commits the government:

. . . to modify its policy of co-operation with the countries of the Third World, abandoning the old model and acquiring a new and more complex comprehension of development, understood as the total realisation of the life expectations of all men, and of the complete individual; to gradually earmark all the financial means available for co-operation with Third World countries in the form of public developmental aid, for the realisation of projects aimed at satisfying the fundamental needs of the poorest strata of the population and creating, in the shortest time possible, mechanisms of endogenous development. Such mechanisms should deal primarily with food production, limiting food aid to foreseeable and unforeseeable emergencies of human or natural origin, and stipulating amount and conditions which would not hinder the full and more rapid development of local food production; to develop, for this purpose, integrated plans for intervention, both occasional and structural, directed at safeguarding human life and promoting self-reliant economic development. Such plans are in keeping with the spirit of the resolution adopted by the European Parliament and by the Manifesto issued by 53 Nobel Prize winners who inspired it, which has been supported by chiefs of state and heads of governments, ministers, members of parliament, directors of international organisations, local administrators, intellectuals, churchmen, men and women in the fields of science and culture, and ordinary citizens of every country; to promote permanent relationships of co-operation for the exploitation of natural resources, with particular regard to forms of energy which are renewable or ecologically adaptable to the infrastructures of service and to information; to take advantage, for the rapid realisation of these plans, of the structures and experience of the international, governmental, and non-governmental organisations, in collaboration with the governments of the interested countries.

This new attitude has already earned considerable praise, both from the countries concerned and from the multi-lateral organisations which closely follow the administrative and financial aspects connected with development: apart from the quantitative aspects, already very significant in themselves, a positive evaluation has been made of the fact that such a task has been assumed and expanded at a time of serious international economic recession, with a concomitant tendency on the part of those states and governments, which up to now have been in the lead, to reduce their contributions to co-operation.

In order to appreciate fully and to render more substantial this choice, Italy has an interest in establishing increasingly closer ties with the Arab financial organisations, whose goal is a policy of active co-operation.

The co-financing of large and medium-sized programmes has now become a necessity for the concurrent initiation of more projects in other countries. This would be both right and opportune in the attempt to use all appropriate resources. Collaboration between governing bodies and financial institutions is the most effective way for the poorest countries to begin to develop.

We naturally do not want, at this point, simplistically to repropose the triangular plan (which has justly given rise to much perplexity) involving the matching of technology from industrialised countries, Arab sources of finance and the needs of the developing countries, but rather a more complex relationship capable of creating real economic integration among countries at different stages of development, in order that each country, on the basis of this collaboration, can maximise its potential and professional capacities.

The co-financing system between Arab and European institutions, in this case Arab and Italian, implies above all common strategic and political choices, keeping in view a reciprocal interest, and tending to make the most of the particular contributions of each country. The principle objective is to initiate a policy of economic development in the less favoured countries with the purpose of increasingly reducing the difference between the incomes of men and women in the North and the South. This difference has been widening over the course of the last decades especially since the recent crisis of the industrialised countries and the world-wide high rate of inflation.

Such development will also contribute to the reinforcement of efforts toward world peace, which remains the noblest aspiration of all mankind. This, however, demands a New International Economic Order. This phrase is repeated too often and, due to the way it has been abused, seems to have lost its true meaning, that of a correct relationship between expanding economies and currencies in a new political equilibrium.

But let us return for a moment to the main discussion from which we have briefly strayed — that of the collaboration of Italian and Arab financial institutions which presupposes a dialogue between the Italian and Arab governments. As a parliamentarian involved in promoting this dialogue, I would say above all that I cannot be satisfied with the point that has been reached. There should be many more connections between Italy and the Arab world, from cultural bonds based on the common traditions of a large part of our literature and science, to political bonds, rooted in our community of geographical interest, as, for example, the problems of the Mediterranean.

The large trade increase of the last few decades, which has made Italy one of the most active partners of the Arab world, does not suffice when speaking of true dialogue and true co-operation: something more is needed, with mutual understanding and efforts to resolve the problems which disturb the peace.

Our dissatisfaction, however, should not lead us to forget the road travelled in the last five years: we cannot talk of relationships between nations in absolute terms, but of positive or negative modifications. It is undeniable that there have been positive modifications and that they have been of great relevance: it is necessary to continue along this path.

I will give a brief example of this. Our country certainly does not have the capability or knowledge of others in organising its own operative presence in the Third World, with all the difficulties which that entails. But Italy has gained experience which can be of great help and I think our Arab friends should bear that in mind. At the beginning of the 1950s Italy was faced with the problem of its own re-equilibrium: that of a country of the industrialised North, which was and is a full member of the developed regions of central Europe, and of the South, which was and is underdeveloped both socially and economically. Human and financial resources were used to overcome this difference and various theories and strategies were put into practice: some showed positive results, others decidedly negative ones. We have learnt from our mistakes and have perhaps reached a stage when we will not repeat them. So I maintain that this experience has been extremely useful and that we can profit from it in order to draw up development plans even in countries different from our own, where we find the same structural causes of imbalance which we recognised and fought in Italy.

Among the industrialised countries Italy is in the best position to explain the problems caused by attempting a guided development scheme and can utilise it in the general interest. This is also true because it has been made possible by an undertaking on the part of small and medium-sized industry: that is, by a pattern of production which is very elastic and adaptable to differing realities. The conference which led to this book is an example to us of a way in which we can bring to the floor questions of financial collaboration when considering a major political objective, such as that of development.

Integration of Europe and the Arab world must continue: this is an old theory, according to which lively synergy is the result of uniting the efforts and potentials of weaker political and economic realities. In this way, Europe and the Arab world could become, for the Third and Fourth Worlds, an economic and political pole of attraction as an alternative to the great powers which still divide the globe into two spheres of influence.

It is particularly important to sustain this at a time when the worsening of the crisis of the industrialised countries is causing a continued reduction in production levels and a consequent fall in demand and prices of raw materials and oil.

The consequence of this is a profound crisis in Third World countries which depend on the exporting of raw materials as their only sources of wealth, and on the OPEC countries which have so far been safe from the effects of the recession. The deciding factor is valid programming, which means economic planning in the Northern countries (here, of course, we mean Europe) in order to face up to the needs of the masses of the Southern countries.

Of course we do not mean, and it is best to repeat this, a mere research of new markets, but, on the contrary, the development of depressed areas so that tomorrow they can become areas of great commercial exchange, by means of a concentrated exploitation of their own resources. This would be impossible without help from the North on a human, technical and financial level. The North needs direct agreements with the South, so eliminating the parasitic mediation of multinational companies and of big financial holdings which either monopolise or control the most important raw materials, thus stabilising the market and the prices of the latter.

Without such direct agreements, which are, above all, political and economic, the South cannot develop, and Europe will continue to lack an essential partner for its development, accepting a subordinate position with respect to other integrated intercontinental economic realities. Even if the Brandt Report can only be accepted with some reservation, we must remember here the basic reasoning which pervades it, even if it does not seem to have been highly respected in Europe. Thus a programme for relaunching the European economy does not solely concern the individual countries of the old continent but also far larger economic and political areas. The Arab states look towards Europe with both anxiety and hope. With anxiety because, unless there is a steady recovery, the conditions for consolidating the phase of development of the Arab countries, at least those which balanced oil returns with investment programmes, will be reduced. But they also look with hope for an ever-greater integration between the two economies.

This is one of the reasons why we gave this book the title *The Role of the Arab Development Funds in the World Economy*. We are convinced that there is much room for co-operation between these two great economic realities and that the first big aid to developing countries can also come from a European recovery, integrated with the Arab world's. And in this case the Funds with which we deal will be able to play an important role.

1 ARAB AID IN THE WORLD ECONOMY

Mohamed Khaldi

The theme proposed in this book is of particular importance at a time when the global economy is going through a crisis which is leading in a direction that nobody can clearly foretell. The presence of contributions from various organisations and experts who are all involved to some degree in international economic co-operation will generate a useful exchange of viewpoints.

Particularly in its public form, development aid is unanimously acknowledged as being a necessity. This is especially true when one considers issues such as the evolution and worsening of the Third World debt, the emergence of reinforced protectionism, the slump in exports and reductions in financial assistance from official sources, in particular of that part known as 'development aid'.

Furthermore, when one looks at the pattern of co-operation and development aid over the past few years one cannot but question oneself as to its meaning and validity. Since a New International Economic Order was called for, the changes and transformations that have occurred in the global economy force one to look even more carefully and fundamentally at international economic relations of which development aid is an important constituent part. The meaning and strategic objectives of this aid must be defined in terms of the prospects for Third World nations which we all know to be very sombre. As a fully-fledged member of the Third World, the Arab world has, and continues to demand, a total reform of North-South economic relations. Despite its own increasing financial needs and the loans obtained from foreign financial institutions, the Arab world already accords, and will continue to accord, great importance to the aid that it grants to other developing countries through its own institutions. The Arab world has always considered that co-operation with the Third World is necessary, even more so now that a convergence of opinion must be reached in the pursuit of a common objective: the establishment of a New International Economic Order. In this context Arab aid appears fundamental, not to say determinant, in the sense that it mitigates the weakness of western aid. One must then ask the question: How far can this aid go? Also, what role should it play in North-South and in South-South relations?

To answer this we must try to situate the importance of Arab aid in the world economy. Having outlined its main features, its volume, distribution channels, etc., we will try to see, from a global point of view, exactly where it fits in.

Arab Aid: Characteristics and Distribution

Be it directly or through international organisations, Arab development aid is particularly important, though diversified owing to the numerous multi-lateral or bi-literal channels used. The very multiplicity of distribution channels used makes it very difficult to pinpoint or even quantify the aid.

Although playing a substantial and important role in the distribution of this aid to developing countries, the Arab Funds are only a part of the total Arab contribution. Other institutions together with non-institutionalised aid should also be taken into consideration when assessing the exact Arab input. Contrary to common belief, it does not date from the 1973–4 period; already in 1960–1 the Kuwait Economic Development Fund was engaged in an important co-operation programme with developing countries.

The 1973–4 oil price readjustments enabled other institutions to be created. Though not followed by the creation of further agencies, the second readjustment allowed for the reinforcement and consolidation of these institutions, and also for the extension of their activities.

These new distribution and allocation networks — mostly made up of regional and multi-lateral organisations — gave a new dimension to Arab Third World aid. The 1973 Funds were specifically designed to supply the organised framework which would enable Arab revenues to be channelled to other Third World countries. Initially designed to promote economic development in Arab countries through programme or development plan financing, the Funds had been created before the 1973 price readjustments. They were now opened up to non-Arab countries, and the new, post-1973 institutions have considerably increased their loan facilities.

Essentially motivated by considerations of solidarity, Arab countries do not consider their aid as a moral obligation. They insist on the particular character of this aid which they claim to be a new historical fact, and, through a number of specific characteristics, to be quite different from the aid dispensed by so-called industrialised countries.

Leaving aside the ideas of moral obligation and solidarity, it is true that Arab aid constitutes a new historical fact in the sense that we are witnessing a transfer of resources from one group of Third World countries to the rest. This is and will continue to be a dynamic element in international economic relations.

A number of characteristics distinguish Arab aid from that granted by industrialised countries. Firstly, it derives from oil receipts which are in part capital and in part revenue since they come from a non-renewable natural resource, i.e., oil. Furthermore the benefit to recipient countries is greater than ever, since, for obvious reasons, these Arab gifts and loans are hardly ever 'tied' to the purchase of goods or equipment.

Except those channelled through international organisations, OECD contributions among others are usually 'tied', just as in the private sector, where export credit is a highly 'tied' flow which constitutes the greatest element of potential surcharge as a result of the 'ties'. Increase of these other public contributions and export credits is more and more dependant on suspensive 'ties' for any support. Against this background, naturally enough Arab aid is not 'tied', unlike CAD country aid. The result for developing countries is a greater freedom of choice for the supplies which are financed by this capital, and this enables them to obtain a better price for services and equipment that are better adapted to their needs.

The Volume of Aid

Since 1973 the Arab contribution has been remarkable. Although the information gathered is still incomplete, progress has been made with regard to establishing statistics on Arab aid such that one can now make comparisons with other donors.

Concerning bi-lateral aid, which is considerable, the Arab contribution has been estimated as $12 billion between 1973 and 1980. But in order better to understand its importance and the extent of the effort involved, it is interesting to examine it in relation to GNP.

On this subject, not only have developed countries contributed a much smaller percentage than the objective they fixed themselves in the OECD, but they have reduced it significantly. Industrialised countries are a long way from the 0.7% of GNP fixed 13 years ago. On the other hand, Arab oil-producing countries have contributed to the tune of 4% of GNP at a time when industrialised countries have provided an aggregate 0.4% of theirs. Aid from certain Arab countries has even reached 10% of GNP. But these comparisons are deceptive as one should also take into account the fact that OPEC countries' aggregate GDP represents only one-fifth of the USA's, and the USA contributes only 0.6% of its GNP. In 1978, the GNP of the 13 OPEC countries stood at $319 billion, which represents 4% of total world revenue and less than the GDP of France ($400 billion), which contributed 0.59% of her GNP in 1979.

Of course, the flow of capital from Western countries has notably increased since the 1970s, but the increases must be interpreted with great caution. In 1975 the capital flows from industrialised countries were estimated at $9,155 million compared with $5,160 million in 1974. However, private capital and resources at prevailing market conditions constituted the greater part. Public aid only increased very slightly, to $619 million exactly.

This financial flow towards the Third World is eaten away by inflation. According to OECD sources, the volume of aid to the Third World for the period 1970–5 went from $6,811 million to $13,585 million, that is approximately double. But the increase was only about 5% since there was an 89.9% increase in the price of products and services during the same period.

Technical aid, which went from $706 million in 1970 to $1,563 million in 1975, did not increase in real terms: 'experts', 'consultants' and 'technicians' who come from Western countries increased their fees by 93.6% over the 1970–5 period.

One could go on multiplying examples to show that in the final analysis, this aid, in all its various forms, is more beneficial to Western countries than to the Third World.

Contrary to what is always said, the oil price readjustments did not aggravate world inflation. In 1979, with inflation running at an average 11 to 12 per cent only 1.5 to 2 per cent could be directly attributed to oil price increases. Nor were these increases responsible for the problems that besiege the economies of the North and the South. Since 1973, one hears and reads that it is the Arab world which, by virtue of its enormous 'oil excesses', 'financial surpluses', etc., is responsible for the wrecking of the entire world, rich and poor alike. Some people have concluded that in the final analysis, Arab countries should come to the rescue not only of developing countries but also of the industrialised countries. This thesis is only a manoeuvre to oppose the Arab world and other developing countries, particularly African countries. For the logical conclusion is that it is the oil-producing countries who are responsible for the worsening crisis in African countries; this in turn is the justification of the aid.

To put the problem in these terms is to obscure the facts. Despite the oil price readjustments, Arab countries are underdeveloped. Their economies remain extrovert and dependent, their internal structures traditional and rudimentary. Furthermore, the problems of the Third World existed before the oil-price readjustments; it is not the price of oil that bears the sole responsibility for the balance of payment deficits and debts. Increases in the price of food products and capital goods explains in great part the worsening of current deficits. The price pattern of principal exports has limited currency revenues and hindered development. Aggravated terms of trade are an eloquent symbol of the unbalanced relations between two worlds that have become antagonistic.

The very nature of the economic problems of the Third World militates against the Arab world's responsibility since it is itself in the throes of the very same problems.

Since the root of the problem is outside the Arab world, the latter does not have the means, and even less the vocation, to assume responsibility for the whole of the Third World, which requires an unprecedented mobilisation of outside capital and a fundamental change of attitude on the part of the financing partners, especially the CAD members whose contribution is still very much lower than what is desirable.

With regard to both economic co-operation and increased financial resources for developing countries, a large share of responsibility falls to the CAD countries who, for the most part, owe most of their growth to their domination and systematic exploitation of Third World countries. In terms of volume of Aid, Arab countries have always done as much as they can but without trying to exploit this problem of responsibility.

One must remember that the wealth of industrialised nations is much more real than that of oil-producing countries. These have to take the calculated risk that, before their reserves are used up, oil revenues will enable them to develop their economies, ensure their economic integration and reduce, if not cancel, their technological, food and even financial dependence on the outside world.

Geographical and Sectoral Spread

Until 1974, Arab aid was essentially granted to Arab countries. Concerning the entire world today, this aid still remains in great part concentrated on certain of these countries. The explanation for this lies mostly in the political situation in the Middle East during this period. Nonetheless, the socio-political scene in certain Middle Eastern countries does oblige them to co-operate with the other countries of the region.

The regular and considerable increase in the number of beneficiaries over the last few years does, however, illustrate how Arab aid has tended to diversify. While in 1973 two-thirds of the aid went to Arab countries, the figure fell to one-quarter in 1976 and even less in 1977. Today, Arab Funds cover 98 developing countries.

Remaining for the most part in line with their initial objectives and charter, the Kuwait, Abu Dhabi and Arab Funds have granted most of their loans to Arab countries. This tendency has been less emphasised in the case of the Saudi Fund and the Islamic Bank; by contrast, the ABAED has granted all of its loans to non-Arab African states.

The change in geographic spread of loans results from a modification to the Charters of the Kuwait and Abu Dhabi Funds enabling them to arrange loans to non-Arab countries. The number of Kuwait Fund loans to Arab countries fell in 1976–7 to reach 48% of the total; the increase in loans to non-Arab countries mostly concerned loans to Asian countries which represented 34% of the total. Similarily, the proportion of Abu Dhabi loans to Arab countries has also fallen and represented 73% in 1976–7. This increase in loans to non-Arab countries shows the extended geographic spread of the aid.

Thus, while the proportion of aid to Arab countries remains high, one should note the substantial increase in the number of non-Arab beneficiaries over recent years: from 42% in 1974, it reached 52% in 1975, 57% in 1976 and 61% in 1982.

The countries most affected by what has been termed 'the energy crisis' received a considerable proportion of the aid: 64% of bi-lateral aid in 1976. In the same way, the Arab contribution to the least advanced developing countries is higher than that of CAD members.

While Arab countries retained a high percentage until 1980, one should remember that the geographic spread was influenced by the aid distributed by the Gulf Organisation for the Development of Egypt. Between 1976 and 1978, 60–80% of Arab multi-lateral aid to developing countries went to Egypt; it received $1.9 billion from

1974 to 1980. So that, leaving aside GODE aid, one sees that Arab aid is geographically balanced out.

One should also stress that, contrary to what is often said, Arab aid does not have any religious character. The geographical spread is practically the same as that of the international organisations. But while the religious connotation should be left aside, as we shall see, the economic, political and diplomatic aspects are often key issues.

Numerous developing countries benefit not only from this increasingly widespread bi- and multi-lateral aid, but also from contributions to traditional multi-lateral organisations. As for the sectoral spread of this aid, it too has evolved considerably.

Whereas in the beginning Arab aid was almost entirely used to remedy balance of payment and external debt problems, and therefore had no direct bearing on the beneficiary's economic development, it has gradually and markedly moved to social and economic projects. Yet Arab aid is concentrated on sectors that, while they may be important for social and economic development, do not, in our opinion, contribute to the attainment of independence *vis-à-vis* industrialised countries. It is all the same noteworthy to see how little and how poor is the quality of aid addressed to the agricultural and, especially, the industrial sectors.

The sectoral distribution of regional Fund loans has remained practically unchanged, but those granted by national institutions have undergone certain changes which can perhaps be explained by policy changes in the granting of loans. The percentage for infrastructural projects granted by the Kuwait and Saudi Funds has considerably increased while those of the Abu Dhabi Fund were reduced. In the case of the Kuwait and Saudi Funds, these increases concerned mostly loans for industrial projects which, on the whole, were to the detriment of agricultural projects.

Lastly, aid to Africa does not concentrate on the economic integration of the region, or at any rate does not particularily favour integration of African countries. The aid should in fact concern vital sectors, such as oil exploration, and the promotion and development of new energy and refining industries. An effort of this type would help, in the long term, the economic integration of African and Arab nations. A coherent, consequent and adapted aid policy would be one that aims at developing sectors which will facilitate a marked integration of Arab, African and other Third World countries in the near future.

In so far as they encourage the transfer of technologies that are unequated to socio-economic realities and therefore transpose development models that have nothing to do with the socio-historical and economic framework of the recipient countries, the projects that Arab Funds are financing in fact facilitate and accentuate the extrovert character of Third World economies.

As to the co-financing of projects, even though this solution presents many advantages with regard to limiting the risks and costs of large-scale projects, Arab Funds help finance projects for which industrialised countries grant supplier credit which is 'tied' aid.

Given the imprecision of the general references guiding these operations and the difficulties of calculating the economic and social returns on infrastructure projects, it is difficult to assess the degree to which these institutions have attained their objectives. The development aid provided would probably have been more effectively distributed if these operations had been better co-ordinated, in a concerted fashion.

Arab aid and North-South Co-operation

Let us now return to the Third World's claims for effective and massive aid. What stage have we reached? What answers do the Northern countries have? Over the last few years, developing countries have continually emphasised that public aid is not the means to effect reconciliation between North and South. Yet, an underlying theme of all international conferences is the increase of public aid.

Third World countries are not only demanding an increase in the volume of aid, they also want qualitative improvements. These should consist of more favourable terms, reinforced aid programmes and the suppression of bi-lateral aid. Greater intervention by multi-lateral organisations, financial facilities that would be more automatically granted with more responsibilities devolved, even allowing an autonomous choice of means, would all greatly improve their situation, they claim.

In the face of these demands, the industrialised countries adopt a strategy that aims at slowing down, or even breaking down, negotiations, by clinging on to questions of detail and refusing to engage in clear and fundamental bargaining. Furthermore, they seek to sow the seeds of discord among Third World nations by opposing countries that are 'poor' in natural resources and others. Feeling that their economic interests are threatened, Northern countries sabotage the negotiations in order to hide their reticence.

Whether oil producers or not, whether endowed with surpluses or poor, Third World countries continue to suffer the effects of the international financial and monetary crisis, and find themselves more and more deeply integrated in the new international division of labour. This is in total contrast to the role they will be called upon to play in future economic, monetary and financial relations.

The slowing down, or rather exhaustion, of international aid is forcing developing countries increasingly to have recourse to international financial markets. The creation of Special Drawing Rights (SDR), which are theoretically a supplement to international liquidity deficiencies, can in no way ensure a reliable source of finance for the Third World in so far as the conditions imposed by the International Monetary Fund submit the countries concerned to often catastrophic choices which will in turn affect national economic policies. In this area capitalist countries, and above all the USA, by using oil surpluses, seek to give the IMF a major role. In turn, by way of the SDR, the IMF will accelerate the integration of Third World countries into the new international division of labour. Thanks to the power resulting from this recycling, it will be able to apply its world strategy which the lending banks seem unable to do on their own. By creating this new mechanism (SDR) and by giving it important financial means (oil surpluses), the role of the IMF will be re-established and it can then destroy at base all attempts at independent, self-centered development.

Confronted for their part with permanent recession, European countries have been trying to build up their position *vis-à-vis* this global strategy. It is in this context that one should understand their overtures to developing countries, particularily those in the Arab world. The new European strategy which consists in opening up peripheral markets calls for a great deal of finance. In fact, European exports to the Third World will hinge on the financial facilities, in the form of aid, that can be offered to the countries concerned.

At a time of stagnating, not to say decreasing global demand, this aid is the only means of controlling Third World markets where there still exists a potential for industrial products. Yet, in the present state of affairs, European capital is tied up in production units and in industrial and technological modernisation.

In this context, Europe considers that Arab aid could enable it to retain a share of trade. Europe's only way of maintaining or increasing its share of the market is to take it away from the competition. Hence the marked tendency, and always with outlets in view, to include Arab aid in its new development strategy. In the present power struggle, Arab development input is Europe's trump card as well as the effective means of creating a genuine demand in African countries who have enormous needs but no purchasing power.

One could even say that this trilogue or tri-lateral co-operation is replacing one form of domination by another. Taking present European strategy into consideration, Arab countries should not expect any substantial changes.

In the framework of these different dialogues, European Community policy is totally concentrated on substituting for its own aid to Third World countries more substantial aid from Arab countries. This is much closer to European interests, which are concerned with obtaining maximum profit from the co-financing mechanisms which are in direct relation with its export industries.

In its present form, Euro-Arab co-operation is aimed entirely at recycling oil revenues in a way that enables European countries to continue to phase out their own contribution to international aid, while retaining their stronghold on Africa, where they have contractual links.

In any event, the basic fact to remember is that Arab resources follow an external circuit which works essentially for the profit of Western countries. The capital outflow into Western monetary and financial markets proves that the national economies are not yet capable of using their wealth in the Arab context; it also facilitates its integration into the global monetary and financial systems. At the end of 1982, the USA alone collected a total of $94 billion from such funds. Between 1974 and 1978, Euromoney deposits were estimated at $118 billion, of which the UK share alone was $76 billion. So that, taken globally, this 're-cycling' process works to the benefit of a small number of countries, essentially the USA, while the rest of the world continues to suffer from lack of capital growth.

Taken in this light, oil revenues do not pose a problem to the international monetary system, but on the contrary, neutralise any adverse effect they could have had on it. While draining these resources into their own economies, Western countries refuse to admit Arab investors as fully fledged partners or to treat them as equals; nor are they disposed to direct these funds to Third World countries. Hence the necessity of a South-South dialogue.

Arab Aid and South-South Collaboration

As a result of the above considerations and in order to confront these strategies, Arab and Third World countries which are faced with the same aggressions, are obliged to co-operate.

The role of Arab aid in this co-operation takes on an essential dimension in so far as it seeks to create economic complementarity between the Arab world and other underdeveloped countries, especially in Africa.

While the Arab world insists on a new division of international labour, it must first of all have a clear vision of South-South collaboration and insert its aid into a strategy designed to accelerate the Third World's access to independence. Once it is recognised that a New International Economic Order is a precondition for the development of the South, the essential problem is to define new forms of co-operation which will truly aim at this objective. Arab Development Funds play a very significant role at this level; being institutions that spring *from* and *for* the Third World, they are in a better position to apprehend priorities and development needs.

In elaborating a new and appropriate strategy, the essential priority is to devise the means of accelerating the process of integration of the Arab world. Thus, the emergence of certain joint projects should be reinforced. It has become clear that where there is a well-managed Arab complementarity, this contributes to the Arab world's disengagement from today's embryonic division of labour. Furthermore, Arab countries cannot confront the problems of dependence and economic construction on an individual basis; it is only through an integrated economic zone that would go beyond empty words of intent that one will arrive at an adequate framework to confront the unequal balance in international relations.

The future of South-South co-operation, or of regional co-operation, will be very dark as long as the countries with wealth do not change their attitude towards strategies that aim at marginalising them.

In order to channel these resources and to reinforce this co-operation one must put into practice the major principles: The Arab world must reinforce South-South exchanges through a strategy that makes better use of its wealth by reducing the flow of resources toward the centre of the system.

It is true that this aid is not tied which is a considerable advantage over Western aid, but it could achieve a great deal more if it were part of a strategy that insisted, from the start, on Third World integration.

In such a context, Arab aid would achieve considerable results for South-South co-operation and the strategy must aim at a united front in order to break the present neo-colonial dependence. At this stage, cohesion and coherence of the Arab world are necessary to redeploy oil surpluses into Arab and Third World economies and thereby avoid falling victim to all opposing concerted manoeuvres. The Arab world must re-examine and review its financial and monetary relations so as to cease financing industrialised countries.

Naturally, this reinforced co-operation, and better deployment of oil 'surpluses' towards developing countries calls for the creation by the latter of the mechanisms to ensure better financial and economic collaboration. The first step in this reinforced co-operation is to create a propitious climate in the beneficiary countries, guaranteeing and protecting the interests of the donor countries. The setting up of the means and financial rules of the economic exchange will encourage the convergence of issues while regulating the interdependence between Arab and Third World countries.

The second stage would be the definition of the type, aims and characteristics of development, to ensure a better utilisation of aid. Development strategy is not concerned with the mere definition of an economic zone but must also address the question of socio-economic development.

To make this aid and co-operation really effective, the two partners must refine their analysis and multiply discussions and meetings, to ensure correct attribution of the most widely adapted solutions to the problems under consideration.

Despite their lack of experience, Arab Funds must draw the obvious conclusions concerning the successes and failures of international aid. Fundamental to success is the improvement of administrative procedures and reinforced co-ordination between Funds.

The Fund Co-ordination Committee must be given sufficient human and financial resources to undertake the research and studies needed to ensure that the recommendations should arrive at concrete results. The lack of forceful co-ordination prevents Arab countries from having a clear strategic aid and co-operation policy.

The creation of research and study centres and of co-ordination control organisations in the field would certainly reinforce the aid's efficacy. Evaluation and study organisations will also enable Arab aid to sidestep the traps of the projects proposed by international organisations. We are convinced that such organisations present a real, even necessary interest to ensure that the projects correspond to the needs of the recipient countries at a time when international organisations evaluate projects according to criteria that are a transposition of models that have little or no bearing on the socio-economic situation of Third World countries. The existence of organisations in the Third World would ensure that projects are better designed than those being elaborated in New York and elsewhere.

Experience has shown that projects put together by local organisations in collaboration with donor organisations are much closer to reality and less theoretical.

In the field of co-financed projects, these study centres could be a great help in that the Funds could then present projects that are properly thought out, far from the promptings of the international organisations.

Political, technical or other more specific co-ordination can only be coherent, adapted and operational if the Arab Funds arrive at concrete proposals through their contacts and meetings and can thereby be on an equal footing with their partners.

This is where Arab Funds have a role to play in South-South co-operation, for thanks to their meetings and discussions, they can bring about important modifications in various aspects of co-financing.

The creation of these delegations in developing countries would present a great advantage to Arab aid institutions in that their delegates could provide the administrative and technical assistance together with the control and follow-up of the projects that are financed or co-financed.

As we have seen above, Arab aid is considerable and Arab countries should have no complexes. The important thing is to arrive at a more imaginative and innovative form of aid, which moves away from international aid and has its own logic and strategy. These are the necessary conditions for reinforced South-South co-operation.

Since the 1970s, Arab aid has undergone considerable development in terms of volume, in terms of geographic spread and in terms of sectoral spread.

In the context of North-South relations, it has replaced Western aid while developing a certain demand for industrial products from capitalist countries. The very importance of this aid has, and continues to command, increased competition among different forms of capitalism to obtain control of its application in the desired direction. For example, in the case of the trilogue, Europe cannot maintain its commitments to Africa; it therefore intends to use Arab aid to better integrate African and Arab states in its new strategy of domination and slavery.

With regard to South-South co-operation, Arab aid cannot be considered as a complement to Western aid since it operates within the context of the industrialised countries' strategy at a time when they are confronted with the staggering Third World debt and with the expansion crisis of the last twenty years. From the above reflections one can conclude that oil revenues play a double role in the world economy being an element of international integration and an important factor in global geo-politics. In the present context, Arab aid is sketching out the first elements of a New International Economic Order, one that strikes us as being totally coherent with the new international division of labour which is in the process of being fashioned.

References

Abdelkader Sid-Ahmed, *Développement sans croissance: l'expérience des économies pétrolières du Tiers-monde* (Publisud, Paris, 1983)

Abdelkader Sid-Ahmed, *et al. Dette et développement* (Publisud, Paris, 1982)

Abdullatif, Sheikh Ahmed, 'A Strategy for Investing the OPEC Surplus', *Euromoney* (August 1980)

Bichara Khader, *Coopération euro-arabe*, Actes du colloque de Louvain-la-Neuve, 3 volumes, (2–4 December 1982)

Bird Graham, *The International Monetary System and the Less Developed Countries* (Macmillan, London 1978)

Bulletin du FMI (12 February 1979)

Borschier V., C. Chase-dunn et R. Rubionson, 'Cross-National Evidence of the Effects of Foreign Investments and Aid on Economic Growth and Inequality: a Survey of Findings and a Reanalysis', *American Journal of Sociology*, vol. 84, no. 3 (1978)

Co-ordination Secretariat of Arab National and Regional Development Institutions, *Statement of Financing Operations* (31 December 1982)

Duhamel Bernard, *La coopération trilatérale* (Editions le Sycomore, Paris, 1982)

Ghalic, Sharif, *OPEC's Cross Foreign Assets and their International Deployment. Arabs Financial Markets*, Euromoney Publications (August 1980)

Ghobal A., Ammons A., Chabane A., *Dépendence et indépendence du Tiers-monde face à la crise mondiale*, Actes du symposium, Sfax, Tunisie (16, 17, 18 April 1981) (Coopérative ouvrière d'impression et de publication Tunisie, 1983)

Grisferi K., 'Foreign Capital, Domestic Saving and Economic Development', *Bulletin of the Oxford Institute for Economics and Statistics* (May 1980)

Guillaumont P., 'Substitution de çontrainte dans le financement international', *Revue économique*, no. 1,625 (May 1979)

OECD, *Economic Assistance by Arab-OPEC Multilateral Development Finance Institutions* (OCD/82.3, Paris 1 June 1982)

OECD, *Examen 1978, 1979, 1980, 1981, 1982* (OECD, Paris)

Observateur (L') de l'OCDE (November 1978)

Wellows P.A., *Les emprunts des pays en voie de développement sur le marché des euro-dollars* (Centre de développement de l'OCDE (OECD), 1977)

Tables

Table 1.1: Basic Data on Arab National and Regional Development Institutions (31 December 1982)

Amount (Millions)

Development Institutions	Date of Commencement of Financing Operations	Capital (US$)		Total Loans Signed (US$)	Total Loans Disbursement
		Authorised	Paid up and Reserve		
1. Islamic Development Bank	1977	2,146	1,296	2,459*	1,635* Islamic Dinar 1,956* US$
2. Abu Dhabi Fund for Arab Economic Development	1974	1,089	693	1,004	2,642 UAE Dirham[1]
3. OPEC Fund for International Development	1976	4,000	2,074	1,629	890[1] US$
4. Saudi Fund for Development	1975	7,289	6,273	3,786	5,481[1] Saudi Riyal
5. Iraqi Fund for External Development	1974	924	616	1,733	279[2] US$
6. Arab Fund for Economic and Social Development	1974	2,800	1,702	1,566	244 Kuwaiti Dinar
7. Kuwait Fund for Arab Economic Development	1962	7,000	3,904	3,866	591 Kuwaiti Dinar
8. Arab Bank for Economic Development in Africa	1976	738	799	472	219[1] US$
Total		25,986	17,357	16,515	

* Including: Loans, Equity, Leasing, Foreign Trade Financing.
1. As on 30/6/1982.
2. AS on 31/12/1981.

Table 1.2: Summary of Development Financing Operations (Loans, Technical Assistance to 21 December 1982)

Amount (Millions)

Development Institutions	Loans		Technical Assistance		Loans Disbursements	
	Local Currency	US$	Local Currency	US$	Local Currency	US$
1. Islamic Development Bank	1,998.97* Islamic Dinar	2,459.08*	15.04 Islamic Dinar	—	1,635.00* Islamic Dinar	1,956.00*
2. Abu Dhabi Fund for Arab Economic Development	3,866.27 UAE (Dirham)	1,004.23	—	0.44[1]	2,641.90[3] UAE (Dirham)	—
3. OPEC Fund for International Development	—	1,628.89	—	132.13	—	890.43[3] (45.61)[3**]
4. Saudi Fund for Development	12,399.15 Saudi Riyal	3,785.89	—	—	5,481.00[3] Saudi Riyal	—
5. Iraqi Fund for External Development	—	1,733.02	—	—	82.49[2] Iraqi Dinar	278.63[2]
6. Arab Fund for Economic and Social Development	448.04 Kuwaiti Dinar	1,565.62	5.20 Kuwaiti Dinar	—	243.67 Kuwaiti Dinar (2.58 KD.: Tech. Ass. Disbur.)	—
7. Kuwait Fund for Arab Economic Development	1,112.76 Kuwaiti Dinar	3,865.58	13.78 Kuwaiti Dinar	—	590.70 Kuwaiti Dinar (7.61 KD.: Tech. Ass. Disbur.)	—
8. Arab Bank for Economic Development in Africa	—	472.28	—	1.58[2]		218.91[3]
Total		16,514.59				

* Including: Loans, Equity, Leasing and Foreign Trade

** Total Technical Assistance Disbursement

1. As on 15 June 1981
2. As on 31 December 1981
3. As on 30 June 1982

Table 1.3: Activities of the Development Institutions up to 1982

Region	Countries	No. of Operations	Amount (US$ M)	%
Arab Countries	18	516	8,464.01	51.3
African Countries	39	434	3,328.33	20.1
Asian Countries	21	256	4,337.04	26.3
Latin American Countries	17	49	315.13	1.9
Other Countries	3	9	70.08	0.4
Total	98	1,264	16,514.59	100.0

Table 1.5: Geographic Distribution of Concessional Net Disbursements from Multi-lateral Aid Agencies

	% of Total			
	1975	1977	1979	1980
Arab Countries	30.2	85.6	49.9	42.4
Egypt	0.2	77.6	16.3	2.9
Jordan	—	0.6	3.6	4.9
Lebanon	—	—	3.1	1.9
Mauritania	—	0.9	0.1	1.0
Morocco	—	0.9	1.8	1.3
Oman	—	0.6	0.1	2.0
Somalia	4.7	0.6	4.1	5.6
Sudan	8.9	1.4	6.1	8.2
Syria	6.8	0.6	3.8	1.6
Yemen AR	1.0	1.0	4.7	4.3
Non-Arab Africa	69.8	7.6	28.7	38.8
Burundi	0.6	0.1	1.7	1.6
Madagascar	1.5	0.3	2.1	4.3
Senegal	4.7	0.2	1.8	3.4
Tanzania	4.5	0.5	0.5	1.5
Zaire	7.8	0.2	1.5	0.1
Non-Arab Asia	—	6.0	9.6	5.8
Bangladesh	—	1.3	4.1	1.5
India	—	2.0	—	0.9
Pakistan	—	1.0	1.9	1.2
Europe	—	—	2.9	2.7
Turkey	—	—	2.9	2.7
Latin America	—	0.7	4.6	6.2
Oceania	—	0.1	0.4	0.5
Unallocated	—	—	3.8	3.6
Total	100.0	100.0	100.0	100.0
LLDCs	49.2	9.7	36.9	46.8
other low-income countries	22.3	84.8	30.3	20.3

Table 1.4: Recipient Countries (31 December 1982)

Arab Countries (in Asia & Africa)	African Countries		Asian Countries	Latin American Countries	Other Countries
1. Jordan	1. Ethiopia	27. Guinea-Bissau	1. Afghanistan	1. Antigua and Barbuda	1. Papua New Guinea
2. United Arab Emirates	2. Central Africa	28. Upper Volta	2. Indonesia	2. Paraguay	2. Cyprus
3. Bahrain	3. Angola	29. Cameroun	3. Pakistan	3. Barbados	3. Malta
4. Tunisia	4. Uganda	30. Congo	4. Bangladesh	4. Brazil	
5. Algeria	5. Benin	31. Kenya	5. Burma	5. Bolivia	
6. Djibouti	6. Botswana	32. Liberia	6. Thailand	6. Jamaica	
7. Sudan	7. Burundi	33. Lesotho	7. Turkey	7. Dominica	
8. Syria	8. Chad	34. Mali	8. Tonga	8. Dominican Republic	
9. Somalia	9. Tanzania	35. Madagascar	9. Solomon Islands	9. St Vincent and The Grenadines	
10. Iraq	10. Togo	36. Malawi	10. Maldives	10. El Salvador	
11. Oman	11. Gabon	37. Mauritius	11. Western Samoa	11. Grenada	
12. Lebanon	12. Cape Verde	38. Mozambique	12. Sri Lanka	12. Guatemala	
13. Libya	13. Comoros	39. Niger	13. China (PDR)	13. Guyana	
14. Egypt	14. Rwanda		14. China (National)	14. Costa Rica	
15. Morocco	15. Zaire		15. Philippines	15. Nicaragua	
16. Mauritania	16. Zambia		16. Vietnam	16. Haiti	
17. Yemen (PDR)	17. Zimbabwe		17. Korea (South)	17. Honduras	
18. Yemen (AR)	18. Ivory Coast		18. Laos		
	19. Sao Tome & Principe		19. Malaysia		
	20. Senegal		20. Nepal		
	21. Sierra Leone		21. India		
	22. Seychelles				
	23. Gambia				
	24. Ghana				
	25. Guinea				
	26. Equatorial Guinea				

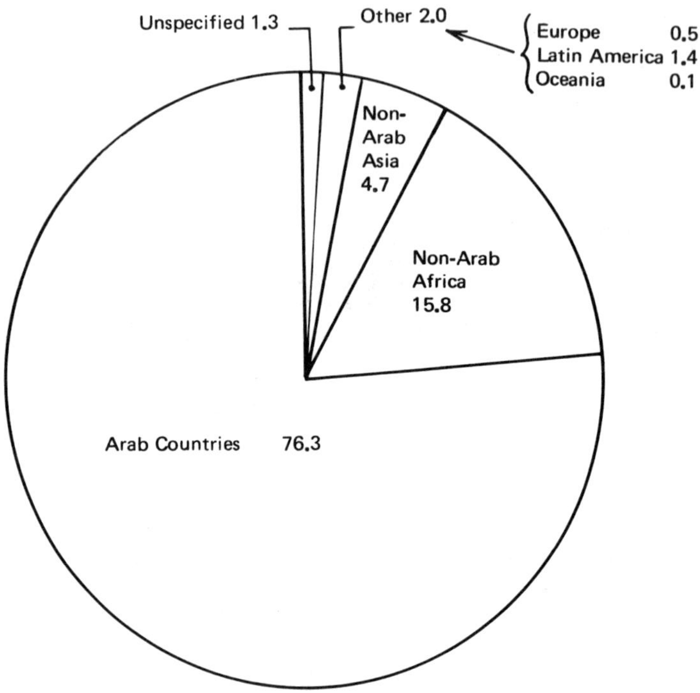

Figure 1.1: Geographic Distribution by Region of Bi-lateral Concessional Net Disbursements from Arab/OPEC Multi-lateral Organisations 1974–80 (%)

Table 1.6: Sectoral Distribution

Sector	Amount (US$ M)	% of Total
1. Infrastructure		
Transport and Telecommunication	3,981.57	24.1
Power (Elect. Oil & Gas)	4,445.97	27.0
Water and Sewerage	835.30	5.0
Sub-total	9,262.84	56.1
2. Productive		
Agriculture and Livestock	2,459.23	14.9
Industry	2,840.73	17.2
Sub-total	5,299.96	32.1
3. Others	1,951.79	11.8
GRAND TOTAL	16,514.59	100.0

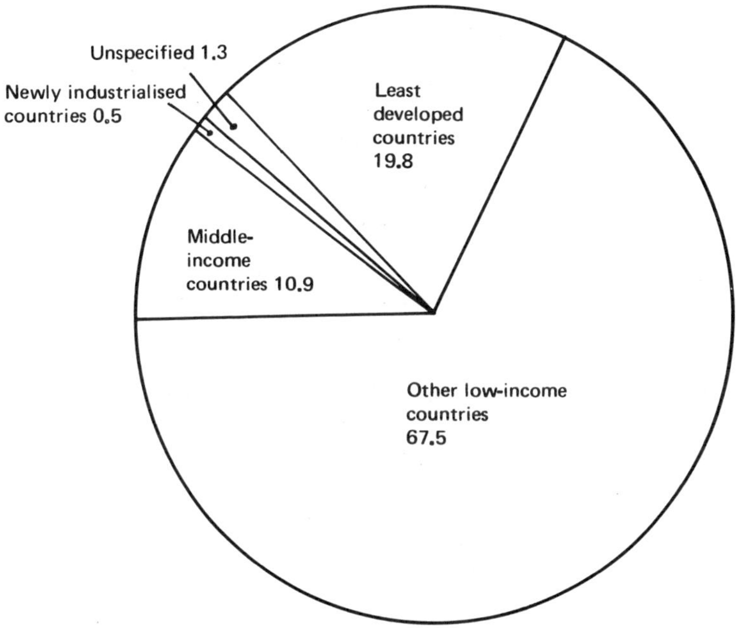

Figure 1.2: Geographic Distribution by Income Group Countries of Bi-lateral Concessional Net Disbursements from Arab/OPEC Multi-lateral Organisations 1974–80 (%)

Table 1.7: Sectoral Distribution of Concessional Commitments by Multi-lateral Agencies (%)

	1975	1977	1979	1980
Non-Project assistance	27.7	77.2	21.4	16.2
Balance of Payments Support	27.7	76.6	21.4	13.5
Emergency Relief	–	0.6	–	0.5
Oil Credits	–	–	–	–
Other	–	–	–	2.2
Project Assistance	72.3	22.8	78.6	83.8
Agriculture	–	0.5	3.6	13.7
Extractive Industries	–	–	10.4	–
Manufacturing	8.9	0.8	5.9	3.5
Energy	–	7.6	22.7	28.3
Transport, Storage and Communications	21.9	10.4	15.5	22.6

Table 1.7 — *Continued*

	1975	1977	1979	1980
Education	—	0.6	3.0	4.0
Health	—	0.3	0.6	1.8
Sewerage, Water, Multi-purpose and others	41.5	2.6	16.9	9.9
Total	100.0	100.0	100.0	100.0

Table 1.8a: Concessional Net Disbursements by Multi-lateral Arab/OPEC Aid Agencies

	$ Million							
	1974	1975	1976	1977	1978	1979	1980	1981
Members of the Co-ordination Group								
AFESD	7	40	64	87	183	106	73	89
BADEA	—	—	2	8	29	42	36	29
Islamic DB	—	—	—	1	10	15	24	27
OPEC Fund	—	—	—	162	85	88	144	254
Sub-total	7	40	66	258	307	251	277	399
Non-Members of the Co-ordination Group								
AFTAAAC	—	—	1	4	7	(4)	(7)	(6)
GODE[1]	—	—	250	825	650	—	—	—
Islamic SF	—	—	6	7	9	10	(10)	(10)
OAPEC Sp.Ac.[1]	79	—	37	—	—	—	—	—
SAAFA[1]	31	118	59	13	—	—	—	—
Sub-total	110	118	353	849	666	14	17	(16)
TOTAL	117	158	419	1107	973	265	294	415
Excluding GODE	117	158	169	282	323	265	294	415

1. No longer operational.

Table 1.8b: Non-Concessional Net Disbursements by Multi-lateral Arab/OPEC Aid Agencies

	1974	1975	1976	1977	1978	1979	1980	1981
	$ million							
Members of the Co-ordination Group								
AFESD	–	1	–	–	38	21	10	22
BADEA	–	–	–	–	27	11	12	3
Islamic DB	–	–	–	20	92	186	90	185
OPEC Fund	–	–	–	–	–	–	16	24
Sub-Total	–	1	–	20	157	218	128	234
Non-Members of the Co-ordination Group								
AAAID	–	–	–	–	–	–	–	31
TOTAL	–	1	–	20	157	218	128	265

Note: The remaining multi-lateral agencies do not extend non-concessional finance

Table 1.9: Summary of Financing Operations (by Year, Region, and Institution)

US$ Million

Region	Development Institutions	No. of Countries	No. of Operations	1962–73	1974	1975	1976	1977	1978	1979	1980	1981	1982	Total	%
1. Arab Countries															
	1. Islamic Bank	16	104	—	—	—	—	64.72	89.50	246.10	235.88	285.32	239.30	1,160.82	
	2. Abu Dhabi Fund	12	43	—	64.29	44.18	117.94	104.22	182.88	138.85	68.24	10.22	27.00	757.82	
	3. OPEC Fund	11	42	—	—	—	7.45	39.40	32.16	26.70	30.20	73.85	53.00	262.76	
	4. Saudi Fund	13	64	—	—	176.69	144.11	428.81	361.87	186.73	55.41	73.36	193.94	1,620.92	
	5. Iraqi Fund	8	33	—	—	—	15.00	25.00	90.00	328.30	326.03	277.00	37.66	1,098.99	
	6. Arab Fund	15	100	—	114.89	193.44	331.59	362.60	—	70.23	111.72	148.40	232.75	1,565.62	
	7. Kuwait Fund	16	130	342.90	138.86	206.24	145.92	202.66	91.45	248.70	98.99	246.07	275.29	1,997.08	
	Total	18	516	342.90	318.04	620.55	762.01	1,227.41	847.86	1,245.61	926.47	1,114.22	1,058.94	8,464.01	51.3
2. African Countries															
	1. Islamic Bank	11	54	—	—	—	—	17.28	35.17	60.37	96.30	114.49	69.17	392.78	
	2. Abu Dhabi Fund	18	23	—	—	—	5.06	12.31	8.27	6.29	5.40	34.66	11.34	83.33	
	3. OPEC Fund	37	145	—	—	—	4.10	82.80	49.55	73.35	101.00	123.35	144.20	578.35	
	4. Saudi Fund	25	58	—	—	29.85	41.71	85.91	138.99	7.52	171.42	66.45	257.55	799.40	
	5. Iraqi Fund	12	17	—	—	—	—	1.30	—	23.00	252.02	37.80	—	314.12	
	6. Kuwait Fund	25	55	—	—	38.80	51.36	76.14	42.00	14.84	97.67	142.81	224.45	688.07	
	7. Arab Bank	36	82	—	—	—	79.40	77.04	66.92	20.20	81.02	69.70	80.00	474.28	
	Total	39	434	—	—	68.65	181.63	352.78	340.90	205.57	804.83	589.26	786.71	3,330.33	20.2

Table 1.10: Summary of Financing Operations (by Region and Institution)

US$ Million

Region	No. of Countries	Islamic Bank Amount	Islamic Bank No.	Abu Dhabi Fund Amount	Abu Dhabi Fund No.	OPEC Fund Amount	OPEC Fund No.	Saudi Fund Amount	Saudi Fund No.	Iraqi Fund Amount	Iraqi Fund No.	Arab Fund Amount	Arab Fund No.	Kuwait Fund Amount	Kuwait Fund No.	Arab Bank Amount	Arab Bank No.	Total	No.	%
1. Arab Countries	18	1,160.82	104	757.82	43	262.76	42	1,620.92	64	1,098.99	33	1,565.62	100	1,997.08	130	—	—	8,464.01	516	51.3
2. African Countries	39	392.78	54	83.33	23	578.35	145	799.40	58	314.12	17	—	—	688.07	55	474.28	82	3,330.33	434	20.2
3. Asian Countries	21	897.44	68	155.85	12	608.69	74	1,277.87	36	229.91	15	—	—	1,159.24	49	—	—	4,329.00	254	26.2
4. Latin American Countries	17	—	—	—	—	175.09	45	55.04	1	85.00	3	—	—	—	—	—	—	315.13	49	1.9
5. Other Countries	3	—	—	7.23	1	4.00	1	32.66	2	5.00	1	—	—	21.19	4	—	—	70.08	9	0.4
Total	98	2,451.04	226	1,004.23	79	1,628.89	307	3,785.89	161	1,733.02	69	1,565.62	100	3,865.58	238	474.28	82	16,508.55	1,262	100.0
%		14.8		6.1		9.9		22.9		10.5		9.5		23.4		2.9		100.00		

Table 1.11: Summary of Financing Operations (by Year and Region)

US$ Million

Region	No. of Countries	No. of Operations	1962–73	1974	1975	1976	1977	1978	1979	1980	1981	1982	Total	%
1. Arab Countries	18	516	342.90	318.04	620.55	762.01	1,227.41	847.86	1,245.61	926.47	1,114.22	1,058.94	8,464.01	51.3
2. African Countries	39	434	—	—	68.65	181.63	352.78	340.90	205.57	804.83	589.26	786.71	3,330.33	20.2
3. Asian Countries	21	254	—	30.00	158.28	440.06	487.98	250.57	616.01	559.29	1,033.32	753.49	4,329.00	26.2
4. Latin American Countries	17	49	—	—	—	—	76.03	14.30	81.90	63.50	64.40	15.00	315.13	1.9
5. Other Countries	3	9	—	—	—	—	3.94	36.00	5.00	9.25	—	15.89	70.08	0.4
Total	98	1,262	342.90	348.04	847.48	1,383.70	2,148.14	1,489.63	2,154.09	2,363.34	2,801.20	2,630.03	16,508.55	100.0
%			2.1	2.1	5.1	8.4	13.0	9.0	13.1	14.3	17.0	15.9	100.0	

Table 1.12: Summary of Sectoral Distribution of Financing Operations (by Region)

US$ Million

Region	No. of Countries	No. of Operations	Transport Telecom. and Storage	Power (Electricity Oil and Gas)	Water and Sewerage	Agriculture and Livestock	Industry and Mining	Others	Total	%
1. Arab Countries	18	516	2,173.70	1,791.30	605.01	1,195.43	1,600.62	1,097.95	8,464.01	51.3
2. African Countries	39	434	1,079.11	591.82	90.56	724.01	374.26	470.57	3,330.33	20.2
3. Asian Countries	21	254	684.70	1,994.91	76.14	523.28	791.81	258.16	4,329.00	26.2
4. Latin American Countries	17	49	10.00	82.94	11.90	15.94	50.00	144.35	315.13	1.9
5. Other Countries	3	9	35.58	—	16.89	13.61	—	4.00	70.08	0.4
Total	98	1,262	3,983.09	4,460.97	800.50	2,472.27	2,816.69	1,975.03	16,508.55	100.0
%			24.1	27.0	4.9	15.0	17.0	12.0	100.0	

Table 1.13: Summary of Financing Operations (by Year and Institution)

US$ Million

Development Institution	No. of Countries	No. of Operations	1962–73	1974	1975	1976	1977	1978	1979	1980	1981	1982	Total	%
1. Islamic Bank	33	226	—	—	—	—	119.34	188.70	498.73	475.39	649.05	519.83	2,451.04	14.8
2. Abu Dhabi Fund	40	79	—	64.29	44.18	163.73	138.82	215.95	145.14	100.61	69.88	61.63	1,004.23	6.1
3. OPEC Fund	81	307	—	—	—	42.70	243.01	155.01	212.80	250.77	400.88	323.72	1,628.89	9.9
4. Saudi Fund	51	161	—	—	282.75	432.58	770.04	561.68	447.01	331.89	348.61	611.33	3,785.89	22.9
5. Iraqi Fund	31	69	—	30.00	—	15.00	26.30	101.20	406.30	743.26	373.30	37.66	1,733.02	10.5
6. Arab Fund	15	100	—	114.89	193.44	331.59	362.60	—	70.23	111.72	148.40	232.75	1,565.62	9.5
7. Kuwait Fund	58	238	342.90	138.86	327.11	318.70	410.99	200.17	353.68	268.68	741.38	763.11	3,865.58	23.4
8. Arab Bank	36	82	—	—	—	79.40	77.04	66.92	20.20	81.02	69.70	80.00	474.28	2.9
Total	98	1,262	342.90	348.04	847.48	1,383.70	2,148.14	1,489.63	2,154.09	2,363.34	2,801.20	2,630.03	16,508.65	100.0
%			2.1	2.1	5.1	8.4	13.0	9.0	13.1	14.3	17.0	15.9	100.0	

Table 1.14: Summary of Sectoral Distribution of Financing Operations (by Institution)

US$ Million

Development Institution	No. of Countries	No. of Operations	Transport Telecom. and Storage	Power (Electricity Oil and Gas)	Water and Sewerage	Agriculture and Livestock	Industry and Mining	Others	Total	%
1. Islamic Bank	33	226	162.09	1,171.94	38.02	134.82	900.69	43.48	2,451.04	14.8
2. Abu Dhabi Fund	40	79	131.31	395.15	16.20	108.66	327.72	25.19	1,004.23	6.1
3. OPEC Fund	81	307	151.69	455.30	27.84	100.54	133.65	759.87	1,628.89	9.9
4. Saudi Fund	51	161	1,445.39	837.06	322.01	681.78	320.32	179.33	3,785.89	22.9
5. Iraqi Fund	31	69	220.75	124.16	5.00	320.70	186.30	876.11	1,733.02	10.5
6. Arab Fund	15	100	562.21	333.70	238.05	212.88	181.78	37.00	1,656.62	9.5
7. Kuwait Fund	58	238	1,113.43	1,088.68	137.51	796.42	690.49	39.05	3,865.58	23.4
8. Arab Bank	36	82	196.22	54.98	15.87	116.47	75.74	15.00	474.28	2.9
Total	98	1,262	3,983.09	4,460.97	800.50	2,472.27	2,816.69	1,975.03	16,508.55	100.0
%			24.1	27.0	4.9	15.0	17.0	12.0	100.0	

Table 1.15: Summary of Financing Operations (by Year and Country)

US$ Million

Country	No. of Operations	1962–73	1974	1975	1976	1977	1978	1979	1980	1981	1982	Total	%
1. Arab Countries													
1. Jordan	59	39.27	8.84	18.50	53.46	108.81	122.73	97.99	122.79	304.94	145.67	1,023.00	6.2
2. United Arab Emirates	2	—	—	—	—	—	5.13	10.00	—	—	—	15.13	0.1
3. Bahrain	13	27.91	10.10	—	40.48	65.12	22.36	3.90	22.79	—	—	192.66	1.2
4. Tunisia	55	40.47	38.82	66.02	20.53	148.79	77.49	141.67	29.94	182.25	118.88	864.86	5.2
5. Algeria	22	28.00	20.46	1.04	—	54.55	37.99	39.50	47.40	86.49	102.04	417.47	2.5
6. Djibouti	12	—	—	—	—	—	—	—	33.55	17.49	51.94	102.98	0.6
7. Sudan	51	67.37	27.28	103.37	73.58	141.72	74.04	115.69	107.87	12.00	14.00	736.92	4.5
8. Syria	32	19.60	65.04	—	126.04	70.53	82.67	39.29	6.40	69.89	23.90	503.36	3.0
9. Somalia	32	—	—	21.38	38.14	109.52	17.66	33.30	67.50	72.31	64.79	424.60	2.6
10. Iraq	2	17.90	—	—	—	—	—	—	—	—	—	17.90	0.1
11. Oman	11	—	—	—	61.35	48.22	171.26	6.20	18.50	14.66	28.62	348.81	2.1
12. Lebanon	8	6.89	—	—	—	55.76	29.09	—	9.75	—	—	101.49	0.6
13. Libya	1	—	—	—	—	—	—	—	11.02	—	—	11.02	0.1
14. Egypt	30	52.49	99.43	278.47	143.61	166.95	21.82	—	—	—	—	762.77	4.6
15. Morocco	50	25.54	8.19	43.10	51.77	100.72	101.82	109.55	254.27	80.00	207.39	982.35	6.0
16. Mauritania	36	—	—	23.93	50.11	5.70	27.76	273.04	17.97	140.44	88.71	627.66	3.8
17. Yemen (PDR)	39	0.93	25.23	28.97	49.38	38.44	15.00	38.98	94.01	61.58	54.29	406.81	2.5
18. Yemen (AR)	61	16.53	14.65	35.77	53.56	112.58	41.04	336.50	82.71	72.17	158.71	924.22	5.6
Sub-total	516	342.90	318.04	620.55	762.01	1,227.41	847.86	1,245.61	926.47	1,114.22	1,058.94	8,464.01	51.3
2. African Countries													
1. Ethiopia	2	—	—	—	—	4.80	0.54	—	—	—	—	5.34	*
2. Central Africa	7	—	—	—	1.75	—	—	4.62	1.60	1.54	10.10	19.61	0.1
3. Angola	4	—	—	—	—	—	—	—	13.00	10.00	12.91	35.91	0.2
4. Uganda	12	—	—	49.68	—	4.55	16.77	—	5.00	10.00	20.46	106.46	0.6
5. Benin	9	—	—	—	8.00	2.00	14.38	4.50	4.50	8.70	—	42.08	0.3

6. Botswana	12	—	—	—	—	10.00	—	4.20	26.62	4.03	32.96	68.81	0.4
7. Burundi	17	—	—	—	2.24	11.81	6.00	4.50	9.47	32.58	8.84	75.42	0.5
8. Chad	5	—	—	—	—	2.40	10.45	1.00	—	—	—	13.85	0.1
9. Tanzania	15	—	—	15.52	5.00	21.60	5.00	—	36.66	64.97	22.00	170.75	1.0
10. Togo	5	—	—	—	—	3.34	—	3.50	10.58	7.40	—	24.82	0.2
11. Gabon	4	—	—	—	—	—	20.77	1.00	2.71	—	27.84	52.32	0.3
12. Cape Verde	11	—	—	—	—	1.55	1.96	1.00	17.58	1.00	1.50	24.59	0.2
13. Comoros	18	—	—	—	6.02	0.50	1.50	10.34	2.57	15.46	30.70	67.09	0.4
14. Rwanda	11	—	—	3.45	5.00	15.05	—	4.50	3.00	8.49	10.00	49.49	0.3
15. Zaire	7	—	—	—	10.00	—	5.00	7.00	69.29	15.00	—	106.29	0.6
16. Zambia	6	—	—	—	—	—	10.00	4.50	—	—	48.61	63.11	0.4
17. Zimbabwe	6	—	—	—	—	—	—	—	—	39.32	44.26	83.58	0.5
18. Ivory Coast	1	—	—	—	—	3.33	—	—	—	—	—	3.33	*
19. Sao Tome and Principe	2	—	—	—	0.35	—	—	—	—	1.00	—	1.35	*
20. Senegal	28	—	—	—	5.70	10.60	53.05	5.79	42.13	62.29	147.14	326.70	2.0
21. Sierra Leone	7	—	—	—	—	7.05	—	1.60	9.50	7.00	5.00	30.15	0.2
22. Seychelles	12	—	—	—	—	0.30	0.30	1.25	1.70	16.80	2.08	22.43	0.1
23. Gambia	20	—	—	—	3.30	26.02	2.60	1.00	35.42	4.94	4.10	77.38	0.5
24. Ghana	10	—	—	—	5.00	84.97	—	3.70	7.50	14.66	—	115.83	0.7
25. Guinea	24	—	—	—	11.58	16.62	5.53	34.80	215.06	5.00	23.00	311.59	1.9
26. Equatorial Guinea	3	—	—	—	—	0.50	—	1.00	—	1.00	—	2.50	*
27. Guinea-Bissau	12	—	—	—	—	1.65	13.97	1.00	15.24	6.50	1.50	39.86	0.2
28. Upper Volta	15	—	—	—	4.50	4.35	7.28	4.75	6.00	22.20	19.26	68.34	0.4
29. Cameroun	17	—	—	—	—	67.69	18.33	9.16	2.30	47.79	8.64	153.91	1.0
30. Congo	12	—	—	—	48.70	—	7.64	1.00	29.09	54.98	—	141.41	0.9
31. Kenya	15	—	—	—	5.00	8.00	30.97	—	58.87	27.81	62.61	193.26	1.2
32. Liberia	8	—	—	—	—	—	38.90	—	5.00	—	8.30	52.20	0.3
33. Lesotho	10	—	—	—	—	1.90	5.14	3.00	17.02	2.50	—	29.56	0.2
34. Mali	30	—	—	—	42.09	23.57	19.14	22.97	41.64	24.55	111.69	285.65	1.7
35. Madagascar	14	—	—	—	5.00	10.43	34.93	10.69	14.37	18.00	10.00	103.42	0.6
36. Malawi	1	—	—	—	—	1.80	—	—	—	—	—	1.80	*
37. Mauritius	8	—	—	—	—	—	—	—	17.55	2.00	31.78	51.33	0.3
38. Mozambique	10	—	—	—	—	6.55	—	18.00	23.76	—	27.50	75.81	0.5
39. Niger	24	—	—	—	12.75	8.50	10.75	35.20	60.10	51.77	53.93	233.00	1.4
Sub-total	434	—	—	68.65	181.63	352.78	340.90	205.57	804.83	589.26	786.71	3,330.33	20.2

* Less than 0.1

Table 1.15 — *Continued*

US$ Million

Country	No. of Operations	1962–73	1974	1975	1976	1977	1978	1979	1980	1981	1982	Total	%
3. Asian Countries													
1. Afghanistan	7	—	30.00	—	—	42.32	—	3.55	—	—	—	75.87	0.5
2. Indonesia	11	—	—	—	70.00	95.38	—	28.10	—	109.30	9.80	312.31	1.9
3. Pakistan	38	—	—	—	93.39	40.52	45.34	166.03	113.65	189.62	114.69	763.54	4.6
4. Bangladesh	45	—	—	30.00	10.12	74.47	58.24	114.61	76.37	219.21	223.98	807.00	4.9
5. Burma	7	—	—	—	—	6.67	6.50	2.00	6.32	—	15.00	36.49	0.2
6. Thailand	11	—	—	—	3.42	27.94	—	28.72	8.00	99.95	18.92	186.95	1.1
7. Turkey	32	—	—	—	—	19.60	25.94	197.72	104.68	151.10	105.17	604.21	3.7
8. Tonga	1	—	—	—	—	—	—	—	—	1.00	—	1.00	*
9. Solomon Islands	3	—	—	—	—	—	1.00	—	—	2.50	—	3.50	*
10. Maldives	20	—	—	—	5.13	0.50	12.23	0.80	37.27	9.65	7.52	73.10	0.4
11. Western Samoa	5	—	—	—	1.60	—	1.00	—	0.75	1.00	1.00	5.35	*
12. Sri Lanka	13	—	—	25.86	13.16	3.15	—	—	13.63	63.95	54.85	174.60	1.1
13. China (PDR)	3	—	—	—	—	—	—	—	—	—	103.80	103.80	0.6
14. China (National)	4	—	—	—	79.58	—	30.89	—	44.91	—	—	155.38	0.9
15. Philippines	7	—	—	—	—	20.46	4.50	3.50	3.83	7.50	20.00	59.79	0.4
16. Vietnam	4	—	—	—	—	—	17.00	10.50	6.43	—	—	33.93	0.2
17. Korea (South)	2	—	—	—	69.70	—	—	—	—	—	—	69.70	0.4
18. Laos	4	—	—	—	—	2.15	5.00	—	1.50	4.00	—	12.65	0.1
19. Malaysia	15	—	—	102.42	8.35	14.73	5.75	28.24	120.35	10.40	—	290.24	1.8
20. Nepal	8	—	—	—	17.10	4.15	3.00	12.24	1.30	11.00	—	48.79	0.3
21. India	14	—	—	—	68.51	135.94	34.18	20.00	20.00	153.41	78.76	510.80	3.1
Sub-total	254	—	30.00	158.28	440.06	487.98	250.57	616.01	559.29	1,033.32	753.49	4,329.00	26.2
1. Latin American Countries													
1. Antigua and Barbuda	1	—	—	—	—	—	—	—	—	—	1.00	1.00	*
2. Paraguay	3	—	—	—	—	—	—	2.90	—	10.00	—	12.90	0.1
3. Barbados	3	—	—	—	—	—	—	1.50	1.50	2.00	—	5.00	*

4. Brazil	1	—	—	—	—	55.04	—	—	—	—	—	55.04	0.3
5. Bolivia	1	—	—	—	—	—	—	5.00	—	—	—	5.00	*
6. Jamaica	6	—	—	—	—	3.00	7.30	50.00	7.00	10.00	—	77.30	0.5
7. Dominica	3	—	—	—	—	—	—	—	0.50	1.00	2.00	3.50	*
8. Dominican Rep.	4	—	—	—	—	2.94	—	5.00	—	10.00	—	17.94	0.1
9. St. Vincent and The Grenadines	1	—	—	—	—	—	—	—	—	1.00	—	1.00	*
10. El Salvador	1	—	—	—	—	1.75	—	—	—	—	—	1.75	*
11. Grenada	6	—	—	—	—	0.35	1.00	—	1.00	7.00	2.00	11.35	0.1
12. Guatamala	1	—	—	—	—	1.75	—	—	—	—	—	1.75	*
13. Guyana	6	—	—	—	—	1.60	6.00	—	35.00	10.00	—	52.60	0.3
14. Costa Rica	2	—	—	—	—	3.00	—	—	—	13.40	—	16.40	0.1
15. Nicaragua	3	—	—	—	—	—	—	10.00	10.00	—	10.00	30.00	0.2
16. Haiti	3	—	—	—	—	3.15	—	4.00	3.50	—	—	10.65	0.1
17. Honduras	4	—	—	—	—	3.45	—	3.50	5.00	—	—	11.95	0.1
Sub-Total	49	—	—	—	—	76.03	14.30	81.90	63.50	64.40	15.00	315.13	1.9
5. Other Countries													
1. Papua New Guinea	2	—	—	—	—	—	3.64	—	—	—	4.00	7.64	*
2. Cyprus	2	—	—	—	—	3.94	—	—	9.25	—	—	13.19	0.1
3. Malta	5	—	—	—	—	—	32.36	5.00	—	—	11.89	49.25	0.3
Sub-total	9	—	—	—	—	3.94	36.00	5.00	9.25	—	15.89	70.08	0.4
Total	1,262	342.90	348.04	847.48	1,383.70	2,148.14	1,489.63	2,154.09	2,363.34	2,801.20	2,630.03	16,508.55	100.0
%		2.1	2.1	5.1	8.4	13.0	9.0	13.1	14.3	17.0	15.9	100.0	

* Less than 0.1

2 OPEC AID TO DEVELOPING COUNTRIES
Awri Al-Ani

OPEC member countries have always considered themselves as an integral part of the developing countries. They share with the group of 77 the same conditions, problems and aims in regard to their economic and social development. OPEC member countries feel, as they have said on many occasions, that it is their obligation to support, with all their weight and capabilities, the rest of the group of developing countries. This support has been proved through the following items:

a. promoting the establishment of a New International Economic Order;
b. giving priority to developing countries in regard to oil supply and undertaking all necessary measures to meet their future needs of this vital energy source;
c. extending development aid to other developing countries on very soft terms;
d. supporting the establishment of institutions whose beneficiaries are developing countries (such as the Common Fund and IFAD), and contributing to existing institutions which extend aid to developing countries (such as the World Bank and the IMF, as well as agencies of United Nations).

I will limit myself to talking about the financial part of OPEC aid.

Facts on OPEC Member Countries

OPEC Countries, which have for some time been thought of as the richest countries of the world, are in fact a group of developing countries whose economic and social indicators do not place them among even the better-off Third World countries:

—Not one of them has yet developed a powerful industrial base or advanced agricultural sector.
—With the exception of one country, all OPEC countries have no

major exports other than oil.

—Gross National Product of all OPEC countries is not more than 5 per cent of the GNP of OECD countries.

—Many of the OPEC Countries now figure among the major Third World borrowers.

—Rates of literacy in OPEC Countries range between 10 and 40 per cent.

—All OPEC countries are food-deficit ones, with some depending almost exclusively on imports for meeting their food needs.

Even when OPEC countries are in a surplus position, their oil revenues could never be equated with the income of industrialised economies where revenues represent recurrent outputs generated from a permanent and renewable productive stock.

In fact, the so-called surpluses of some OPEC countries have resulted from the extraction of their depletable natural resources at a rate which exceeded their financial needs at the time of production. The resulting liquidity should not therefore be mistaken for additional wealth. It is simply a monetary realisation of a pre-existing asset.

One may easily argue that the transformation of a depletable natural resource into cash which cannot be converted immediately into real investment, and thus real wealth, may make the country poorer rather than richer in the long run. Because of this major difference in the nature of revenues between OPEC and industrialised countries, the GNP of the former cannot be calculated on the same basis as that of the latter.

Facts on OPEC Aid

In spite of the facts mentioned above in regard to the economic circumstances of OPEC member countries, their aid record compared with the aid of industrialised countries is very impressive. Note the following facts:

1. The rate of 0.7 per cent of GNP, which was adopted by the UN as a target for development aid, was exceeded by OPEC, not recently and not after the so-called 'oil price revolution', but as far back as 1973. The official development aid by OPEC member countries from 1973 to 1980 ranged between 1.46 and

2.9 per cent of their GNP. In the same period the official development assistance (ODA) of OECD amounted to between 0.30 to 0.35 per cent of GNP, with a declining trend for the future.

2. In spite of the fact that the GNP of OPEC countries does not exceed 5 per cent of the GNP of OECD countries, the official development assistance by OPEC countries in the period 1970–81 was more than $27 billion compared with OECD aid ($115 billion) for the same period.
3. The OPEC aid agencies constitute today significant channels for external financial assistance. The total authorised capital of all these agencies amounts to $27.6 billion; by the end of 1981 their paid-up capital reached $14.3 billion, with reserves of $2.8 billion.
4. The development aid of OPEC countries is not designed as compensation for oil price increases. Firstly, many OPEC aid institutions were established before the oil price adjustments took place; the Kuwait Fund was established in December 1961, the Abu Dhabi Fund in July 1971 and the Arab Fund in 1968. Secondly, there is no relation between oil imports by developing countries from OPEC and OPEC aid received by these countries. Otherwise, OPEC should have channelled 75 per cent of its aid to only 10 developing countries, which buy 75 per cent of all OPEC oil supplied to such countries. On the contrary, the majority of these countries has not benefited from any OPEC aid, because most of them have relatively advanced economic structures.
5. OPEC aid has a wide geographical distribution. Until now, 83 developing countries have benefited from OPEC aid. OPEC member countries do not consider any political or geographical limitation in the process of extending development aid. In fact, many of the recipient countries do not even have diplomatic relations with many OPEC member countries.
6. OPEC countries do not use or even consider their aid as an instrument to promote trade among them and other developing countries. Therefore recipient countries are allowed to procure food and services provided through the provisions of OPEC aid from any supplier in the world, with only one condition: international bidding. In this regard, OPEC aid is not tied to any sources of supply, unlike OECD aid, which is mainly tied to procuring goods and services from the country which has provided the loan.

The OPEC Fund for International Development

One of the multinational aid institutions of OPEC member countries is the OPEC Fund for International Development. This Fund was created in 1976 in line with the desire of OPEC countries to establish a collective financial facility to consolidate OPEC's assistance to other developing countries in addition to the existing bi-lateral and multi-lateral channels through which OPEC countries have individually extended financial aid to the Third World.

The objective of the Fund is to reinforce financial co-operation between OPEC countries and other developing countries.

Concerning the policy and operations of the OPEC Fund, the following facts should be emphasised:

1. The OPEC Fund started in 1976 as a temporary one, with an initial allocation amounting to $800 million; by 1980 the Fund had become a permanent international legal entity, with a target of resources amounting to $4 billion.
2. At the end of 1982, the approved amount for commitments reached $2.9 billion; actual commitments were $2.6 billion and disbursements reached $1.7 billion.
3. The operations of the Fund can be divided into the following categories:
   a. to meet the short-term needs of developing countries through providing concessional loans for balance of payments support;
   b. to meet the long-term needs of developing countries through providing concessional loans for the implementation of development projects;
   c. to finance technical assistance activities in the form of grants.

   In figures:
   —the OPEC Fund has extended $919.5 million for financing 141 project loans;
   —the OPEC Fund has provided $661.9 million for 159 loans to support the balance of payments;
   —the OPEC Fund has provided $47.5 million for 7 programme loans and
   —extended grants to the amount of $106 million.
4. The majority of the project loans are interest-free with a 20 year maturity including a 5-year grace period; the interest

rate for balance of payments support loans ranges from interest-free to 4 per cent. Except in very few cases, the maturity period for these types of loan is 10 years, including a 3-year grace period. The calculation of interest depends on the per capita income of the recipient country.

5. Recipient countries of OPEC aid are *all* developing countries. A special and preferential treatment is given to least developed countries. Therefore the OPEC Fund aid shows a very wide geographical distribution. As of December 1982, 83 developing countries have benefited from OPEC Fund aid as follows:

Africa	173	loans totalling	$760 million
Asia	89	loans totalling	$693 million
Latin America	45	loans totalling	$175 million

6. The Fund has no priority for the financing of projects in specific sectors. The needs and priorities of each country are taken into account. In this sense the Fund has financed:
   45 projects totalling $457 million in the energy sector
   33 projects totalling $145 million in the transport sector
   22 projects totalling $116 million in the agricultural sector
   33 projects totalling $191 million in other sectors
7. The Fund is giving the time factor in approving loans great importance. Therefore it has established very simple and quick procedures to evaluate, approve, sign and disburse loans to recipient countries. To save time, the Fund decided to accept appraisal reports of other international organisations for its consideration to approve loans for co-financed projects.
8. Procurements of loans provided by the OPEC Fund are not tied and are only subject to international biddings. However, and upon the request of the beneficiary countries, preferential treatment could be given to supplies and suppliers from developing countries.

Promoting Co-operation with Developing Countries

The promotion of economic co-operation among developing countries is a major part of the Fund's policy. The following activities are to be highlighted in this regard:

a. The Fund has contributed $455 million to the initial resources of the International Fund for Agricultural Development

(IFAD), so helping to establish this institution.

b. $37 million are allocated by the Fund to cover the contribution of 35 low-income developing countries to the Common Fund, which is designed to stabilise the prices of primary commodities.
c. The Fund gives preferential treatment to the procurement of goods and services from developing countries. It has initiated the creation of some other institutions to the benefit of the developing countries. These include the African Fertiliser Center and the International Development Law Institute. In addition, it supports many international organisations like UNDP, UNRWA, CGIAR etc., whose beneficiaries are developing countries.
d. The Fund gives preferential treatment to financing projects in co-operation with developing countries.

The revenues of OPEC member countries are declining because of the fall in oil prices and the reduction of production. According to some sources, OPEC member countries have closed the year 1982 with a deficit for the first time since 1973. If this development continues, it is doubtful that OPEC member countries and the OPEC Fund, as the multinational agency of these countries, will be able to commit themselves to the same amount of aid as hitherto.

3 THE ROLE OF THE ARAB FUND FOR ECONOMIC AND SOCIAL DEVELOPMENT

Mahmoud El-Helw

The objective of this chapter is rather limited. It is intended to introduce to those who are not acquainted with it the Arab Fund for Economic and Social Development, and to touch upon some of its activities which may not be common to, or at least priorities of, other similar institutions.

The Arab Fund is a regional agency created to participate in the development of its member states through financing economic projects of an investment character by means of loans granted on easy terms to governments and public or private institutions, giving preference to such joint projects as are vital to the Arab entity and its closer unity. The Fund is also required to encourage, directly or indirectly, the investment of public and private capital in such a manner as to ensure the development and growth of the Arab economy. Finally, the Fund provides expertise and assistance in the various fields of economic development.

The Arab Fund mandate is confined to Arab countries which are also its members. At present, all twenty-one independent Arab states, and Palestine, have joined the Fund. The land area covered extends from the boundaries of Mauritania at the Senegal River, north to Morocco, and east to cover the whole southern Mediterranean coast, the Nile Valley, Somalia and Djibouti and, in Asia, the Fertile Cresent and the Arabian peninsula — a land mass with a total area of almost 14 million square kilometres, or one-and-a-half times the size of the USA, with a population of about 150 million.

The Fund's resources consist of its subscribed capital and reserves. The Fund is also authorised to raise loans through the issuing of bonds or obtaining credits from public and private Arab institutions, or from individuals or international institutions. Its authorised capital currently stands at 800 million Kuwaiti Dinars which, at the prevailing rate of exchange, is equivalent to about US$2.8 billion, of which about US$1.4 billion has been paid and the remainder is being paid through annual installments, the last of which is due by February 1986. Paid-up capital and reserves now amount to US$1.7 billion. The Fund has not yet resorted to raising loans through bonds or credits.

The top management of the Fund is vested in a Board of Governors, the Director-General/Chairman of the Board of Directors and the Board of Directors. The Board of Governors is equivalent to a legislative authority and is composed of a Governor and an Alternate Governor appointed by each member state for a renewable period of five years. Governors and their alternates are high-ranking officials of the member states and are usually Ministers of Finance. The Board meets once a year and considers such matters as membership of the Fund, the status of its resources and operations, formal agreements with regional and international bodies and other issues of a similar nature brought to its attention. The Board of Governors appoints the Director-General/Chairman of the Board of Directors and the members of this Board, who are now six in number (with six alternate members), each representing a group of member countries and voting on their behalf. The Board of Directors is charged with all activities of the Fund in general within the limits defined by the Board of Governors.

The Director-General is the Chief Executive of the Fund and is assisted by professional and administrative staff organised in such a way and including such members as he considers necessary for the efficient running of the Fund. At present, the Fund's staff numbers about 140 of whom about 40 are professionals and work through 4 departments — Operations, Finance, Legal Affairs and Administration. One Unit is concerned with research, and the identification and study of projects of an inter-Arab character.

The origins of the Arab Fund date back to, perhaps, twenty years ago, but, for all practical considerations, it became an operational entity with the appointment of its first Director-General in 1972. Thus the Fund must be considered a product of the seventies and the special characteristics it developed have undoubtedly reflected the happenings and mood of that decade. This was a period of fundamental changes in the relations between the Arab world and other nations, particularly in the West. These changes had already been in progress but were given greater momentum by increased oil revenues. We had great expectations that here, at last, the Arab world had within its grasp the tools it needed to implement basic structural changes in all spheres of its economic and social life, from the better control and utilisation of its resource base to the diversification of its economies through industrialisation and the more intensive use of modern technologies, to the realisation of a better standard of living for its citizens. Having attained political independence, the Arab world was, in effect, asserting its economic and, to a certain extent, intellectual and cultural independence and self-reliance. In this context, the Arab Fund was conceived of as an important instrument and catalyst of change.

By the end of 1982, just eight years after the start of its operations, the Arab Fund has granted 108 loans with total commitments of about US$1.63 billion in support of 80 projects whose total cost has been estimated at over US$10 billion. Some 70 per cent of this was for infra-structural projects in transport and telecommunications (36 per cent) energy (18 per cent) and drinking water supply and sewerage (15 per cent). Among the productive sectors, mining and industry received 16 per cent and agriculture 14 per cent. The relatively low share of agriculture should not be interpreted as lack of interest in this very important sector. It resulted from late Arab Fund intervention which has since gathered momentum, and this sector is currently receiving an appreciably higher proportion of our lending allocations. There is no need to dwell on this statistical aspect, as these are covered in the tables at the end of this chapter.

While the Arab Fund is primarily a development lending agency, its operations have some special features which reflect a basic policy orientation, embodied in its Charter and translated in its operational guidelines and procedures. Foremost among these is the priority given to all actions leading to Arab economic integration, particularly the promotion of Arab inter-country projects, and the special attention accorded to the social aspects in all Arab Fund operations.

Regional or Inter-country Projects

From the start of its operations, the Arab Fund has actively supported all actions considered conducive to strengthening inter-Arab ties and interdependence. Because they are particularly suited to this purpose, and also create bonds that are hard to break, joint projects and ventures have received preferential treatment in AF operations. This orientation has required a thorough look at the region's physical infrastructure and resources in order positively to influence the volume and quality of goods and services exchanged within it.

The Fund identified, at an early stage, the availability of well studied inter-country projects suitable for financing as a key element for the success of its promotional endeavours in this area. For this purpose, it collaborated with the UNDP in creating a special programme designed to identify and prepare Arab inter-country projects. In this instance, the Arab Fund was a partner, a partial beneficiary and an executing agency. The initial undertakings of the Joint Programme (JP) focused on surveys to identify potential projects, while its later work was directed towards feasibility studies. The JP operated for the six years 1976–81, during which nine surveys and a number of feasibility studies were completed or started in the areas of transportation, telecommunications, industry, agriculture and education (Table 3.3). Its work is being continued by the Arab Fund as an important function of its Research Unit.

Equally important is the Fund's actual participation in financing Arab inter-country projects. Table 3.4 gives details of all regional projects supported by Arab Fund loans up to the end of 1982. They cover a number of sectors, of which the most prominent has been telecommunications. National networks have been, or are being, improved, expanded and linked. In the Maghreb countries, work is in progress from Morocco to Libya; and in the Mashrek countries projects are under way to connect the telecommunications systems of Syria, Jordan, Iraq, Saudi Arabia, the two Yemens, Djibouti, Somalia and Sudan. To help access to the services of the ARABSAT, the Fund is also financing receiving earth stations in ten member countries. Other regional projects have been in transportation, industry and rural water supply. Out of 108 loans granted by the Fund over the period 1974–82, 32 were in support of projects in this category which received some US$231 million, or 15 per cent of Arab Fund total commitments. This level is, in our view, rather modest, but the Arab Fund is committed to continue its efforts to attain a better balance in its portfolio between national and regional projects. In the pipeline are a number of projects for power interconnection, the studies of which are already in progress. There are also huge possibilities in the fields of transportation (roads and railways), industry (iron ore, agricultural machinery, pesticides), natural resources, training and technical education.

The Social Aspects in Arab Fund Operations

The importance that the Arab Fund accords to the social sector is manifest in its mandate and reflected in its name. In this chapter I merely intend to show how the Fund has addressed itself to problems in this sector through its lending and technical assistance operations.

There are social sub-sectors which, by their nature, are generally considered eligible to borrow. These are usually administered by financially independent public organisations which are able to generate income from the services they sell to the public. Provision of safe drinking water and electricity to both urban and rural populations is an example of social services in this category. The Fund is supporting some 20 operations to expand and improve the water facilities in member countries. Total commitments to this sub-sector at the end of 1982 stood at some US$245 million or about 15 per cent of all Arab Fund commitments. In the electricity sub-sector the Fund is supporting 17 projects for the generation and distribution of electricity for which it has committed some US$300 million or about 18 per cent of the total. Of this amount some 50 per cent was for the electrification of houses.

'Soft' social sub-sectors produce services offered either free or for nominal fees, including health, education, training and housing. Here, the Fund's support is often provided as a grant or as a component of a production project. This latter mode is made possible through the comprehensive approach we follow in project formulation and preparation. One or more of these social components appears in almost all Arab Fund-supported projects. It has been estimated that the value of these 'soft' components amounts to about US$100 million, representing on average 10 per cent of the individual loan. Together with lending to the first category of social projects, the total share of social projects adds up to nearly US$500 million or about 30 per cent of all loans granted by the end of 1982. (Table 3.5).

With regard to technical assistance, the Fund has financed on a grant basis some 68 operations with total commitments reaching about US$18 million. (This does not include allocations under the Joint Programme (JP).) Of these operations, 37 were in support of social activities (either directly or indirectly) for which the grants amounted to about US$5 million or some 27 per cent of the total. Training of manpower, especially in the Arab LDC's, claimed most of the grants in this group. (Table 3.6).

Although AF allocations (grants and loans) to the social sub-sectors may appear modest, it should be remembered that they constitute only a part of the total investment involved. For the period

1974–82, this has been estimated at some US$2400 million or about 25 per cent of total lending by the Fund.

The above estimates touch only upon those social aspects of Arab Fund operations which could be expressed in money values. There are, however, other important facets which, though equally important, are difficult to quantify. Examples are primary and secondary employment generation from the AF-financed projects. One estimate has put the primary employment generation from all AF projects at nearly 200,000. The transfer of technology is another spin-off of developmental projects financed by the Fund, with obvious social connotations. In the longer run, such benefits may equal, if not surpass, the immediate quantifiable benefits.

Other Special Features

Because it is owned by all Arab states, the AF has proved to be a suitable vehicle for certain activities which go beyond its immediate mandate. Examples of such activities are:

a. *Co-ordination Secretariat:* The AF has been elected as the Technical Secretariat for co-ordination between the Arab national and regional development financing agencies. The nature and mechanisms of this co-ordination are set out in a separate chapter (chapter 7). Suffice to say here that the principal duties of the Secretariat include preparations for regular meetings, follow-up of recommendations, and publication of the quarterly reports on the lending and technical assistance operations extended by members of the Co-ordination Group.
b. *Administration of IFAD operations in the Arab countries:* The International Fund for Agricultural Development (IFAD) entered in 1980 into a Co-operation Agreement with the AF by which the latter undertakes on behalf of IFAD the appraisal and loan administration of projects financed by IFAD in Arab countries. The AF has appraised and is administering six operations under this Agreement. In line with all IFAD projects, these are basically rural development projects, helping small farmers to increase their productivity in general and raise food production in particular.
c. *Technical Secretariat for AGFUND:* The Arab Gulf Programme for the Support of UN Specialised Agencies, created

and funded by seven Arab Gulf States, has entrusted the AF with all technical work related to its operations. This includes the evaluation of project proposals submitted by the UN agencies for financial support and the preparation of technical reports and legal documents. During its first year of operation, the AGFUND has committed about US$45 million in support of 42 projects whose total cost is about US$400 million. These projects, which were selected from 160 proposals, are benefiting 46 developing countries and are directed towards the poor segments of the population in the fields of health, child and motherhood care, rural water, agricultural extension, community development and environment.

d. *Co-operation with other Arab organisations:* It is to be expected that an entity, such as the Arab Fund, owned jointly by all Arab Countries, would work closely with the Arab League Secretariat and its specialised agencies in all economic and technical matters that fall within its competence. Examples of this wider area of interest are: the co-operation with the Arab Monetary Fund and the Arab League Secretariat to issue the *Unified Arab Economic Report* on an annual basis; the organisation of the two Arab Energy Conferences with OAPEC; and the study of the flow of Arab private investments in the Arab world with the Kuwait Fund, and the Inter-Arab Investment Guarantee Corporation.

This has been a brief review of the structure and function of the Arab Fund. Nevertheless, I trust that it has brought out its main characteristics.

Table 3.1: The Arab Fund for Economic and Social Development: Activities 1974–82 (KD Million)*

LOANS	1972	1973	1974	1975	1976	1977	1978	1979	1980	1981	1982	Total position as at 31 December 1982
Number of Loans	–	–	8	11	14	15	–	6	8	15	31	108
Total Amount	–	–	33.700	56.100	97.000	103.900	–	26.200	24.800	50.600	73.200	465.500
Average Amount of Loan	–	–	4.200	5.100	7.000	6.900	–	4.400	3.100	3.373	2.240	4.310
Total Disbursements	–	–	1.809	11.753	18.285	24.681	61.822	36.967	25.458	36.055	26.845	243.615
Repayments	–	–	–	–	–	–	0.155	2.071	3.433	5.989	9.524	21.172
TECHNICAL ASSISTANCE												
Amount	–	–	0.125	0.115	0.628	0.805	0.366	0.200	0.474	1.196	1.293	5.202
Disbursements	–	–	0.125	0.112	0.159	0.623	0.278	0.169	0.215	0.243	0.655	2.579
UNDP/AFESD JOINT PROGRAMME												
Fund's Allocation	–	–	–	–	1.600	–	–	–	–	–	–	1.600
Amount Disbursed	–	–	–	–	0.115	0.093	0.122	0.051	0.090	0.133	–	
Authorised Capital	100.000	–	102.500	400.000	–	–	–	–	–	–	800.000	800.000
Subscribed Capital	81.010	–	18.850	2.190	87.460	180.930	–	14.700	9.970	0.010	354.980	750.100
Paid-up Capital	15.400	6.291	14.219	16.079	47.618	32.227	33.001	37.775	58.017	56.833	56.717	374.217
Total Income	0.593	0.984	2.924	3.706	5.929	10.277	11.331	14.697	22.130	26.777	36.752	136.100
Total Expenditure	0.045	0.562	0.831	0.928	1.449	2.107	2.199	1.997	2.204	2.120	2.397	16.839
Income Surplus	0.548	0.422	2.093	2.778	4.480	8.170	9.132	12.700	19.926	24.657	34.355	119.261
General Reserves	0.055	0.042	0.197	0.266	0.448	0.817	0.913	1.270	1.993	2.466	3.435	11.902
Additional Reserves	0.493	0.380	1.536	2.397	3.011	4.211	6.526	10.602	17.380	20.796	29.449	96.781
Foreign Currencies and Investment Reserves	–	–	0.235	–	0.278	2.244	1.204	0.625	(0.642)	0.103	0.113	4.160
Technical Assistance	–	–	0.125	0.115	0.743	0.898	0.488	0.203	0.527	1.292	1.357	5.748
No. of Member Countries	17	17	17	20	21	21	21	21	21	22	22	22
No. of Beneficiary Countries	–	–	7	8	10	11	–	6	8	11	15	15
No. of Technical Staff	–	18	26	30	43	56	48	30	32	29	31	31

* KD = Kuwaiti Dinar = approx. US$3.50

Table 3.2: Sectoral and Country Distribution of Loans 1974–82 (KD Million)

Sectors	Jordan	Tunisia	Algeria	Sudan	Syria	Egypt	YAR	Lebanon	Morocco	PDRY	Bahrain	Djibouti	Somalia	Mauritania	Oman	Total	%
Electric Power	16.9	2.0			6.0	12.0	21.7	6.0		4.0	5.0		2.0	8.4		84.0	18.1
Water and Sewerage	2.1	3.3			17.0	18.0	14.0			3.5			5.0			62.9	13.5
Roads	5.0			33.6									11.5	8.5		58.6	12.6
Ports		3.8	18.0			12.0		5.0		6.9		1.5				47.2	10.0
Telecommunications				4.8												4.8	1.0
Storage					2.0											2.0	0.4
Total	24.0	9.1	18.0	38.4	25.0	42.0	35.7	11.0		14.4	5.0	1.5	18.5	16.9		259.5	55.6
Cement Industry and Building Materials						6.7			9.0							15.7	3.4
Textiles Industries						10.0										10.0	2.1
Petroleum and Gas Industries		4.0													9.0	13.0	2.8
Mining														10.0		10.0	2.1
Fertiliser					2.2	9.2										11.4	2.5
Sugar				6.0												6.0	1.3
Total		4.0		6.0	2.2	25.9			9.0					10.0	9.0	66.1	14.2
Agriculture and Settlement		7.0		2.5					22.0				5.2			36.7	7.9
Development of Livestock and Animal Resources					2.0								1.6			3.6	0.8
Multi-purpose									14.0	7.7						21.7	4.7
Total		7.0		2.5	2.0				36.0	7.7			6.8			62.0	13.3

Services Sector		7.0	5.0													12.0	2.6
Inter-Arab																	
Telecommunications	6.0	4.7	5.8	1.3	3.7		1.4		4.0	2.5		2.1	2.9	1.2		35.6	7.7
Airports			2.0													2.0	0.4
Roads					6.0		3.8			6.5						16.3	3.5
Cement Industry	5.0															5.0	1.1
Rural Water	0.7	0.6		1.8			0.7		1.3	1.5				0.4		7.0	1.5
Total	11.7	5.3	7.8	3.1	9.7		5.9		5.3	10.5		2.1	2.9	1.6		65.9	14.2
Grand Total	35.7	32.4	30.8	50.0	38.9	67.9	41.6	11.0	50.3	32.6	5.0	3.6	28.2	28.5	9.0	465.5	100.0
%	7.7	7.0	6.6	10.7	8.3	14.6	8.9	2.4	10.8	7.0	1.1	0.8	6.1	6.1	1.9	100.0	

Table 3.3: Surveys and Feasibility Studies Financed by the Regional Programme*

Project	Countries Involved	(KD Thousand) Cost	RP Contribution
A. Studies Completed			
1. Inter-Arab Telecommunications Link Sub-region III	Egypt, Iraq, Jordan, Kuwait, Saudi Arabia, Syria	83	83
2. Equipment Study for the Arab Maritime Transport Academy (AMTA)	All Arab States	23	23
3. Management Information System for AMTA	All Arab States	19	19
4. Pan Arab Shipping Co. (PASCO)	All Arab States	29	29
5. Preliminary Study on Status and Prospects of Agriculture, Machinery and Equipment	All Arab States	36	20
6. Arab Long-term Regional Model	All Arab States	18	10
7. Educational Television Programme for Children (Open Sesame)	All Arab States	280	80
8. White Cement Project Study	Jordan, Syria	72	72
9. Educational Television Programme on Child Rearing	All Arab States	28	20
10. Unified Geologic and Water Resource Mapping	YAR, PDRY	32	32
11. Iron and Steel Industry	All Arab States	100	30
12. Development of Pesticide Industry	All Arab States	60	60
13. Natural Resources Survey	YAR, PDRY	19	19**
14. Arab Passenger Airlines Reservation System	All Arab States	23	23**
15. Advanced Medical Training Programme	All Arab States	13	13**
16. Manual for Preparation of Arab Inter-country Projects	All Arab States	6	6
17. Transport Section in the Arab World	All Arab States	15	15
B. Studies Under Preparation			
1. Engineering Industries II	All Arab States	48	48
2. Production of Teaching Aids	All Arab States	28.5	20
3. Integrated Development of Hamad Basin	Syria, Jordan, Iraq, Saudi Arabia	224	140

4. Experimental Year of the Regional Training Programme for Water Technicians at Wad El Magboul Institute	PDRY, ARY, Sudan, Somalia	340	114
5. Production of Grain, Fodder and Vegetables in Al-Hella Region	Iraq + Gulf States	60	60
6. Manufacture of Fishing Gear	All Arab States	82	77
7. Preparation of Prototype Post-literacy Books	All Arab States	31	23
8. Regional Arab System for Labor Market Information	All Arab States	580	217
9. Development of Paper Industries***	All Arab States	40	40
10. Development of Low-cost School Buildings and Equipment***	YAR, PDRY, Sudan, Djibouti, & Mauritania	260	260
11. Educational TV Programme for the Eradication of Illiteracy***	All Arab States	38	38

* A Joint AFESD/UNDP Program for the Identification and Preparation of Inter-country Investment Projects and Related Feasibility Studies 1976–81. Studies undertaken in the context of this programme are financed on a 50–50 basis by AFESD and UNDP.

** Financed completely by the Arab Fund.

*** Supported by the Fund outside the RP.

Table 3.4: Arab Inter-country Projects Financed by the Arab Fund, 1974–82 (KD Million)

Project	Countries Involved	Year	Amount of Loan
1. Telecommunication Interconnection I	Algeria-Morocco	1975	3.3
2. Aden-Taiz Road	YAR-PDRY	1976	10.3
3. Algeria/Aerial Navigation Aid Inspection	All Arab States	1980	2.0
4. Telecommunication Interconnection II	Jordan-Syria	1980	7.7
5. Telecommunication Interconnection III	Somalia, Djibouti, YAR, PDRY, Saudi Arabia	1981	5.4
6. Telecommunication Interconnection IV	Algeria-Tunisia	1981	8.2
7. White Cement	Jordan-Syria	1982	5.0
8. Rural Water Supply	Jordan, Tunisia, Sudan, Morocco, Mauritania, PDRY, YAR.	1982	7.0

Table 3.4 — *Continued*

Project	Countries Involved	Year	Amount of Loan
9. Lathequia-Tartous Highway	Syria, Lebanon, Gulf States	1982	6.0
10. Telecommunication V (Earth Stations)	Syria, Jordan, PDRY, Djibouti, Somalia, Sudan, Tunisia, Algeria, Morocco, Mauritania	1982	11.0
	TOTAL		65.9
	About US$		240.0 M

Table 3.5: Social Components in Arab Fund Loans Operations, 31 December 1982 (KD Million)

	Total		Share of Social Components	
Sector	Loans	Investments	Loans	Investments
1. Water[1]	70	350	70	350
2. Electricity[2]	84	560	42	280
3. Health and Housing[3]	12	30	12	30
4. Training[3]	17	30	17	30
Total	183	970	141	690

Notes: 1. Includes Sewerage.
2. 50% of the investment is related to electrification of houses.
3. Represents social component in production and infrastructural projects.

Table 3.6: Social Components in Arab Fund Technical Assistance Operations, 31 December 1982 (KD thousand)

	Total Allocations		Share of Social Components	
Activity	Grants	Investments	Grants	Investments
Feasibility Studies	1,813	2,175	180	220
Research Studies	812	1,625	100	200
Training	796	1,000	796	1,000
Institution-building	1,483	2,000	300	400
Special Programme	299	500	24	40
TOTAL	5,203	7,300	1,400	1,860

4 THE KUWAIT FUND FOR ARAB ECONOMIC DEVELOPMENT: THE LOAN GRANT POLICY AND PROCEDURE IN FAVOUR OF DEVELOPING COUNTRIES

Bader Al-Humaidi

The Kuwait Fund is a development aid agency established in 1961 by the developing state of Kuwait for the benefit of other developing countries. The objective of the Fund is to assist the developing countries in their efforts towards economic development, and its function is the provision and administration of such assistance.

The Fund is an autonomous public body with a juristic personality, having administrative and financial independence. It is administered by a Board of Directors. The rules, policies and procedures of the Fund were basically designed to serve the developmental interests and efforts of the recipient countries, and to encourage possible co-operation among the developing countries themselves.

The Fund provides financial assistance in the form of concessionary loans and technical assistance grants, and co-operates closely with recipients to ensure that the aid-supported projects and programmes contribute effectively to their development efforts and goals.

All developing countries are in principle eligible for financial assistance from the Fund. Up to the end of 1982 the Fund was able to co-operate with some 61 countries with a broad spectrum of political and economic systems. Cumulative loan commitments reached Kuwaiti Dinars (KD) 1104 million at the end of 1982, distributed over 58 countries, of which 16 are Arab, 25 African, 14 Asian, with 3 other countries (Cyprus, Malta and Papua New Guinea). Technical assistance grants totalled some KD 14 million at the end of the same year, benefiting 30 countries and 4 development bodies. The recipients comprise 10 Arab countries, 14 African, 5 Asian, and one other country — Malta.

In accordance with its initial mandate, the Fund confined its operations to the Arab countries until 14 July 1974 when the original mandate was extended to include non-Arab developing countries as well. Concomitant to this geographical extension the authorised capital of the Fund was raised five-fold to reach a level of KD 1,000 million. In March 1981 the Law and Charter of the Fund were amended, giving effect, on the one hand, to enlarging the Fund's powers and scope of operations, and on the other, to increasing the authorised capital of the Fund by 100 per cent, to reach KD 2,000 million. The amendment enables the Fund to contribute to the capital stock of corporate bodies, development finance institutions and other organisations whose aim is not confined to commercial profit-making, and whose operations have a developmental dimension and could contribute effectively to the development goals of the developing countries.

The function of the Fund is not only the provision of financial assistance but also technical assistance, to ensure that the developmental objectives of the Fund-financed projects are achieved. Normally, the co-operation between the Fund and recipient countries involves the participation of third parties who supply goods or services needed for the implementation of projects. Such third parties often include consulting firms, contractors, or suppliers from the developed countries. The Fund policies and procedures were basically designed to ensure close co-operation with recipients and to give effect to equitable and balanced relationships with third parties. In dealing with the parties involved, the Fund follows general guidelines of policies and procedures which take account of the special circumstances of particular situations.

Recipient Countries

As already indicated all developing countries are in principle eligible for financial assistance from the Fund. It has been its general policy, however, to extend its operations, within the limits of its financial and other resources, to those countries of the developing world which are more in need of assistance than others. Fund loans are granted at concessionary terms for development projects and programmes in such sectors as agriculture, power, transport and communications and storage, and other infrastructure projects, as well as industry. Loans were also made to national development banks to assist them in strengthening and expanding their development operations.

Fund loans as indicated above have been granted to recipient countries on soft terms. Such terms are differentiated from others on the basis of general criteria which take into account mainly such factors as a country's per capital income level, prospective balance of payments position, and debt-servicing capacity, as well the nature of the financed project and its earning capacity.

In selecting projects to be financed by the Fund, due consideration is given to the development plans of the prospective recipients. No special application forms are required to be submitted to the Fund. Preliminary inquiries relating to development co-operation in general may be initiated by the country concerned or by the Fund itself. Once a certain development potential is identified, it is then pursued through close collaboration between the Fund and the prospective recipient country throughout its subsequent stages.

A loan is granted to a developing country only after the Fund assesses the technical soundness and economic and financial viability of the proposed project and its beneficial impact on the economy of the recipient country. Procedurally, a request for a loan should be addressed to the Fund by the competent authorities of the applicant country. The latter is usually expected to indicate the priority level it attaches to the project submitted for consideration, pertaining to the significance of the project in the context of the borrower's economy. It is the Fund's general policy to respect, in principle, the priorities set by the countries themselves, especially if such priorities were determined in accordance with a well-prepared and rational development plan.

A Project is considered for financing by the Fund only after ascertaining that its feasibility studies are satisfactory, and were prepared by a competent body, be it an agency of the borrower or a consultant. On the basis of such studies and other information and data made available, the Fund may proceed to evaluate the project.

If, however, the Fund finds that a country's capacity to absorb more development investments is constrained by a lack of well-prepared and well-conceived projects, which is the case in many developing countries, especially the least developed ones, it would then consider providing technical assistance to that country for the study of candidate projects.

Project appraisal is considered by the Fund an essential and important activity. Not only because a project which fails the rigorous technical, economic and financial evaluation is rejected, but also because both the Fund and the recipient co-operate very closely during appraisal to seek ways and means for optimising projects, and to identify possible problems and obstacles that might impede their orderly and timely implementation.

The loan agreement negotiated with the borrowers embodies more than just financial terms relating to disbursement and repayment of the loan. It is designed to ensure that favourable conditions will exist for the proper implementation and management of the project, and as such it often includes provisions aimed at enhancing the technical capabilities of the agency in charge of the project and promoting the efficient and economic conduct of its operations. Thus, depending on the circumstances of each case, the provisions of the loan agreement may require strengthening the organisational set-up of such an agency through acquisition of staff or training, the rationalisation of its financial affairs and the observance of appropriate performance criteria.

After evaluation of a project, a loan agreement is negotiated with the recipient country. Following that the project appraisal report together with the draft loan agreement are submitted to the Board of Directors for consideration and approval.

Third Parties

As regards consultants, contractors and suppliers, the Fund adopts policies and procedures that will serve and safeguard the interests of recipients. To this effect, such policies and procedures are kept flexible to ensure harmony and consistency with the desired objectives.

Consultants

The nature and type of services rendered by consulting firms depends on the circumstances of each project. Such services may, however, include pre-investment, pre-feasibility and feasibility studies, detailed engineering designs and tender documents, and supervision of project implementation, as well as other services.

The selection and appointment of consultants by recipients is normally made in close consultation with the Fund. Whenever certain type of services are required, a 'short-list' comprising a limited number of qualified and competent consulting firms is prepared, and the final version is normally adopted after consultation between the Fund and the recipient. A letter of invitation is sent to each of the short-listed and approved consulting firms requesting the invitee to submit a proposal for undertaking the required services.

Draft terms of reference and other background information agreed between the Fund and the recipient country are normally dispatched with the letter of invitation.

The consulting firms invited are requested to submit their proposals within a reasonable period of time, and in accordance with the required information spelled out in the letter of invitation. They concern: any comments on or amendments deemed appropriate by the consultants to the draft terms of reference; experience and qualifications of consultants, and their relevance to the work required; the general approach and the proposed plan of work; an estimate of time to be spent by the consulting firm in the field as well as in the home office; an estimate of the man-months required, and an allocation of these among the individual team members; and biodata on the individuals to be assigned to the work.

In addition to the above information to be provided in the proposal submitted by a consulting firm, the latter is also requested to furnish as part of the proposal a detailed cost estimate of the services required, preferably in a separate sealed envelope.

Proposals submitted are analysed and compared by the Fund on the basis of the consultants' technical capabilities, experience, proposed work plan and approach. Remuneration for the required services is considered only after evaluating the technical proposals. Both the Fund and the recipient country co-operate closely on the evaluation of proposals, by informing each other of the procedures to be used and the criteria to be applied, and by exchanging views, making comments and suggestions.

Realising the need to obtain the services of the most suitable and competent consulting firms, the Fund is also keen on promoting the technical capabilities and the performance level of consulting firms and improving their expertise in the developing world. Therefore, it is the policy of the Fund to encourage the participation of consultants from developing countries, particularly through the collaboration of such consulting firms with others from the developed world.

A contract for the work to be accomplished is normally signed by the recipient country and the consulting firm selected. However, during negotiations, and depending on the issues to be considered, the Fund could be actively involved in assisting the recipient country in this respect. In any case, contracts negotiated between the recipient country and a consulting firm should be submitted to the Fund for comments and approval.

The Fund and the recipient country co-operate closely in

supervising the work of the consulting firm, which in any case should submit a report in draft form for comment on, and approval by, the Fund and the recipient country.

Contractors and Suppliers

Financial assistance provided by the Fund is untied and free from any strings attached as to the source of procurement of goods or services. Therefore, it is the Fund's policy that contracts for the implementation of Fund-financed projects should be based on international competitive bidding. Such policy is designed to give recipient countries the maximum advantage possible in importing goods and services from the lowest-cost source.

Often a recipient country is assisted by a consulting firm in the implementation of projects. Whether the services of such a consulting firm are financed by the Fund or not, the recipient country is requested to seek the approval of the Fund for the appointment of such consultants. Details of the policies and procedures favoured by the Fund in dealing with consulting firms have already been given. However, it is important to note in this respect that the services of a consulting firm for the implementation phase of a project are normally more diverse and wider in scope than those relating to prefeasibility and feasibility studies. They generally include detailed engineering design, preparation of tender documents, and supervision of project implementation, as well as assisting the recipient country in the pre-qualification of bidders, and bid analysis and evaluation. Designs, tender documents, supervision schedules, prequalifications and the bid evaluation report should be submitted to the Fund for comments and approval.

The Fund's favoured procedure leading to the award of major contracts requires that the recipient country places an advertisement notification of the intended works in some internationally recognised and widely circulated newspapers and magazines, and/or that it uses other channels suitable for transmitting the notification to as many prospective bidders as possible. Responses from interested bidders are then analysed by the recipient country with the assistance of the consulting firm, and a list of pre-qualified contractors submitted to the Fund for comment and approval. All pre-qualified bidders are then invited to bid in accordance with the prepared and approved tender documents. Bids received are analysed and compared by the recipient country and the consulting firm. The bid analysis and evaluation report, and the recommendations made are submitted to the Fund for comment and approval.

Upon approval by the Fund of the recommended contractor, negotiations between the recipient country and the contractor may be initiated. During negotiations, the Fund may render assistance to the recipient with the view to ensuring that the agreement reached will serve the interests of the project and maintain a sound and balanced relationship between the two parties. In any case, all contracts to be financed by the Fund must be submitted for its approval.

The procedure for the supply of goods or execution of works depends on the size and complexity of the goods or works required, and while open international competitive bidding is generally required, pre-qualification of bidders is normally considered desirable for big contracts. For small and simpler contracts, quotations may be solicited from a reasonable number of well-known suppliers from various countries. In any case, the notification or the letter of invitation to bid, the bidding documents, and the report or analysis and evaluation of bids, all have to be submitted by the recipient country to the Fund for comment and approval.

Although the Fund requires that goods and services be obtained, as a general rule, on the basis of international competitive bidding, there may be particular instances where international competitive bidding is not the most desirable method for implementing the project or certain components thereof, and therefore other methods may be more economical and efficient, especially in cases where goods and services could be procured locally. In such cases the procedures to be followed are normally agreed in advance between the Fund and the recipient.

As it is the policy of the Fund to pay special attention to the promotion of local expertise and enterprise in developing countries and foster collaboration among the developing countries themselves, due regard is given by the Fund to encouraging bidders from developing countries to participate in aiming for the whole or part of the project. At the request of the recipient country, domestic contractors may be granted a margin of preference when comparing domestic with foreign bids. Such an arrangement is subject to conditions and procedures to be agreed between the Fund and the recipient.

Co-financiers

Often the implementation of projects requires co-operation with other donors, especially in cases of large-scale projects. In this respect, the Fund welcomes co-operation not only with sister institutions in the Arab world, but also with donors from the developed countries, as well as multi-lateral development agencies and other organisations involved in co-operation for development.

Being a development aid agency whose purpose is to assist the developing countries in their efforts towards economic development, and being uninfluenced by any commercial interests, the Fund's general policies and procedures, characterised by a significant degree of flexibility, are always applied with a view to accelerating development in the recipient countries, and to achieving the objectives of economy and technical soundness with respect to procurement.

As there are normally third parties involved in these efforts, the Fund's main concern is to ensure and safeguard the interests and rights of the recipient countries, and to assist them in reaching and sustaining sound and balanced contractual dealings with such third parties.

5 THE ACTIVITIES OF THE SAUDI FUND FOR DEVELOPMENT

Saleh H. Humaidan

For the last several years, the Kingdom of Saudi Arabia has played a leading role in providing financial assistance to the developing countries. For example, during the second half of the last decade when the development assistance from the industrialised countries (OECD members) was below 0.7 per cent of their Gross National Product, that of Saudi Arabia amounted to almost 6 per cent of its GNP. In 1981 alone, the Kingdom provided 5.798 billion dollars in financial assistance, an amount larger than that provided by any other country of the world during the same year.

Qualitatively as well, the financial aid from Saudi Arabia differs in many respects from that of the industrialised countries. Most of the time the industrial countries offer tied and selective financial assistance in view of self-interest, wishing to sell the goods and services of their respective countries. On the other hand, Saudi financial assistance is untied and is offered on soft terms. It also has a weighted grant element of 50 per cent or more. The assistance enables the recipient country to acquire goods and services from the world market at competitive prices. Saudi assistance to the developing countries in fact also benefits the industrialised countries by creating markets for the services and goods produced by them. During the last couple of years the growth in the GNP of developing countries, primarily a result of external loans and financial assistance, has helped the industrialised countries by mitigating the intensity of their economic recession.

Saudi Arabia's financial assistance to the developing countries is routed through various channels. Most of the financial assistance is provided on a bi-lateral basis but at the same time the Kingdom is a major contributor to a number of regional and international financing institutions, such as the OPEC Fund for International Development, the Islamic Development Bank, the Arab Fund for Economic and Social Development, the Arab Fund for Economic Development in Africa, the African Development Bank, the World Bank, the International Monetary Fund, the International Fund for Agricultural Development, and the specialised agencies of the

United Nations. The Kingdom's national organisation for providing and administering the bi-lateral financial assistance is the Saudi Fund for Development.

The Saudi Fund for Development (SFD)

The Saudi Fund was established through a Royal Decree in September, 1974, and started its operations in February 1975. The Fund, under its Charter, is an autonomous organisation 'with a legal entity and autonomous financing status' and is administered by a Board of Directors, chaired by HE the Minister of Finance and National Economy, The Vice-Chairman and Managing Director is the Executive Head responsible for execution of the decisions of the Board of Directors.

The basic objectives of the Fund are to establish financial cooperation links with other developing countries by assisting them in the implementation of their development programmes, and to promote regionally balanced economic and social development. In order to achieve these objectives the Fund participates in the financing of development projects, by providing loans on concessionary terms. It does not provide grants or involve itself in equity participation.

The authorised capital of the Fund, set orginally at 10 billion Saudi Riyals, was raised to 15 billion in 1979, and to 25 billion Saudi Riyals in 1981.

The scope of the Fund's activities is worldwide, as the Charter of the Fund has not put any restrictions relative to countries which may qualify to receive loans.

Criteria Generally Followed in the Granting of Loans

Prior to the granting of a loan, the Fund, like other similar institutions, evaluates the expected benefits of the loan taking into account the following:

1. the significance of the project with regard to its priority over other projects and its integration with the overall economic base of the country;
2. the availability to the borrowing country of funds required for execution in addition to the amount of the loan.

In pursuing this approach, the SFD also takes into account the development priorities and objectives of the borrowing country and assesses the impact of assistance on the country's economy in terms of output, employment generated, savings of foreign exchange, and, in particular, the eradication of poverty.

In implementing its lending programme, the Fund has tried to focus the benefits of its assistance predominantly on the poorest countries, those having very low per capita income, for whom the need for concessional loans is the greater. For example, in Africa, the sub-Saharan countries have received a large share of the Fund's commitments. Commitments to sub-Saharan countries stand at present stand at about 34 per cent of the total. Similarly, in Asia, 56 per cent of the assistance provided has been for the thickly-populated regions of the south-east, those with a relatively very low per capital income.

Co-financing of projects is another aspect of the Fund's policy. This emerged due to practical necessity and its inherent benefits. Firstly, by its Charter, the total amount of loan for a project cannot exceed 50 per cent of the cost of the project, and secondly, the predominant constraint in the execution of development projects is not the shortage of resources but the lack of technical know-how and insufficient project execution capacity. Co-financing helps both with regard to providing additional finances to meet the cost of the project, and monitoring by more than one lending institution is an added security for successful completion. In fact, out of the 18,118 million Saudi Riyals committed by the SFD to the end of the last financial year, 11,728 million were for projects where other colenders were also involved.

Since the start of its operations in 1975 the Fund has followed a policy of special emphasis on the financing of infrastructure and social projects rather than commercial or industrial ones. This policy has been followed for two reasons. Firstly, for any meaningful economic growth to take place in a country, a minimum base of infrastructure facilities is a prerequisite. Secondly, the commercial and industrial projects can, without much difficulty, attract financing from international financing sources. Therefore, up until now the loans provided for housing, education, health, transportation and energy projects represent 75 per cent of the Fund's total commitment.

In many countries, infrastructure facilities having been improved, the Fund's financing policy in the future may show a gradual shift towards greater financing for projects in the productive sectors.

Current Level of SFD Loans and Commitments

Since the start of operations the Fund has maintained a high level of lending and, as a result, its current total commitments are more than those by many other similar institutions during the same period. Also, consistent with the increase in its authorised capital, the yearly commitments of the Fund have over the years shown an upward trend. For example, during the year 1974–5, the total commitments made amounted to 1,725 million Saudi Riyals, while during the financial year 1981–82, commitments made amounted to 3,666 million.

The Fund has now committed 18,860 million Saudi Riyals for the financing of over 250 projects spread over 59 countries in Africa, Asia, Latin America and Oceania. Of the total commitments, loan agreements amounting to 12,952 Saudi Riyals have been signed, while for the remaining commitments of 5,908 million, agreements will be signed in due course.

The split in the total commitments between Africa and Asia is about equal. The percentage of total commitments for Asia and Africa is now 49 and 48 per cent respectively. The remaining 3 per cent is for other countries in Latin America and Oceania. To illustrate further the way that the SFD has directed its efforts towards the world's poorest countries, it needs to be said that a large portion, 70 per cent, of its assistance to Africa has been for sub-Saharan countries, where the per capita income has not grown for a decade.

The allocation figures presented above only illustrate one important facet of SFD policy, i.e., directing its concessionary loans towards the poorest countries. The emphasis on infrastructure development will be apparent from the sectoral distribution of the commitments, which will now be presented.

Sectoral Distribution of SFD Loans

The Fund's aid strategy relative to the allocation to various sectors has been aimed at:

1. helping the country in building an economic base through infrastructure development,
2. improvement in productivity through better housing, education and health facilities,
3. facilitating the growth of the core sector of the economy, which in most cases is agriculture.

Infrastructure

In line with the criteria enumerated above, SFD loans have been directed mainly towards the development of infrastructure projects, with the knowledge that such projects receive little private capital as these investments do not generate attractive short-term economic returns. Lack of infrastructure facilities in the less developed countries is one of the major constraints to rapid economic development, and emphasis on this aspect is a prerequisite for rapid and sustained growth. In fact in many countries basic infrastructure was in large areas non-existent. In line with its policy of special emphasis on infrastructure projects the Fund's current commitments for the infrastructure sector therefore include transportation, ports, telecommunications and energy projects; these stand at 59 per cent of the total commitments.

Agriculture

For most of the developing countries, agriculture is the productive sector of the economy, as almost 70 per cent of the population in such countries is dependent for their livelihood on this sector. Therefore, growth in the agriculture sector translates to a better economy and improved standards of living for the people. Unfortunately, in Africa, export crop production has stagnated over the past few decades. An increase in production registered during the 1960s was wiped out by a decline of similar proportion during the 1970s.

Becaue of its overriding importance, the Fund has consistently accorded a higher priority to agriculture. Currently, SFD assistance for agricultural projects stands at 14 per cent of its total commitments. The agricultural projects in Africa received almost 20 per cent of the commitments for that continent. Asian countries, which are agriculturally more advanced, received 8 per cent of the total commitments for that continent.

Social Sector

The loans for the development of the social sector, housing, education, health and water supplies, aiming at the improvement of productivity of the population, amount to 2,899 million Saudi Riyals, or 15 per cent of the total commitments. Based on commitments for Africa and Asia considered separately, the percentage allocated to this sector for each continent is almost the same. Comparatively lower levels of contribution towards this sector are explained by the fact that investments in the social sector are usually from national budgets, in pursuance of social, ethical and political goals, and these considerations minimise the need for funds from external sources.

Industrial Sector

Here, SFD commitments have been basically towards agro-based industries and industries necessary for the agricultural and construction sectors, such as fertiliser and cement factories. The Fund has also provided assistance in funding mining projects having identifiable export potential and an impact on the economy of recipient countries. Currently, loans for the industrial sector represent 11 per cent of total commitments.

Future Directions

To achieve direct contact with problems that impede development in the borrowing countries, the Fund has lately adopted a system of division of tasks based on multi-disciplinary working units, each specialising in a specific geographic region. Six working units have been set up within the Technical Department of the Fund. It is hoped that such division of tasks will enable the fund's technical staff to gain a thorough knowledge of the needs of recipient countries and help the Fund gear its contributions to projects that play a major role in their development, at the same time providing much-needed technical advice.

We firmly believe that the Third World countries have the potential to overcome the problems that impede their development. The Fund in years to come hopes to work hand in hand with the international community in the belief that by working together we shall achieve better standards of living for the people of developing nations.

6 THE CO-FINANCING OPERATIONS OF THE ISLAMIC DEVELOPMENT BANK

Suleiman Al-Salem

Important as the promotion of co-financing arrangements between international, regional and national financing institutions is, an attempt is made in this chapter to highlight issues related to the co-financing operations of the Islamic Development Bank in association with national development funds and regional development financing institutions, known as the Co-ordination Group. This comprises the following: the Arab Fund for Economic and Social Development, the Abu Dhabi Fund for Arab Economic Development, the Arab Bank for Economic Development in Africa (BADEA), the Kuwait Fund for Arab Economic Development, the Libyan Company for External Investments, the OPEC Fund for International Development, the Iraqi Fund for External Development, the State of Qatar, the Saudi Fund for Development, and the Islamic Development Bank. Because of the availability of more information, the experience of the Islamic Development Bank (IDB) will be used to illustrate the general experience.

The founders of the Islamic Development Bank were realistically aware of the dire need for member countries to obtain external resources to speed the pace of their economic development. They foresaw the catalytic role of the Bank for mobilising these external resources and, accordingly, made provision for this role in the Articles of Agreement.

For the IDB and members of the Co-ordination Group, co-financing was the quickest strategy for becoming operational. Indeed, the introduction to the policies and procedures for financing operations of the Bank states:

> While the Islamic Development Bank is fully aware of the need for making initial arrangements for establishing a sound organisational structure and appointment of competent professional staff, in which task it is currently engaged, it is equally anxious that its resources be utilised for the development of its member countries as early as possible on a sound basis and in line with the bank's objectives.

With this objective in view, the Bank has decided to move in the direction of joint-financing arrangements with other co-lenders which would enable it to make the quickest possible start.

Types of Co-financing

There are, as most of us are aware, two types of co-financing operation:

1. *Parallel Financing*
   Under this strategy, the entire project is divided into a number of identifiable components. Each co-financing institution selects one or more components for financing. Each institution is then responsible, unless it entrusts this function to another, for the supervision of the implementation phase of the project it is financing. From experience, so far, this is the strategy preferred by the IDB.
2. *Joint Financing*
   Under this alternative strategy, funds from all co-financiers are pooled for financing certain services and the procurement of a set of goods in pre-agreed proportions associated with each of the financiers. This method is easier when the group has co-ordinated and synchronised procedures.

Advantages of Co-financing

The numerous advantages of co-financing operations for the implementation of projects include the following:

1. Co-financing arrangements have the effect of providing additional resources to augment what is available through the IDB for transfer to its member countries. It is important for this additionality criterion that those who invite participants do not see these potential contributions as substitutes for their own effort. However, through co-financing, the IDB is assisted in the implementation of one of its main objectives, that of ensuring the enlargement of the aggregate flow of resources to its member countries.
2. Through this strategy, the Bank is able to participate in

relatively large projects which the Bank would have found very difficult to undertake alone from its own resources. Therefore, the participation in these schemes permits the IDB to play the catalytic role for which it was intended.

3. Co-financing contributes toward the diversification of operations and widening of the sphere and impact of project financing. In this instance, co-financing institutions, which lack the expertise and administrative experience or infrastructure for certain projects, stand to benefit from co-financing facilities that more effectively channel their funds into sound and viable projects of a priority order. The availability of such co-financing channels can result in cost saving for the participants who have not yet developed the necessary expertise and administrative infrastructure for project appraisal and implementation.
4. Further cost saving arises when, by mutual agreement, one of the co-financing institutions undertakes the role of loan administor. This relieves the recepient country of the burden, as well as the associated costs, of directly dealing with various institutions. Simultaneously, the co-financiers are spared the associated costs of duplicating each of the procedures associated with loan administration.

Some Issues that may Arise and Possible Approaches for Resolving Them

Satisfactory results that may flow from co-financing depend, to a large extent, on the degree of co-ordination and the harmonisation of various procedures of the participating institutions. Some of the suggestions presented here are already being implemented by our various institutions. However, there is room for improvement.

Period of Time for Appraisal

If the period of time during which the appraisal of the project has to be conducted should differ among each of the participating financiers, this could lead to otherwise avoidable delays in project implementation, and to unnecessary cost overruns. Therefore, it is imperative that there be either joint appraisals or the co-ordination of the separate missions during the appraisal phase. The total information that is obtained can then be harmonised.

Standardisation of Basic Documents

Sources of difficulty arise from the lack of standardisation in the basic documents such as: *The Loan Agreement; The Procurement Guidelines;* and *Procedures for the Disbursement of Funds.* Co-financing operations can be enhanced through any attempts at standardisation, to the extent that this is possible.

Centralised Loan Administration

As is widely appreciated, numerous centres for loan administration for any single project can be a source of difficulty. Therefore, it is normally cost-effective to have, by mutual agreement among the co-financiers, one of them appointed as the loan administrator on behalf of the entire group involved in a particular project. The functions of the loan administrator would include the approval of contracts, the processing and clearance of disbursement requests, and the processing of procurement documents, for example, the establishment of letters of credit, etc. Obvious benefits flow from this co-ordinated loan administration. In the first place, duplication of procedures on the part of the entire group of participants is eliminated. Secondly, documents are more speedily processed, thereby enhancing project implementation and the flow of benefits to the recipient country.

Cross-effectiveness

Avoidable delays can easily arise in any situation whereby the loan-effectiveness of one institution is conditional on others being loan-effective. Definitely, any improvement in co-ordination and closer co-operation among co-financing institutions for any given project would be most helpful.

Additionality Criterion must be Real

Where resources are scarce in relation to the demand, there could be the temptation for some institutions to consider the potential contributions of others as substitute for their own effort. Certainly, the more real the additionality criterion, the greater the impact in any co-financing arrangement, especially when this is within a coherent country programme rather than on some piecemeal basis.

Cognisance of Priorities of Co-financiers

Since the priorities of each co-financier may differ from those of the others, this can adversely affect participation. Therefore, liaison is needed with prospective co-financiers right from the start as the project is being developed. Simultaneously, awareness of the priorities of potential co-financing institutions can enhance the extent of participation and the volume of external resources that can be generated.

Adequate Credit for Participation

It is relatively easy for credit to be denied to the less well-known participants while all the credit goes to the seasoned and more well-known institutions for any participation that has occurred. Obviously, appropriate credit must be given to the less well-known partners in any co-financing operation.

Joint Follow-up Procedures

By mutual agreement among the co-financing institutions, there could either be joint follow-up missions or reliance on the follow-up reports of one suitable institution entrusted with this responsibility of project supervision. There are, under this procedure, obvious cost savings, and the benefits which arise from the pooling of relevant information.

The Experience of the Islamic Development Bank

Co-financing operations of the Islamic Development Bank have, thus far, been very satisfactory. Therefore the Bank attaches a great deal of importance to this strategy for the mobilisation of ever-increasing external resources for meeting the developmental needs of its member countries. The importance that the IDB attaches to co-financing, in co-operation with the members of the Co-ordination Group and other development financing institutions in the region is demonstrated by the fact that the first project financed by IDB, in October 1976, was with the Co-ordination Group, along with certain European financing institutions. This project is the Songloulou Hydro-power Plant in the Republic of Cameroon, at a total cost of US$219.12 million. Other co-financiers were: the Saudi Fund, the Kuwait Fund, the European Investment Bank, the CCCE, and European banks. The pattern of this strategy of investment, for the period 1977–82, is presented in Table 6.1, while Table 6.2 shows the distribution of the projects, along with the sums of money involved, by the various beneficiary countries.

The funds committed by the IDB to co-financing operations have been modest, but they are expanding. These external resources are bound to be expanded further, in recognition of the importance of this strategy for accelerating the flow of funds to member countries.

Manner in which Funds are Employed in Co-financing Operations

The principal modes of financing undertaken by the Islamic Development Bank consists of loans, the acquisition of equity and leasing. Each of these lends itself to different forms of outside participation. Thus far, the Bank has participated in the co-financing of 62 projects out of a total of 150 projects financed in its member countries. The total amount of funds committed in this fashion amounts to just over US$400 million, to enable the completion of projects whose total value comes to US$8.4 billion. Other participations in these co-financing operations have been multilateral financial institutions, bi-lateral institutions, and private institutions including those providing suppliers' credits.

The IDB's co-financing operations have employed funds mainly through two channels:

1. *Direct loans*

   Under this category, the Bank has provided concessional loans for infrastructure projects. The period for loans repayment varies up to 40 years, and, depending upon the level of development of the beneficiary country, the service fee charged by the Bank ranges between $2\frac{1}{2}$ per cent and 3 per cent.

   These loans have tended to create an atmosphere conducive for inducing other concessional and semi-concessional loans for the completion of the various projects affected. Within a period of six years, the IDB has approved 49 loan operations that involved a total sum of US$332.08 million. The Bank considers co-financing through loans as the best of all existing alternatives in this sphere, for participation with the Co-ordination Group.
2. *Acquisition of Equity*

   Under this alternative means, the IDB acquires equity in industrial and agro-industrial projects. As a policy, the Bank restricts its participation to relatively smaller percentages of the total cost of the project, never exceeding one-third of the total share capital. Here, the Bank's role is catalytic for attracting other institutions which may participate in the venture through loans or through the acquisition of equity, depending upon the policies and procedures of the participating institutions and the country concerned.

The IDB has acquired equity positions in 34 companies, involving a contribution of US$190.53 million. The Bank, through the respective National Development Banks, has also taken part, by way of equity shares, in 25 medium and small-size industrial companies, committing a total sum of US$21.7 million.

Viewed under prevailing recession-affected world economic conditions, the record of the Co-ordination Group in co-financing projects in the developing countries can be considered commendable. The total amount of financing approved and the associated agreements signed by the members of the Co-ordination Group, as at 30 June 1982, comes to US$15.3 billion and the total disbursement that has been made is US$8 billion.

One of the serious factors that adversely affect co-financing activities is the shortage of adequately prepared, viable and bankable projects, especially in the least developed member countries. In order to overcome this constraint and to promote co-financing, the IDB is intensifying its technical assistance for project preparation, implementation and, sometimes, operation. Such effort should also cater to the needs of potential co-financiers.

Co-financing which members of the Co-ordination Group has become a regular feature of the IDB's financing operations in its member countries. A most important feature, that has enhanced excellent co-operation between the IDB and the Co-ordination Group, has been the absence of some of the problems which were mentioned earlier in this chapter. The basic documents and procedures of the members of the Co-ordination Group and the IDB have been harmonised and synchronised.

Prospects for the Future

Under current world economic conditions and, to the extent that it is humanly possible to hazard any projections into the future, it is the view of the IDB that co-financing has come to stay, as a very important feature of the mobilisation of international funds. The developmental needs of the less developed countries seem to be expanding at a faster rate than that of the ability of the international community to generate and mobilise enough of the required funds. This situation of demand exceeding supply of needed external resources will continue to persist.

These circumstances call for intensified joint effort by all funding institutions for the continued exploration of both active and potential sources, as well as seeking other ways for the mobilisation of additional external resources. Co-financing appears increasingly to be the best strategy for this co-ordinated effort by the international community for the implementation of projects and programmes in the less developed countries of the world community. One such area of co-ordination is with commercial groups, private financial institutions and other agencies involved in providing suppliers' credits. The IDB is already actively involved in this sphere and is co-operating with private Islamic banks in its member countries.

A large scope for co-financing exists in technical assistance programmes for sector studies as well as in institution-building. In this regard, it is not the volume of financing that needs to be co-financed. Here what is needed is closer co-operation and the involvement of various institutions for designing a comprehensive development programme for reaching the target population, instead of the current piecemeal approach. Positive impact will result from co-financing arrangements oriented toward institution-building in low-income countries as a vehicle for project generation, implementation, supervision and, in appropriate circumstances, management, through joint technical assistance programmes.

Yet another issue that warrants very serious consideration is the need to involve potential co-financiers with the projects right from the beginning and right through the appraisal, instead of waiting for invitations to be extended mainly to fill gaps requiring funding. The expanding role that co-financing will play necessitates that there be more co-ordination and harmonisation of basic formalities and procedures, to the extent that this is practicable.

The IDB's co-financing operations, in association with those of the Co-ordination Group, were and continue to be motivated by the desire to increase the flow of external resources for the developmental needs of the less developed member countries. Co-financing is attractive in yet another sense: it is a strategy which permitted the Bank and members of the Co-ordination Group to be operational within the shortest possible period of time. We are steadily improving upon our respective capacities for the independent generation of economically feasible and bankable projects. It is hoped that, as our institutions within the Co-ordination Group make

Table 6.1: IDB Co-financing with Co-ordination Group and other Sources from Member Countries of IDB (1977–82)

	Amount (US$ Million)											
	Co-ordination Group								National and Regional			
Year	IDB	Abu Dhabi Fund	Arab Fund	BADEA	Kuwait Fund	Saudi Fund	OPEC Fund	Sub-Total	Regional and National	Private Sector	Sub-Total	Total
1977	85.47	20.00	79.35	10.00	38.00	118.50	3.50	354.82	6.20	—	6.20	361.02
1978	62.32	29.27	35.90	12.80	45.00	21.20	14.51	221.00	78.44	—	78.44	299.44
1979	62.20	20.00	49.50	10.00	53.00	102.34	7.00	304.04	65.36	55.70	121.06	425.10
1980	108.03	—	33.00	10.00	42.30	32.60	43.36	269.29	—	—	—	269.29
1981	81.57	92.27	8.00	17.00	120.91	183.30	15.00	518.05	40.00	4.00	44.00	562.05
1982	102.88	10.13	15.00	—	20.24	69.29	2.50	220.04	—	14.43	14.43	234.47
Total	502.47	171.67	220.75	59.80	319.45	527.23	85.87	1,887.24	190.00	74.13	264.13	2,151.37
As % of Co-financing	23.36	7.98	10.26	2.78	14.85	24.50	3.99	87.72	8.83	3.45	12.28	100.00
As % of Co-ordination Group	26.62	9.10	11.70	3.17	16.93	27.94	4.55	100.00				

strides in this direction, other project financing institutions, with whom we have co-operated up to now, will reciprocate our invitations to co-finance projects identified by us. The IDB and members of the Co-ordination Group, within the context of the issues raised in this chapter, welcome the co-operation of all other institutions, both public and private, for the co-financing of projects in member countries.

Table 6.2: Country Distribution of Co-financing by Co-ordination Group (1977–82)

US$ Million

Country	No. of Projects	Funds from Co-financiers
Bangladesh	3	152.18
Cameroon	3	112.44
Chad	1	18.75
Comoros	1	34.39
Djibouti	1	35.72
Egypt	1	144.20
Gabon	1	30.55
Guinea	1	40.00
Guinea Bissau	1	13.75
Jordan	6	277.18
Mali	2	60.70
Maldives	1	22.18
Mauritania	3	290.60
Morocco	3	73.27
Niger	1	13.88
Oman	1	13.01
Pakistan	1	20.42
Senegal	2	44.96
Somalia	2	20.01
Sudan	3	73.78
Syria	3	94.29
Tunisia	1	9.30
Yemen, Arab Republic	2	32.51
Yemen, Peoples Democratic Republic	2	41.50
OMVS (Mali, Mauritania, Senegal)	1	322.35
Total	47	1,991.92*

* Note: The total cost of the projects includes participation by institutions which are not considered as members of the Co-ordination Group: the Arab Mining Company, the Arab Investment Company, a consortium of Kuwaiti banks and the Sheikh Kamel Group.

7 CO-OPERATION AMONG ARAB DEVELOPMENT FINANCING AGENCIES*

Mahmoud El-Helw

During the last ten years, considerable progress has been made in co-operation for development between the Arab countries, as an important donor group, and the developing countries of the Third World. This is a new and uncommon phenomenon in international economic co-operation. Although they are developing countries themselves, the Arab donors are sharing their relatively greater wealth with most developing countries, and Arab aid has so far reached some 96 countries.

While much of this aid has been channelled through bi-lateral and other existing institutions, new Arab institutions have been set up to handle part of the aid. With large capital, financial independence and global geographical coverage they have quickly developed to occupy an important place in the field of international development finance. From the start, the new institutions recognised the importance of close co-ordination for their efficient performance, and have responded well to this need.

At the initiative of the Kuwait Fund for Arab Economic Development, the oldest Arab aid agency, representatives of three Funds, the Abu Dhabi Fund for Arab Economic Development, the Arab Fund for Economic and Social Development and the Kuwait Fund for Arab Economic Development, met in Kuwait on 24 February 1974 to discuss ways and means of possible co-ordination and harmonisation of their respective activities.

The first formal co-ordination meeting followed on 20 September 1975, again at the invitation of the Kuwait Fund, and was attended by the Directors of Operations of the three Funds which were represented in the preparatory meeting, and the Saudi Fund for Development which had been established in that year. On this occasion it was agreed to convene meetings at this level twice annually and to call for a higher-level meeting (at the Director-General/President level)

* This chapter is an updated version of a paper entitled 'The Arab Co-ordination Effort' presented to the 4th Annual Meeting of DAC Members and Arab-OPEC Aid Agencies, held in Paris, 11–13 June 1981.

when the need arose. It was further decided to entrust the Arab Fund with the responsibilities of the Co-ordination Secretariat to service these meetings and act as the channel for the exchange of information and the preparation of documents.

Subsequent meetings continued to be held regularly as originally intended and membership continued to expand until, by the seventh meeting held in Khartoum in January 1979, it had grown to its present number of ten (Table 7.1). Altogether, four meetings at the Head of Organisation level and fifteen at the Director of Operations level have been held. The sixteenth meeting in the latter series was held in May 1983 and was hosted by the Abu Dhabi Fund in the Emirates (Table 7.2).

Member institutions of the Co-ordination Group fall into three categories:

1. *National Institutions:* These have been established and are wholly funded by their governments. They are the Abu Dhabi Fund for Arab Economic Development, the Iraqi Fund for External Development, the Kuwait Fund for Arab Economic Development, the Saudi Fund for Development and the Libyan Arab Company for Foreign Investment which recently took over the activities.of the Libyan Arab Foreign Bank. The representatives of the government of Qatar may also be included in this category.
2. *Multi-lateral Arab Institutions:* These are the Arab Fund for Economic and Social Development and the Arab Bank for Economic Development in Africa. (There are other Arab multi-lateral financing institutions which are not members of the Co-ordination Group because of their specialised activity. These include the Arab Monetary Fund (AMF), the Arab Agricultural Authority (AAAID), the Inter-Arab Investment Guarantee Corporation and the joint Arab investment/banking companies.)
3. *Multi-lateral Institutions with mixed Arab and non-Arab Participation:* These are The Islamic Development Bank and the OPEC Fund for International Development. Arab participation in the capital of these two institutions is about 85 per cent and 50 per cent respectively.

It is worth pointing out at this juncture that nine of the ten member Co-ordination Group have combined authorised capital of some US$28 billion and that their lending capacity is at least twice this amount. Loan commitments by eight members of the Group by the end of 1982 have been estimated at about US$17 billion, or almost 65 per cent of their authorised capital (Table 7.3).

Achievements within the Group

The progress made so far in the co-ordination effort within the Group, can, perhaps, be best gauged through a brief review of a few indicative parameters, as follows.

Procedures

Aware of the importance of unified procedures as a prerequisite for effective co-operation, the Co-ordination Group, early in its work, gave priority to the question of the standardisation and harmonisation of operational procedures followed by its members. Over the period 1975–6 technical sub-committees prepared models for a number of basic documents, including a standard Loan Agreement, Procurement Guidelines and Disbursement Procedures. These models have been broadly adopted by the member institutions, with the result that the Group is now using identical or near-identical procedures in these areas.

The advantages of the above achievements for both the lending institutions and the aid recipient countries, need hardly be dwelt upon. On the one hand they have enhanced the chances of joint financing of projects and, on the other, have helped in speeding up loan processing, particularly by the recipient country, which has minimised the onerous burden of coping with diverse rules, regulations and documents.

Co-financing

A standard item on the agenda of all co-ordination meetings is the exchange of information on new projects. Under this key item, each fund presents its new projects on a country-by-country basis. Where interest is shown, agencies can follow-up details in side meetings and, occasionally, through special meetings called for the purpose. One advantage of the system is that it offers an opportunity for checking loan applications submitted to more than one institution for the same project, for pooling fragmentary and incomplete information available to individual institutions, and agreeing on financing plans. The percentage of co-financed projects by the Group has increased substantially over time and now ranges between 30 and 70 per cent of the commitments of the members; in most cases joint financing has been the rule.

Joint Preparation, Appraisal and Supervision

It is not uncommon for members of the Co-ordination Group to undertake joint operational missions. Arrangements for these are often made during the ordinary meetings. The increasing acceptance of joint operational missions is helping both lenders and borrowers economise in effort and time. Invariably, appraisal and supervision reports and other relevant information are interchanged by interested members of the Group.

Loan Administration

One important aspect of co-ordination which is receiving increasing attention from the Group is the delegation to one or the other of its members of most of the tasks involved in loan administration of jointly-financed projects. The delegated powers include approval of contracts, checking disbursement applications and, at times, opening letters of credit and actual disbursement on behalf of the co-operating sister institutions.

This relationship between the loan administrator and the co-financiers is now regularised by a standard loan administration letter exchanged between co-financiers. This document has been agreed upon by all members of the group and, because of its obvious advantages, the procedure has been welcome to borrowers, contractors, consultants and the banking community.

Exchange of Operational Experience

The regular meetings of the Co-ordination Group are an important forum for the exchange of technical experience gained by the member institutions. Invariably, meetings include a discussion of one or more issues of an operational nature, the discussion often being supported by specially prepared working papers. Examples of the issues discussed and documented by technical reports during the past few years are:

a. The contracting industries in the recipient countries: their problems and the duty of the lending agencies in solving them.
b. Approaches to supporting agricultural projects.

c. Approaches to supporting the National Development Banks.
d. Cost overrun in jointly-financed projects.
e. Exchange rate fluctuations on commitments guaranteed by letters of credit.
f. The letter of credit for jointly-financed projects.
g. The case for small and medium-sized projects.
h. Performance bonds and insurance policies for jointly-financed projects.

Loan Reporting

Since 1977, the Co-ordination Secretariat has been publishing a quarterly *Summary of Loans and Technical Assistance Granted to Developing Countries* by members of the Group. This has undergone several changes to make it more comprehensive and informative. It is now widely distributed all over the world. An annual report comprising a summary of the four quarterly reports is also prepared and distributed in the same manner. The Secretariat has recently completed a comprehensive report on all operations undertaken by members of the Group since the start of business until the end of 1981, and it is being updated to the end of 1982. An English summary has been issued which is available to all concerned with aid to developing countries.

Co-ordination with Non-Arab Groups

The first co-ordination meeting with a non-Arab group took place in 1978 with the DAC Secretariat and members of the OECD. Because of the positive results which were satisfactory to both Groups (Arab-OPEC and DAC Members), it was agreed to continue such meetings on an annual basis. So far there have been five meetings, attended by all aid agencies in the OECD as well as in the Arab-OPEC countries. The sixth Meeting was scheduled for June 1983.

Co-ordination between the Arab Group and the EEC (the European Development Fund and the European Development Bank) started in 1980; the fourth of such meetings again was held in June 1983. Parallel to these annual meetings which examine both policy and operational matters, there has been a number of technical meetings on procedures.

Bi-lateral co-ordination between individual members of the Arab Group and the World Bank has existed for a long time to the satisfaction of all concerned. It is, however, planned to have a joint co-ordination meeting between the Arab and World Bank Groups this year. It is envisaged that this meeting will focus primarily on issues of global interest, such as strategies, procedures and practical operational problems which arise during the project cycle. The Secretariat is at present working with the World Bank on an agenda and other organisational matters.

The move towards a common approach in processing and following up the lending operations of members of the Co-ordination Group has, undoubtedly, met with success. This has been possible through the convergence of certain features that characterise the structure and mode of operation of the network of Arab development finance agencies. Among the more evident contributing elements are:

a. The Arab aid institutions have not been hampered in their common development efforts by any political, historical or self-serving economic considerations. The relief from such considerations provided, on the other hand, the basic elements of success in the co-ordination mechanism.
b. The co-ordination effort has consistently received the support and blessing of the top management of the Co-ordination Group. Indeed, many of the more ambitious objectives have been suggested by the Heads of Organisations themselves.
c. Some Board members of the regional organisations, e.g., the Arab Fund, BADEA and the OPEC Fund, are drawn from national sister agencies. This linkage has been immensely valuable in bridging differences in the approaches of Co-ordination Group members.
d. The 'recommendations' of the Group are not mandatory. Paradoxically, this has led to a speedier arrival at a consensus and greater readiness to accept recommendations.
e. Being operation-oriented, the serving members of the Group have the advantage of similar experience which is conducive to narrowing divergence in their outlook or approaches.
f. The funding agencies in the Co-ordination Group are relatively small and decision-making within them takes shorter routes. They are, thus, more flexible and readier to make such adjustments as circumstances may dictate.

The above is not intended to convey the impression that the Arab Co-ordination Group has resolved all problems of joint action or that it has attained perfection. We are still learning and evolving in the full knowledge that we have to continue in this direction for a long time to come. There are also new avenues that we have only lately started to explore. Foremost among these is parallel co-ordination with sister non-Arab organisations. Our growing contacts with them have not revealed any divergence in basic orientation and approach that goodwill and commonsense cannot overcome. We are confident that the objective of the fullest co-operation between all the organisations active in the area of development is not beyond reach.

Table 7.1: Co-ordination Secretariat between Arab National and Regional Development Financing Institutions: Members of the Co-ordination Group

1. Abu Dhabi Fund for Arab Economic Development
   PO Box No. 814, Abu Dhabi, UAE, Telex: 22287-AH
2. Iraqi Fund for External Development
   PO Box No. 2257, Baghdad, Iraq, Telex: 2651 IFED-IK
3. Kuwait Fund for Arab Economic Development
   PO Box No. 2921, Safat, Kuwait, Telex: 22025 ALSUNDUK-KT
4. Libyan Arab Foreign Investment Co.,
   PO Box No. 4538, Tripoli, Libya, Telex: 20598 NIC-LY
5. Saudi Fund for Development
   PO Box No. 1887, Riyadh, Saudi Arabia, Telex: 201145 SUNDOQ-SJ
6. Representative of Qatar
   Office of HE the Minister of Finance and Petroleum
   PO Box No. 2233, Doha, Qatar, Telex: 4233 QATFIN-DH
7. Arab Bank for Economic Development in Africa
   PO Box No. 2640, Khartoum, Sudan, Telex: 22248 BADEA-KM
8. Arab Fund for Economic and Social Development
   PO Box No. 21923, Safat, Kuwait, Telex: 22153, 22143 INMARABI-KT
9. Islamic Development Bank
   PO Box No. 5925, Jeddah, Saudi Arabia, Telex: 401137 BISLAM-SJ
10. OPEC Fund for International Development
    PO Box No. 995, 1090 Vienna, Austria, Telex: 131734 FUND-A

The Co-ordination Secretariat
Dr Mahmoud El-Helw, Deputy Director, Operations Department and Honorary Secretary,
Arab Fund for Economic and Social Development,
PO Box No. 21923, Safat, Kuwait, Telex: 22153, 22143.

Table 7.2: Co-ordination Secretariat Between Arab National and Regional Development Financing Institutions: Meetings of Co-ordination Group

Sequence	Date	Location	Host
	At the Director of Operations Level		
1st Meeting	20/9/1975	Kuwait	Kuwait Fund
2nd Meeting	10–12/1/1976	Abu Dhabi	Abu Dhabi Fund
3rd Meeting	5–6/6/1976	Riyadh	Saudi Fund
4th Meeting	13–16/2/1977	Khartoum	BADEA
5th Meeting	1–3/11/1977	Kuwait	Arab Fund
6th Meeting	5–7/6/1978	Taif	Islamic Development Bank
7th Meeting	10–12/1/1979	Khartoum	BADEA
8th Meeting	9–10/6/1979	Kuwait	Kuwait Fund
9th Meeting	15–16/12/1979	Abu Dhabi	Abu Dhabi Fund
10th Meeting	15–16/6/1980	Riyadh	Saudi Fund
11th Meeting	12–13/11/1980	Kuwait	Kuwait Fund
12th Meeting	8–10/6/1981	Vienna	OPEC Fund
13th Meeting	12–15/12/1981	Kuwait	Arab Fund
14th Meeting	5–6/6/1982	Jeddah	Islamic Development Bank
15th Meeting	14–17/12/1982	Khartoum	BADEA
16th Meeting	28–30/5/1983	Abu Dhabi	Abu Dhabi Fund
	At the Director-General/President Level		
1st Meeting	5/6/1976	Riyadh	Saudi Fund
2nd Meeting	13/4/1977	Kuwait	Kuwait Fund
3rd Meeting	16/4/1980	Doha, Qatar	Arab Fund
4th Meeting	15/11/1980	Kuwait	Kuwait Fund
5th Meeting	27/4/1983	Jeddah	Islamic Development Bank
OECD			
1st Meeting	June 1978	Paris	OECD
2nd Meeting	June 1979	Paris	OECD
3rd Meeting	June 1980	Paris	OECD
4th Meeting	June 1981	Paris	OECD
5th Meeting	June 1982	Paris	OECD
6th Meeting	June 1983	Vienna	OPEC Fund
EEC			
1st Meeting	June 1980	Brussels	EEC
2nd Meeting	June 1981	Brussels	EEC
3rd Meeting	June 1982	Brussels	EEC
4th Meeting	June 1983	Brussels	EEC
IBRD			
1st Meeting	1983		

Table 7.3: Co-ordination Secretariat Between Arab National and Regional Development Financing Institutions: Basic Data on Members of the Co-ordination Group

		US$ Million		
		Capital		
Institution	Date of Commencement of Operations	Authorised	Paid-up and Reserves	Total Loans (Signed)
A. National Funds				
Kuwait Fund	1963	7,000	3,904	3,866
Abu Dhabi Fund	1973	1,089	693	1,004
Saudi Fund	1975	7,289	6,273	3,786
Iraqi Fund	1978	924	616	1,733*
Libyan Arab For. Bk	1973			
Libyan Arab Inv.	1981	1,685	807	na
		17,987	12,293	10,389
B. Multi-lateral				
Arab Fund	1974	2,800	1,702	1,566
BADEA	1975	738	944	795**
Islamic Devl. Bank	1975	2,146	1,296	2,459
OPEC Fund	1975	4,000	2,074	1,629
		9,684	6,016	6,449
Total		27,671	18,309	16,838

* Includes some operations on behalf of the government (bi-lateral loans)
** Includes loans granted by the old Arab Special Fund for Africa

8 ARAB AND THIRD-WORLD RELATIONS: GENESIS OF SOUTH-SOUTH CO-OPERATION AND SOLIDARITY

Hamid Chabar

First of all, two points must be made clear:

1. The Arab world is not an economic power. Evaluated in terms of certain socio-economic indicators used by the World Bank and other international institutions, this power should be qualified. The aggregate GNP of all the states in the Arab League is inferior to that of most industrialised countries taken separately. OPEC's GNP is very slightly higher than that of a country like Holland.[1]
2. Among Arab countries, the majority (16/22) are confronted with chronic social and economic underdevelopment problems. In some cases, their very survival is due to the financial assistance resulting from the oil manna (political humours permitting).

Since 1973 Arab members of OPEC have undertaken a huge effort in co-operation and development aid not only in favour of Arab countries but also in favour of the Third World as a whole. Since the 1973 adjustments to oil prices, their commitment to the Third World has become a real factor in international economic relations.

This chapter is divided into two parts. The first presents the Arab world today, with its contradictions, obstacles and all its existing differences. Does it have any new advantages today? Will they be mastered? Are the conditions right? How will it have to develop tomorrow? It is only through self-centered development in the context of South-South regional co-operation that one can arrive at advantageous possibilities: development based on a redefinition of needs and priorities, and founded on a different axis of solidarity. In this spirit, the second part of the chapter examines Arab OPEC members' financial commitments in favour of developing countries. These now cover the whole of the Third World and have put OPEC second only to the CAD countries as aid contributors. Aid is channelled through a multitude of bi-lateral and multi-lateral institutions, most of which have come with into existence in the 1970s.

I do not pretend to give a detailed analysis of this whole problem area, which has only recently attracted the interest of university circles. Nonetheless I would like to contribute to a clarification of the new forms of solidarity that must be put in place and which, though still only embryonic, carry the hopes of a new type of co-operation between developing countries in an international context that is marked by the increasing North-South divide.

The Different Situations in Arab countries, Economic Dissemination and Integration into the World Capitalist System

By the Arab World we mean the group of 22 'state' entities which make up the members of the Arab League. Covering the vast geographical area of 13.7 million km^2, i.e., 10 per cent of the earth's surface, this zone is made up of 168 million inhabitants (4.2 per cent of the world's population) spread in very unequal proportions between different countries.

Yet, while representing a vast geographical area, important human potential and an undeniable historical cultural and socio-demographic unity, the Arab World is a long way from representing a single economic power, and is even further from being a political one. Since gaining their independence, the Arab states have all evolved separately, more often than not with their backs turned on one another, with the result that they have privileged vertical links to the detriment of horizontal ones. Precedent has been given to developing a confined nationalism that emphasises local particularities over and above the projects of solidarity, often inflationary, that have punctuated the leaders' declarations. We are thus confronted with countries of differing size and importance that are isolated, divided and integrated into the world capitalist system on a one-to-one basis.[2] The entire areas is characterised by a sickening state of economic and social underdevelopment. One should therefore be wary of attributing to it the great economic power that has become the fashionable view since the 1973 oil price increases.[3] When one looks carefully at the Arab region, one is struck by the disparity between the various component parts. Four sub-groups can be distinguished:

1. *The Gulf States and Libya:* In this group, oil is the principal

industry and dictates the orientations and realities of the producing state's political and social life. These countries account for only 10 per cent of the entire Arab population, while possessing 55 per cent of its GDP. Agriculture remains undeveloped and accounts for only 1–3 per cent of GNP according to country. For example, in Saudi Arabia where the agricultural sector employs 60 per cent of the working population, it only generates 2 per cent of GNP. Only Libya has undertaken a serious effort to modernise agriculture and aims at reaching food self-sufficiency in 1985.

2. *Iraq and Algeria:* Semi-populated and semi-oil producing countries, in these countries all financial surpluses are ploughed back into ambitious industrialisation projects, to the detriment of agriculture in the case of Algeria.
3. *Morocco, Tunisia, Jordan, Egypt and Syria:* Populated non-oil producing countries, this group accounts for 51 per cent of the population. The economic structures of this group vary enormously. Agriculture contributes 23 per cent to this group's GDP and accounts for some 56 per cent of overall agricultural production in the area.
4. *Mauritania, Sudan, the two Yemens, Somalia and Djibouti:* In these less advanced countries the average per capita income does not exceed $300, and this is essentially generated through agriculture which employs an overwhelming majority of the workforce. Industrial development in these countries is next to nothing.[4]

Examining certain economic fundamentals of the Arab world, one can extract a few features that are common to all the countries concerned, despite the differences in individual situations:

1. The agricultural sector provides employment to an important percentage of the working population, between 35 per cent and 80 per cent according to country, with the exception of Kuwait and Libya.
2. An increasingly important part of the economy (between 30 per cent and 80 per cent according to country) is taken up by service industries.
3. A private consumption/GNP ratio which oscillates between 61 and 83 except in the case of those countries where there is great imbalance between oil revenues and absorption capacity (the

Gulf States and Libya, and where the ratio is around 40, which remains all the same noteworthy).

4. There are serious disparities between the countries of the area, and they seem likely to increase. The Gulf States, Libya, Algeria and Iraq provide 90 per cent of total Arab exports while representing only 30 per cent of the population, and the remaining countries, that is 70 per cent of the Arab world's population, only provide 10 per cent of export volume and are always in chronic deficit in their balance of payments schedule with trading partners.

Per capita GNP in the oil producing countries is at the top of the pyramid with a record $15,000 in certain countries, while the base of the pyramid regroups the majority of countries where there is great poverty compounded by a very high birth-rate. The average increase in GNP which is often held up as an example hides a number of differences: performance is a great deal less spectacular when one discovers that it is essentially due to the increase in oil output.[5] This in turn has engendered capital surpluses among the beneficiaries, i.e., the developed Western nations. So the present Arab context is in fact marked by an economic underdevelopment which can be summarised in three words: integration, subordination, and disarticulation:

1. *Vertical integration of the Arab economies in the world capitalist system and active absorption in the international division of labour:* For Samir Amin, this absorption is measured in terms of the equation between exports and imports related to GNP.[6] This ratio is 60 per cent for the Arab world, 22 per cent for sub-Saharan Africa and 13 per cent for Latin America. The Arab world is the region most integrated into the international division of labour.
2. *The predominance of oil in the region's exports:* Only a small share of the GDP comes from industry, meaning food dependence for the ovewhelming majority of countries concerned.
3. *Unsatisfactory distribution of resources and production facilities so that no one country really disposes of the elements needed for its development, resulting in structural disarticulation:* One thinks of Egypt, Sudan, Morocco where the manpower exists but not the capital resources. In the Gulf States and Libya, however, there are enormous financial resources

> but no labour force. This partial possession of the elements necessary for each country's development has resulted in a structural disarticulation which impedes the achievement of complementarity between sectors, or any coherence in production factors.

Arab economies are becoming primary, disjointed and marginally industrialised ones. Imports consist mainly of manufactured goods, followed by food products. 1981 figures show agricultural product deficits in the overwhelming majority of Arab countries whereas in 1973, three countries showed trade surpluses (Egypt of $40.578 million, Syria $4.23 million and Morocco $5.574 million).

The Need for Regional Integration: Targets for Tomorrow

My conclusion is that, as things at present stand, Arab countries cannot hope to attain economic and social development on an individual basis. The main obstacle is the fact that they are splintered into isolated groups. Regional integration is not just a necessity, it is a question of survival. Integration should not be simply limited to trade liberalisation, nor to a customs treaty such as the Maghreb countries have already unsuccessfully tried.[7] The lack of success is not particular to Arab countries, for other developing countries have also been through the same bitter experience. Hence the need to investigate and move in other directions. Not only for the Arab world but for other Third World countries too, the first step must necessarily be a profound reassessment of their development policies and then a restructuring of production structures.

The objectives must be defined in terms of their polarity:

1. Attainment of Food Self-sufficiency

The present situation is disastrous. Nearly all Arab countries have to import agricultural products from the OECD to feed themselves. These imports cost Saudi Arabia $4 billion in 1981, the United Arab Emirates where the total population is less than 800,000 people, $3.2 billion. Self-sufficiency ratios have fallen in the case of the principal products: cereals: 55 per cent; wheat: 37 per cent; sugar: 23 per cent.

Table 8.1: Agricultural State of Balance in Arab States, 1981 ($ billion)

Morocco	−0.40	Lebanon	−0.47
Algeria	−2.05	Syria	−1.49
Mauritania	−0.03	Iraq	−1.74
Tunisia	−0.37	Kuwait	−0.89
Libya	−1.17	Saudi Arabia	−4.36
Egypt	+0.185	UAE	−3.20
Sudan	+0.11	Qatar	−0.69
Somalia	+0.04	Bahrain	− −
Djibouti	−0.125	North Yemen	−0.39
Jordan	−0.40	South Yemen	−0.21
		Oman	− −

Note: The statistics showing deficits have been double-checked and we have only retained figures that appear in more than one source

In a general manner, trade balance of agricultural and food products show a growing extenal dependence and per capita deficit. Indeed, the aggregate agri-food balance in Arab countries has worsened considerably: 101 per cent in 1961–5; 81 per cent in 1970–2; 20 per cent in 1978–80. In almost all countries agri-food imports have increased much faster than exports.

Whereas in the 1961–5 period eight countries had a balance of trade surplus, in the 1978–80 period, with the exception of Somalia and the Sudan, all countries were net importers of agricultural products and twelve countries showed a coverage ratio of under 10 per cent. As to the per capita deficit, it has moved from $0.2 dollars to $3.4 to reach $74 in the last period under discussion. Yet self-sufficiency is possible, particularily when one takes into account the extraordinary agricultural potential of the area. What progress, for instance, has been made with the project to redevelop Sudanese land potential? On its own, this country could satisfy the entire area's needs.[8]

2. Mobilisation of Human and Financial Resources

This is necessary to build a solidary regional environment that can answer the basic needs of a population that will double by the year 2000. Taking an average annual population growth of 3 per cent (Arab world average), we are looking at a population of 300 million souls. Integration is not a luxury, it is a matter of survival.

3. Promotion of Democratic Ideals

This will allow the masses to participate in the economic and political management of their countries instead of being kept so decidedly

Table 8.2: Arab Countries According to their Agri-Food Balance of Trade Deficits

	1961–5		1970–2		1978–80	
Balance	No. of Countries	% of Population in Arab Countries	No. of Countries	% of Population in Arab Countries	No. of Countries	% of Arab Countries
100 b	8	75.2	6	59.6	2	13.6
10 b 100	7	18.7	9	32.7	7	52.3
b 10	6	6.1	6	7.7	12	33.6
Total	21	100	21	100	21	100

Source: Institut Agronomique Méditerranéen de Montpellier, 'Agri-food Development in Arab Countries and their Relations with Europe', Lecture given at the Euro-Arab Discussion Forum, *Analysis and Prospects*, held in Louvain-la -Neuve, Belgium, 2–4 December 1983. The forum's reports are available from CERMAC, 3 Place Montesquieu, B–1348 Louvain-la-Neuve, Belgium.

aside. Each political regime swans in a feeling of self-admiration, considering that it holds the absolute truth outside which there is no salvation. What of individual freedom and the rights of man? Political regimes that are maintained through sometimes bloodthirsty repressions and permanent violation of the most elementary freedoms can in no way contribute to the emergence of a responsible society capable of controlling its destiny. I am convinced that the economic integration of Arab countries, some of which benefit from important financial surpluses, will contribute not only to the achievement of the aims already discussed but will also turn the Arab world into a new reality which will be a model for other developing countries. Prospective studies show us that mini-states have no future. The majority of Third World countries can have little or no hope of solving their problems within the confines of narrow territorial frameworks. It is large aggregates and regional groupings that hold the future. To be able to confront the large open entities of the USA, USSR, China, EEC, Comecom or AELE, which dictate the international economy and impose their rules of the game,[9] is essential.

Next to these large economic realities, Third World countries are fragmented; dominated and without resources. Their place in the present world economy is marginal and subject to the international division of labour which works to their disadvantage and only increases their dependence. The two Development Decades have put an end to any illusions one could have harboured with regard to their economic take-off. This is why serious consideration is now being given to the advantages of encouraging economic harmonisation of developing countries and South-South co-operation in the hope of establishing, in the long run, a New International Economic Order. The Arab world would appear to have the financial means to contribute to the development of the Southern countries. Are they prepared to do so? What exactly is the position regarding these flows of aid? This is what I shall now examine.

International Co-operation and the Third World

The Role of the Arab Oil Producing Countries

The resounding failure of the two so-called Development Decades (1960–70 and 1970–80) besides sweeping aside any illusions still left concerning a possible take-off of Third World countries, also marks the failure of North-South co-operation. Third World resentment has many foundations:

a. The relatively low volume of net aid (considering need);
b. The corollary constraints of this aid;
c. The pressures, manipulations and blackmail imposed by the donors;
d. The Diktat of international organisations (World Bank, IMF etc.);
e. The accompanying character of the aid;
f. A current account deficit which is increasingly alarming, having moved from \$11.5 billion in 1973 to \$97.5 billion in 1981 (see Table 8.6)
g. The staggering debt, estimated at \$600 billion at the end of 1982, of which half concerns Latin American countries, where there are many loans given to certain countries to finance the repayment of interest on previous loans (see Table 8.5).

Impact on the Third World of the Oil Price Hikes: Taking the Myth out of the Problem

An unfortunately common idea is that all the problems of developing countries stem from the huge hike in oil prices and its negative impact on the world economy as a whole. It is certainly true that the oil bill (readjusted in 1973 and 1979) has contributed to Third World oil importers' current deficits; but other elements that are usually left unmentioned have worsened the situation in a much more significant way. For example:

a. The price increase of OECD-sourced manufactured goods.
b. The worsening terms of trade with developing countries coupled with the slow growth of the industrial nations.
c. High interest rates prevalent internationally and the accompanying balance of trade deficit stemming from the repayment to industrialised countries of non-concessional loans, and the servicing of those loans.

It is all these factors together which have aggravated the balance of payment deficit of developing countries. (See Table 8.4 taken from A. Sid Ahmed's work).

A. Sid Ahmed notes that the impact of the oil price hike becomes negligible from 1975 onwards; oil only represents $1.9 billion out of a total $12.9 billion excess deficit from 1974–5, while manufactured goods count for $11.8 billion in the same period, i.e. 91 per cent of the deficit's increase. He goes on to ask how, in 1978, the year of the oil freeze, non-oil-producing developing countries reached a deficit that the WMF estimates at more than $40 billion? (See Table 8.6).

This is why the worsening of the situation in other developing countries cannot be apportioned solely to the oil producers. OPEC members' financial commitments to Third World countries should not be considered as the retribution to atone for harm caused by the former to the latter. In the present state of developing countries, it is the dominating relations between a united and powerful centre and a fragmented and weak periphery that constitute the root of the problem. So that the option to work towards South-South co-operation and solidarity must be understood as a step towards the reversal of these dominating relations which are the greatest barrier to an economic take-off of the Third World.

The Weight of OPEC

Today, everyone recognises the catalysing role of OPEC in the Third World's struggle to revise the value of its raw materials and to reverse, or at any rate attenuate, the characteristically dominant nature of North-South relations as they have been practised since the

Second World War. We are in fact speaking of putting an end to one of the hallmarks of the present world economic order, which is the unequal distribution of profits generated by international trade. The worsening of trade terms which has continued over the past three decades has resulted in a transfer of wealth from developing countries to the Northern industrial ones. OPEC's action will show the way for other Third World countries to become aware of their potential *vis-à-vis* this dominated relationship, but only on the condition that they unite. This is why OPEC's fight is to be seen in a global context: the struggle of the Third World to obtain revalued prices for its raw materials and to arrive at a New International Economic Order. As A. Sid Ahmed has emphasised, the effort of OPEC members to obtain a revised valuation of their wealth is one and the same as other developing countries' struggle.[10]

OPEC members' intense activity and intransigeance at meetings of the UN and other international institutions are the proof of the oil producers' intention to globalise North-South issues. The early 1960s marked the start of South-South solidarity actually evolving beyond the discussion stage. The result, as I shall examine later, has been some concrete and sincere acts on the part of the Arab oil producing countries for the benefit of other developing countries. It is in this context that one should consider Arab OPEC members' aid to developing countries. The 1973 OPEC resolution XXXIV noted:

> The economic conditions prevalent in most developing countries as a result of their lack of access to industrial nations' technology and markets are a limiting factor for OPEC and Third World nations' development. This resolution serves only to register the OPEC countries' exhortation to reinforce co-operation between and with other developing countries whose efforts are compromised for lack of funds.[11]

The extraordinary speed with which numerous bi-lateral and multi-lateral institutes have been created[12] is a further proof of the unfailing desire to help countries in need.

Arab Development Funds and Banks

In the main we are concerned with Arab institutions[13] as the other oil producing countries such as Venezuela and Nigeria are more concerned with their own geographical area.

The Kuwait Fund for Arab Economic Development (KFAED)

Created in December 1961 with a capital of $3.4 billion (March 1974), the Fund lends over periods between 10 and 35 years at interest rates of 2.5 to 4 per cent, or even with no interest on very long-term loans (50 years) that carry a 0.5 per cent service charge. The release clause varies from 30 to 85 per cent. Limited to Arab countries in the beginning, the Fund extended its activities to non-Arab countries from 1974.

The Abu Dhabi Arab Economic Fund

Created in 1971 with a capital of $126 million, then increased to $500 million in 1974, this dealt only with Arab countries until 1975, but now arranges loans to African and Asian countries. Limited to 10 per cent of the capital and never financing more than 50 per cent of a given project, the loans vary from 10 to 25 years with a grace period of 3 to 5 years and carry interest rates varying from 3.5 to 5.5 per cent.

The Saudi Development Fund

Created in 1974 with a capital of $845 million, later increased to $2.8 billion, the Fund arranges Saudi Riyal loans to Arab and non-Arab countries, particularily for agricultural and infrastructural projects. Limited to 5 per cent of the capital and not exceeding 50 per cent of the project's total cost, the loans carry a usual interest rate of 4 per cent. Recently the Fund has toughened loan conditions with the release element being raised from 74 to 92 per cent.

Iraqi External Development Fund (IEDF)

Created in 1974 with a capital of $170 million, increased to $340 million in 1979, this Fund finances long-term loans for Arab and non-Arab development plans, and provides pre-investment studies and technical aid.

Arab Fund for Economic and Social Development (AFESD)

This Fund was created after the Khartoum Summit of 1968. Starting with a capital that was increased from $347 million to $1.36 billion, it established its headquarters in Kuwait. It finances 15 to 25 year loans with deferment periods of between 4 and 6 years carrying interest rates of 4 to 6 per cent. The loans are granted to Arab League countries only.

Special OPEC Account

Created in 1974 with a capital of $80 million and managed by the AFESD, this account is designed to aid non-oil producing Arab countries. In 1975, all member states except Iraq decided to reconstitute the account, which serves mainly for balance of payment problems.

Islamic Development Bank (IDB)

Created in Riyadh in 1974 with 24 members, by the end of 1979 there were 35 members. The initial capital was fixed at $2.4 billion, and the Bank loans carry no interest but only a service commission. By the end of 1978, facilities and loans for a total of $492.7 millions had been granted. At that time, the principal activities were loans (18), equity stakes (15), leasings (2), export finance (21), technical assistance projects (8).

Arab Bank for Economic Development of Africa (BADEA)

Positioned as the privileged organisation for Arab-African co-operation, this bank was founded in 1973 at the Arab Summit in Algiers. It became operative in January 1975 and now has a capital of $738 million. The Bank's objective is to reinforce economic, financial and technical co-operation between Arab and African states. With long-term loans for economic development and incentives to Arab Funds to participate in economic development projects, the BADEA lends only to non-Arab League countries in Africa.

Special Arab Fund for Africa (SAFA)

This Fund was created in January 1974 in Cairo by the OPEC oil ministers and the OAU's Oil Committee, with a capital of $200 million. On 20 March 1976, the Arab League placed this Fund under the administration of the BADEA.

Arab-African Technical Assistance Fund (AATAF)

Decided on in 1973 by the Arab League Economic Council, this Fund for the exchange of technical assitance became operative in August 1975. A total of $7 million has been committed to ten countries, nine of which are African.

Special OPEC Fund

Aimed at providing technical assistance to its own members and other developing countries, the Fund was ratified by all OPEC member states in early 1976. The resources committed were fixed at first at $800 million, and augmented in early 1980 to $2.4 billion. In fact, in January 1980 the Fund was transformed into an International Development Agency.

Arab Aid to the Third World: Some Characteristics

As witnessed by the numerous institutions created since 1973, Arab aid to Third World countries has been spectacular since that year. One can sum up the effort in two elements: on the one hand, the number of these organisations, and on the other, the sums distributed annually by the oil producing countries (see Table 8.7). Only among these countries is the UN-backed objective of 1 per cent of GNP for development aid far exceeded. The proportion is 4.28 per cent for the Gulf States, 1.08 per cent for Iraq, Algeria and Libya in 1980. By comparison, the ration is 0.38 per cent for CAD countries and 0.15 per cent for the CAEM countries in the same year (see Table 8.8). The volume of development aid fell in 1981 when it reached $25.6 billion against $27.3 billion in 1980, a fall of 7 per cent. Of the total volume of $25.6 billion, OPEC countries accounted for a total of $7.8 billion, of which OAPEC countries represented $7.6 billion (see Table 8.8). Thus some 30 per cent of world development aid originates from donors other than CAD members, mostly from oil producing Arab countries, and to a lesser extent CAEM countries. Saudi Arabia alone provided 75 per cent of the total OPEC contribution in 1981. According to the OECD, that country contributed $353 million to multi-lateral organisations and $5.445 million to bi-lateral aid in the same year. Four (Arab) OPEC countries contributed over 90 per cent of 1981 OPEC aid as against 80 per cent in 1980.

Characteristics of Arab Aid

Arab aid is not suspensive to any clauses for the simple reason that the Arab world has no technology to sell. The aid serves to finance the beneficiary countries' purchases from industrialised countries. So that, by extension, Arab aid benefits Western countries who have the technology to sell. The lack of return from this aid constitutes a very real loss for the donor countries.

Arab aid is granted under liberal conditions, that is to say with an inbuilt share of at least 25 per cent gift equivalent (see table 8.9).

This aid comes from oil producers that are part of the Arab entity. The majority of member countries suffer from chronic economic and social underdevelopment and have great capital needs, thus emphasising the element of sacrifice involved. One must not forget that the Arab states have their own problems which have a logical priority, if only because it is not in the Third World countries' interest to arrive at the situation twenty years hence, when the oil reserves are exhausted, where the oil-producing countries will be paralysed. Even if only partially substituting CAD countries' contribution, Arab aid can enable Third World countries to break away from the vertical links that are both imperialist and customer-orientated, while continuing to develop:

> This presupposes that aid to developing countries will be quite distinct from international aid to date which is trapped in Western models of development. Failing this, the result will be the same incapacity to develop anything other than monetary profits for private investors. Failing this, those with the technological power will continue to retain the power to direct the accumulation of profit towards the centre to the detriment of the periphery. Indeed, it is in this sense that Europe can back up the idea of trilateral co-operation (Arab World, Europe, Africa).[14]

Towards a Collective Autonomy of the South

Implicit in Third World countries' desired independence from the world capitalist market is their determined intention to utilise their natural, human and financial resources to attain freedom. It is a question of survival. Urgently, these countries must develop their agriculture where, given the right courage and determination, not only could they become self-sufficient but could even generate export potential in foodstuffs. An industrialisation programme should be envisaged which takes into account, not international objectives, but rather those that are dictated by and designed in accordance with local consumer needs. Collective autonomy of the South is not simply a means of moving from state X to state Y (considered better), but also a means of reinforcing what is termed 'bargaining power' *vis-à-vis* the North. It is in these terms that one should place attempts at co-operation and solidarity which are beginning to emerge as a pattern linking developing countries. This is why Southern countries have to define their priorities in the framework of collective and national development and to act together in order to sway the world system in the direction of a better adaptation to the South's development needs.

Regional programmes (Arab region, sub-Saharan Africa, etc.) must be drawn up in the mould outlined above. The whole problem is to know whether South-South co-operation, now in its infancy and sometimes held back by the negative behaviour of its protagonists, can in the long run form the foundation of a Third World capacity to assume its own destiny. Is this not the right moment to initiate a strategy of real collective autonomy? The present context, which is marked by a deep crisis in the North, and the emergence of certain Southern countries (OPEC, newly-industrialised countries) is perhaps the ideal spring-board for systematic and joint actions by the developing countries.

Notes

1. B. Khader, 'Arab Funds in Africa', lecture given at the Amman Conference, December 1982.
2. S. Amin, 'Contemporary Arab Economy', various documents (Editions Minuit, 1980) p. 2.
3. One must distinguish between wealth (financial) and development (economic power), as the first does not necessarily imply the second.
4. We have taken this classification both from S. Amin and also from F. Oulalou, 'Monde Arabe CEE, globalisme ou différentiation', paper given at Rabat Conference, April 1981.
5. Taking the period 1968–74, this annual rate of increase was 84.12 per cent for Saudi Arabia.
6. S. Amin, p. 18.
7. H. Chabar, 'Attempts at Integration in the Arab World: the Maghreb Experiment', *Cermac* (June 1980) Louvain-la-Neuve, Belgium.
8. A. Brahimi, 'Dimensions and Prospects of the Arab World', *Economica* (1977) p. 258.
9. M. El Mandjara, 'Horizon 2000 et dans 20 ans?', *Jeune Afrique*, special no, (January 1982).
10. A. Sid Ahmed, 'OPEC, Past, Present and to Come', *Economica* (1980) p. 367.
11. Quoted by A. Sid Ahmed, p. 368.
12. By these we understand institutes that have been created and financed by Arab countries.
13. We have taken the list established by X. Authie, 'L'aide des pays arabes à l'Afrique noire', *Afrique contemporaine*, no. 110 (July 1980).
14. B. Duhamel, *La Coopération Trilatérale* (Editions le Sycomore, Paris, 1982).

Table 8.3: Cereal Production and Deficit in Arab Countries

Country	Cereals				Wheat				Barley				Rice				Other Cereals			
	1961–5		1975–9		1961–5		1975–9		1961–5		1975–9		1961–5		1975–9		1961–5		1975–9	
	Prod.	Deficit	Prod.	Deficit	Prod.	Deficit	Prod.	Deficit	Prod.	Deficit	Prod.	Deficit	Prod.	Deficit	Prod.	Deficit	Prod.	Deficit	Prod.	Deficit
Algeria	1,771,067	310,830	1,623,741	2,220,155	1,254,017	361,024	1,147,966	1,879,645	475,673	54,433	403,189	199,264	6,943	2,000	1,116	11,455	34,434	2,239	71,470	129,791
Morocco	3,582,566	217,421	4,230,076	1,439,784	1,516,400	290,110	1,744,762	1,377,854	1,513,700	10,983	2,002,400	29,439	19,600	2,884	22,994	8	532,866	80,788	459,320	32,483
Tunisia	692,589	195,081	1,021,340	612,588	495,134	146,388	763,000	467,380	144,898	37,831	230,020	43,956	0	2,280	0	2,085	52,557	8,582	28,320	99,167
Libya	126,318	145,759	272,104	638,024	36,521	126,901	75,587	520,232	87,076	9,315	194,308	62,338	0	9,264	0	40,534	2,721	279	2,209	14,920
Egypt	6,076,155	1,669,339	8,129,971	4,814,188	1,458,781	1,766,577	1,896,400	4,431,220	137,070	220	121,945	600	1,844,800	326,998	2,371,296	155,673	2,635,504	229,980	3,738,330	539,041
Jordan	251,181	187,571	62,418	387,796	179,703	143,132	49,492	255,052	62,472	11,156	11,433	30,016	0	22,297	0	25,147	9,006	10,986	1,493	77,581
Lebanon	91,490	325,393	61,052	563,816	63,649	229,767	48,000	379,512	12,540	47,900	9,600	56,600	0	17,735	0	17,744	15,301	29,991	3,452	109,960
Syria	1,798,960	235,778	2,203,041	381,775	1,092,952	14,173	1,505,408	296,398	648,714	246,319	623,118	37,490	1,206	29,307	1,359	78,709	56,088	4,593	73,156	44,158
Saudi Arabia	400,094	255,459	285,740	1,162,717	142,980	74,028	129,838	558,899	9,540	32,946	14,657	105,423	2,774	117,078	3,000	271,909	244,800	31,407	138,245	226,486
Iraq	1,853,544	82,675	1,892,942	1,358,183	848,680	150,365	1,048,960	936,570	851,322	116,860	592,660	117,670	141,504	49,720	175,748	244,098	12,038	550	75,574	59,845
Kuwait	0	90,840	28	255,743	0	57,371	0	132,561	0	14,850	25	41,163	0	17,829	0	55,830	0	790	3	26,189
Bahrain	0	–	0	46,804	0	–	0		0		0		0		0		0		0	
Oman	3,103		5,772	104,412	1,504		3,453		25		191		0		0		1,574		2,128	
Qatar	0		0	36,398	0		0		0		0		0		0		0		0	
United Arab Emirates	0		0	200,766	0		0		0		0		0		0		0		0	
North Yemen	1,104,000	5,503	957,600	303,251	20,800	2,303	59,400	294,239	140,800		63,000		0	3,200	0	7,312	942,400		835,200	1,700
South Yemen	69,811	71,710	108,118	144,634	14,780	59,267	23,028	96,630	3,231	92	2,241		0	8,800	0	44,996	51,800	3,551	82,849	3,000
Sudan	1,613,353	28,848	2,864,977	144,438	35,723	113,451	284,840	209,950	378		0		1,209	4,405	10,697	2,459	1,576,013	89,010	2,569,140	67,380
Mauritania	97,709	44,261	39,460	138,207	97	12,504	200	41,344	202		160	130	590	9,760	3,780	35,907	96,820	22,000	35,300	60,826
Somalia	242,500	46,365	229,000	116,460	0	14,962	1,200	46,500	0		0		0	24,159	5,800	34,232	242,500	7,244	222,000	35,720
Arab Countries	19,774,440	3,544,377	23,870,381	15,065,347	7,161,721	3,589,775	8,783,534	12,119,331	4,087,641	251,008	4,268,966	661,860	2,018,626	29,479	2,597,970	882,060	6,506,452	176,131	8,222,091	1,402,096

Source: FAO

Table 8.4: Elements Contributing to Current Account Deficits among Non-Oil Producing Developing Countries, 1974–5 (billion dollars)

	1974	1975	1974–5 %
Current Account Deficits[1]	33.5[2]	45.2	
Increase in Deficit Attributable to:	21.3	11.7	100.0
1. Price Variations[3]	14.3	17.5	96.4
a. Import Price Increases	36.0	12.9	148.2
i. Oil	18.5[4]	1.9	61.8
ii. Food products	3.1	−0.5	7.9
—imports from OECD countries	(1.7)	(−0.3)	(4.2)
—imports from other countries	(1.4)	(−0.2)	(3.5)
iii. Other raw materials	1.8	−0.3	4.5
—imports from OECD countries	(0.9)	(−0.2)	(2.1)
—imports from other countries	(0.9)	(−0.1)	(2.4)
iv. Manufactured Goods	12.6	11.8	73.9
—imports from OECD countries	(10.1)	(9.5)	(59.4)
—imports from other countries	(2.5)	(2.3)	(14.5)
b. Export Price Decreases (Increase = −)	−21.7	4.6	−51.8
i. Exports from OECD countries	15.6	3.3	−37.3
ii. Exports from other countries	−6.1	1.3	−14.5
2. Volume Variations	7.5	−9.8	− 7.0
a. Imports (Decrease = −)	10.2	−8.4	5.5
i. From OECD Countries	12.2	−6.1	18.5
ii. From Other Countries	−2.0	−2.3	−13.0
— including oil	−3.0	−1.0	−12.1
b. Exports (Increase = −)	−2.7	−1.4	−12.4
i. From OECD Countries	−1.9	−1.0	− 8.8
ii. From Other Countries	−0.8	−0.4	− 3.6
3. Other net elements	−0.5	4.0	10.6
a. Increase in payments for services and private transfers	−1.9	1.6	− 0.9
b. Increase in payments for private investment revenue	1.4	2.4	11.5

Source: ENUCED secretariat estimates.
Table reproduced in A. Sid Ahmed, 'OPEC, Past, Present and to Come', *Economica*, 1980.
1. Based on the figures for 113 Developing nations and territories.
2. The corresponding figure for 1973 is $12.2 million.
3. Calculated by applying price changes on preceding years' trade volume.
4. The value of crude oil and of all oil products has been calculated on the 1974 prices. Insofar as oil delivered to developing countries was done so at price levels fixed in 1973, this figure overestimates the price.

Table 8.6: Balance of Payment Current Accounts (Excluding Public Transfers) of Non-Oil Exporting Developing Countries

	1967–72	1973	1974	1975	1976	1977	1978	1979	1980	1981
Deficit										
In billion $	49.9	11.5	37.1	46.5	33.0	28.6	37.5	57.6	82.1	97.5
% Goods and Services Exported	17.0	10.5	21.5	31.0	18.5	13.5	15.5	18.5	22.0	n.a.
% GDP	2.0	2.0	5.0	5.8	3.7	3.0	3.2	4.0	4.8	4.9
Annual Variation (%)										
GDP	5.8	6.3	5.6	4.0	5.4	4.8	5.5	4.9	4.4	5.0
Trade Terms	1.0	6.5	−7.0	−9.0	2.0	6.5	−5.5	−0.5	−3.0	−2.5
GDP of Principal Trading Partners	5.0	6.3	0.3	−1.0	5.4	3.8	4.0	3.5	1.2	1.1
Export Volume	9.3	10.1	1.5	0.3	13.9	3.9	11.2	9.2	7.9	6.8

Non-oil exporting developing countries include WMF member states other than OECD countries (except Greece, Portugal, Turkey) and OPEC countries (except Ecuador and Gabon) and Oman.

Table 8.5: The Twenty Developing Countries with Highest Debt-Servicing Payments

Countries in Order of Average Debt Servicing Payments, 1979–80	Debt Servicing (Payments Made)				Debt at Year End (Amount Paid)			Total Year End Reserves		GNP Rate of Increase	Per Capita GNP
	1978	1979	1980 prelim.	1981 estimated	1978	1979	1980 prelim.	1978	1980	1970–79	1979
	$ M									% p.a.	$
1. Brazil	8.1	10.8	13.4	16.0	44.2	50.6	56.6	11.9	5.9	8.7	1,687
2. Mexico	7.0	11.0	9.0	12.2	30.5	34.5	42.4	1.9	2.9	5.1	1,592
3. Venezuela	1.6	2.8	5.1	6.8	9.7	11.6	13.2	6.6	7.1	5.9	3,135
4. Algeria	2.0	3.3	4.2	4.6	14.7	17.4	17.8	2.2	4.0	5.9	1,578
5. Spain	3.0	3.2	4.1	4.9	13.1	15.0	18.2	10.3	12.5	4.0	4,338
6. Saudi Arabia	1.8	2.9	(3.5)	(4.0)	2.3	3.1	4.0	19.4	23.6	11.4	7,373
7. South Korea	2.0	2.9	3.3	4.0	12.5	15.6	20.5	2.8	2.9	9.9	1,501
8. Yugoslavia	1.8	2.5	2.9	3.5	11.3	13.3	15.0	2.5	1.5	6.5	2,430
9. Argentina	2.2	1.8	2.8	3.6	7.8	11.3	14.0	5.2	6.9	2.7	2,281
10. Indonesia	1.6	2.3	2.3	2.7	14.5	15.6	17.0	2.6	5.5	6.9	376
11. Chile	1.5	1.6	1.9	2.5	5.3	7.1	8.8	1.2	3.2	3.2	1,781
12. Iran	2.4	1.9	(1.4)	(6.5)	10.6	(9.9)	(9.5)	12.1	10.0	6.4	2,028
13. Peru	0.8	1.1	1.9	2.1	6.0	6.8	6.9	0.4	2.0	2.6	726
14. Egypt	1.4	1.2	1.7	2.0	10.3	12.0	12.7	0.6	1.2	7.5	455
15. Philippines	1.3	1.3	1.5	2.0	6.2	7.2	9.5	1.8	2.9	6.3	601
16. Greece	0.9	1.2	1.6	2.0	4.8	5.6	6.5	1.2	1.3	5.1	3,890
17. Taiwan	0.9	0.9	1.3	1.6	3.5	3.9	4.9	1.5	2.4	9.9	1,802
18. India	1.1	1.1	1.1	1.3	15.9	16.6	16.7	6.8	7.3	3.1	191
19. Morocco	0.6	0.9	1.2	1.6	5.4	6.6	7.5	0.7	0.4	6.1	740
20. Thailand	0.8	1.0	1.1	1.4	2.6	3.7	5.6	2.1	1.7	7.4	592
Total	42.8	55.7	65.3	85.3	231.2	267.4	307.3	94.3	105.2		
% of Overall Total for all Developing Countries	76	76	72	76	69	67	67	62	51		

Among countries with only slightly lower debt servicing, one finds Turkey (whose initial debt servicing obligations, over $2 billion in 1980, slightly reduced by alleviation measures), Israel (military debt excluded) Ecuador, Libya and Portugal.

Table 8.7: The Twenty Developing Countries with Highest Debt-Servicing Payments

Countries in Order of Importance of Debt Servicing 1980	Debt Servicing (Payments Made)				Debt at Year-End (Amount Paid)			Total Year-End Reserves		GNP Rate of Increase	Per Capita GNP
	1979	1980	1981 prelim.	1982 estimated	1979	1980	1981 prelim.	1979	1981	1970–80	1980
					$ M					annual %	$
1. Brazil	11.4	13.7	17.3	18.5	50.8	57.0	65.6	9.0	6.7	8.7	2,050
2. Mexico[1]	11.4	9.3	13.4	15.2	37.6	43.5	54.4	2.2	4.2	5.4	2,135
3. Venezuela[2]	2.8	4.7	6.0	7.8	12.3	14.7	14.9	7.8	8.7	4.8	3,631
4. Spain	3.0	3.7	5.0	5.7	16.3	20.7	25.1	13.9	11.4	3.7	5,345
5. Algeria[2]	3.2	3.9	4.4	4.8	17.0	17.2	17.0	2.9	3.9	5.9	1,924
6. Iran[2]	2.0	2.0	(6.1)	(1.6)	10.5	(10.3)	(8.5)	15.4	(3.5)	2.9	1,937
7. Yugoslavia	2.7	3.3	4.2	4.7	13.5	15.1	16.8	1.3	1.7	6.2	2,623
8. Korea	2.9	3.3	4.0	4.8	15.5	17.6	20.8	3.0	2.7	8.1	1,523
9. Argentina	2.1	2.8	3.7	(4.9)	12.6	15.6	20.0	9.6	3.4	2.5	2,395
10. Saudi Arabia[2]	2.9	3.1	3.4	3.9	3.2	3.3	3.5	19.5	32.4	13.6	11,265
11. Chile	1.7	2.2	3.1	3.3	7.1	9.0	12.3	2.0	3.3	3.9	2,160
12. Indonesia[2]	2.2	2.0	2.7	3.4	15.1	16.6	18.2	4.1	5.1	7.0	422
13. Egypt[1]	1.3	1.8	2.2	2.4	12.2	13.8	14.0	0.6	0.8	7.0	582
14. Peru[1]	1.1	1.6	2.0	1.9	6.5	7.1	7.3	1.6	1.3	3.0	935
15. Greece	1.1	1.3	1.7	2.1	5.6	6.9	7.6	1.5	1.2	4.7	4,522
16. Morocco	1.0	1.3	1.5	1.9	6.7	7.3	8.0	0.6	0.3	5.9	864
17. Nigeria[2]	0.8	1.2	1.6	1.9	4.2	5.5	6.0	5.6	3.9	7.3	1,009
18. India	1.1	1.4	1.4	1.7	16.5	18.0	19.4	7.8	5.0	3.5	237
19. Turkey	0.9	1.1	1.6	1.9	11.6	14.5	15.5	0.9	1.4	5.1	1,457
20. Philippines	1.3	1.1	1.6	2.1	7.4	8.5	9.5	2.3	2.3	6.4	717
Total	56.9	64.8	86.9	94.5	282.2	322.2	364.4	111.6	103.2		
% of total	(75)	(75)	(80)	(72)	(70)	(69)	(69)	(68)	(55)		

[1] Net oil exporter
[2] Member of OPEC
[3] Among the countries that follow are the Emirates, Portugal, Taiwan, Iraq and Thailand. China's Debt Servicing for 1980 is provisionally estimated at $1.4 billion.
Source: OECD.

Table 8.8: Concessional Aid by OPEC Member States, 1970–81

% of GNP

	1970	1971	1972	1973	1974	1975	1976	1977	1978	1979	1980	1981
Gulf States												
Kuwait	6.21	3.45	4.39	8.62	5.33	7.40	3.64	8.20	5.64	1.79	2.04	1.98
Qatar	n.a.	n.a.	n.a.	15.62	9.26	15.59	7.95	7.76	3.75	6.03	4.25	2.64
Saudi Arabia	5.60	5.04	6.57	14.80	9.32	7.76	6.47	5.33	8.45	6.12	5.09	4.77
United Arab Emirates	n.a.	(3.82)	(4.62)	12.67	7.04	11.69	8.88	7.27	6.27	5.09	3.38	2.88
Total	5.86	4.28	5.57	12.76	7.78	8.56	6.33	6.20	7.51	5.05	4.28	3.92
Other Arab Donors												
Algeria	n.a.	n.a.	n.a.	0.28	0.37	0.27	0.33	0.24	0.18	0.89	0.17	0.16
Iraq	0.13	0.23	0.27	0.21	3.98	1.63	1.44	0.33	0.76	2.53	2.13	(0.37)
Libya	2.01	1.60	1.49	3.33	1.26	2.29	0.63	0.63	0.85	0.45	0.92	0.37
Total	1.10	0.97	0.94	1.21	1.76	1.31	0.80	0.39	0.56	1.40	1.08	0.29
Non-Arab Donors												
Iran	0.03	0.03	0.02	0.01	0.87	1.13	1.16	0.29	(0.37)	(0.03)	(0.01)	—
Nigeria	n.a.	n.a.	n.a.	0.03	0.05	0.04	0.19	0.13	0.07	0.04	0.05	0.17
Venezuela	0.01	0.04	0.21	0.11	0.23	0.11	0.34	0.15	0.29	0.22	0.21	0.10
Total	0.02	0.02	0.06	0.04	0.48	0.55	0.68	0.21	0.25	0.08	0.07	0.03
Grand Total	1.18	1.10	1.43	2.25	2.53	2.92	2.32	2.03	2.46	1.88	(1.74)	(1.46)

Note: GNP statistics were provided by the World Bank, except for those in brackets which are OECD Estimates.

Table 8.9: Concessional Aid by OPEC Member States

$ M

	1970	1971	1972	1973	1974	1975	1976	1977	1978	1979	1980	1981
Gulf States												
Kuwait	148	108	153	356	631	946	532	1,309	991	477	645	685
Qatar	—	—	—	94	185	338	195	194	109	280	284	175
Saudi Arabia	173	214	366	1,118	2,153	2,756	3,033	3,138	5,507	4,674	5,944	5,798
United Arab Emirates	—	50	74	289	510	1,046	1,021	1,060	891	967	906	799
Total	321	372	593	1,857	3,479	5,086	4,781	5,701	7,498	6,398	7,779	7,457
Other Arab Donors												
Algeria	—	—	—	25	47	41	54	47	44	272	65	65
Iraq	4	8	11	11	423	215	231	61	173	847	829	143
Libya	68	64	69	215	147	259	94	113	146	105	282	105
Total	72	72	80	251	617	515	379	221	363	1,224	1,176	313
Non-Arab Donors												
Iran	4	3	3	2	408	593	753	221	278	25	7	−150
Nigeria	—	—	—	5	15	14	83	64	38	30	42	149
Venezuela	1	5	28	18	60	31	108	56	115	109	125	67
Total	5	8	31	25	483	638	944	341	431	164	174	66
Grand Total	398	452	704	2,133	4,579	6,239	6,104	6,263	8,292	7,786	9,129	7,836
Total at constant 1981 prices	1,026	1,097	1,537	4,158	8,076	9,540	9,056	8,603	9,895	8,239	8,855	7,836

Source: OECD

Table 8.10: OPEC Members' Concessional Aid, 1980

$ M

Donor Country	Commitments			Net payments			
	Bi-lateral	Multi-laternal	Total	Bi-lateral	Multi-lateral	Total	In % of GNP
Gulf States							
Kuwait	537.8	203.0	740.8	487.5	157.9	645.4	2.04
Qatar	279.0	35.3	314.3	250.2	33.3	283.5	4.25
Saudi Arabia	5,142.2	344.2	5,486.4	5,668.0	276.4	5,944.4	5.09
United Arab Emirates	1,023.7	69.0	1,092.7	847.0	59.2	906.2	3.38
Sub-total	6,982.7	651.5	7,634.2	7,252.7	526.8	7,779.5	4.28
Other Arab Donors							
Algeria	(60.1)	48.6	(107.7)	(22.0)	42.6	(64.6)	0.17
Iraq	1,061.7	87.8	1,149.5	774.8	54.6	829.4	2.13
Libya	(662.5)	(81.9)	(774.4)	(217.9)	64.0	(281.9)	0.92
Sub-total	1,784.3	218.3	2,002.6	1,014.7	161.2	1,175.9	1.08
Other Arab Donors							
Iran	–	57.7	57.7	(−25.4)	32.7	(7.3)	(0.01)
Nigeria	18.4	56.7	75.1	9.1	32.6	41.7	0.05
Venezuela	15.0	192.5	207.5	5.0	120.3	125.3	0.21
Sub-total	33.4	306.9	340.3	−11.3	185.6	174.3	0.07
Total	8,800.4	1,176.7	9,977.1	8,256.1	873.6	9,129.7	1.74

Excluding $487.1 million for Jordan and Syria under the Baghdad Convention which Kuwait does not consider as an Arab developing country.

Table 8.11: OPEC Members' Concessional Aid, 1981

$ M

Donor Country	Commitments			Net payments			
	Bi-lateral	Multi-lateral	Total	Bi-lateral	Multi-lateral	Total	In % of GNP
Gulf States							
Kuwait	1,038.0	461.2	1,499.2	513.4	171.5	684.9	1.98
Qatar	(240.7)	104.0	(344.7)	(156.7)	18.5	(175.2)	2.64
Saudi Arabia	5,231.2	1,057.0	6,288.2	5,445.1	352.8	5,797.9	4.77
United Arab Emirates	748.3	232.7	981.0	748.7	49.9	798.6	2.88
Sub-total	7,258.2	1,854.9	9,113.1	6,863.9	592.7	7,456.6	3.92
Other Arab Donors							
Algeria	(20.3)	108.8	(129.1)	(22.3)	42.7	(65.0)	0.16
Iraq	(176.6)	212.1	(388.7)	(117.1)	25.8	(142.9)	(0.37)
Libya	(121.6)	(196.6)	(318.2)	(41.6)	63.8	(105.4)	0.37
Sub-total	(318.5)	(517.5)	836.0	(181.0)	132.3	313.3	0.29

Table 8.11 — *Continued*

$ M

Donor Country	Commitments			Net payments			
	Bi-lateral	Multi-lateral	Total	Bi-lateral	Multi-lateral	Total	In % of GNP
Non-Arab Donors							
Iran	—	(88.4)	(88.4)	(−150.0)	0.4	(−149.6)	—
Nigeria	(2.5)	267.6	(270.1)	(8.5)	140.5	(149.0)	0.17
Venezuela	(4.5)	(178.3)	(182.8)	(4.5)	62.7	(67.2)	0.10
Sub-total	(7.0)	(534.3)	(541.3)	(−137.0)	203.6	(66.6)	0.03
Total	(7,583.7)	(2,906.7)	(10,490.4)	(6,907.9)	928.6	(7,836.5)	(1.46)

Source: OECD.

Table 8.13: Financial Conditions by Developing Country, OPEC Member States' Commitments, 1981

Low-income and Least-developed Countries	ADC total	Gifts		Liberality Element	
		Gifts	Loans	APD Loans	Total ADC
		$ M		%	
Developing Countries					
Afghanistan	1.0	1.0	—	—	100.0
Angola	2.0	2.0	—	—	100.0
Bangladesh	77.6	5.9	71.7	63.2	65.9
Botswana	3.9	—	3.9	39.9	39.9
Burundi	15.3	—	15.3	51.0	51.0
Central African Republic	1.5	—	1.5	47.3	47.3
Comores	22.5	12.7	9.8	59.8	82.5
Djibouti	32.5	19.9	12.6	54.5	82.4
Egypt	4.5	4.5	—	—	100.0
Ethiopia	14.5	14.5	—	—	100.0
Gambia	10.5	10.5	—	—	100.0
Ghana	14.4	—	14.4	30.9	30.9
India	136.2	15.1	121.0	41.9	48.3
Indonesia	108.0	10.0	98.0	41.1	46.6
Kenya	24.4	—	24.4	44.2	44.2
Maldives	6.9	1.8	5.1	51.6	64.3
Mali	8.2	—	8.2	49.9	49.9
Mauritania	71.2	14.0	57.1	53.5	62.7
Mozambique	2.0	2.0	—	—	100.0
Niger	29.2	2.0	27.2	42.8	46.7
Pakistan	142.0	28.4	113.5	47.2	57.8
Rwanda	8.4	—	8.4	47.0	47.0
Senegal	7.6	—	7.6	55.3	55.3
Somalia	56.7	18.7	38.0	63.9	75.8
Sri Lanka	49.2	0.0	49.2	53.3	53.3
Sudan	104.0	4.0	100.0	67.2	68.5
Tanzania	63.8	—	63.8	44.5	44.5

Table 8.12: Public Development Aid from CAD Countries to Developing Countries and Multi-lateral Agencies

	Average 1971–3		1976		1977		1978		1979		1980		1981	
Country	$ M	% GNP	$ M	% GNP	$ M	% GNP	$ M	% GNP	$ M	% GNP	$ M	% GNP	$ M	% GNP
Australia	266	0.54	377	0.41	400	0.42	588	0.55	629	0.53	667	0.48	649	0.41
Austria	23	0.11	50	0.12	108	0.22	154	0.27	131	0.19	178	0.23	313	0.48
Belgium	191	0.52	340	0.51	371	0.46	536	0.55	643	0.57	595	0.50	575	0.59
Canada	457	0.42	887	0.46	991	0.50	1,060	0.52	1,056	0.48	1,075	0.43	1,189	0.43
Denmark	100	0.46	214	0.56	258	0.60	388	0.75	461	0.77	481	0.74	403	0.73
Finland	21	1.42	51	0.17	49	0.16	55	0.16	90	0.22	110	0.22	135	0.28
France	1,286	0.63	2,146	0.62	2,267	0.60	2,705	0.57	3,449	0.60	4,162	0.64	4,177	0.73
Germany	881	0.32	1,593	0.36	1,717	0.33	2,347	0.37	3,393	0.45	3,567	0.44	3,181	0.47
Italy	159	0.13	226	0.13	198	0.10	376	0.14	273	0.08	683	0.17	666	0.19
Japan	711	0.23	1,105	0.20	1,424	0.21	2,215	0.23	2,685	0.27	3,353	0.32	3,171	0.28
Netherlands	282	0.59	728	0.83	908	0.86	1,074	0.82	1,472	0.98	1,630	1.03	1,510	1.08
New Zealand	21	0.23	53	0.41	53	0.39	55	0.34	68	0.33	72	0.33	68	0.29
Norway	64	0.40	218	0.70	295	0.83	355	0.90	429	0.93	486	0.85	467	0.82
Sweden	211	0.50	608	0.82	779	0.99	783	0.90	988	0.97	962	0.79	916	0.83
Switzerland	53	0.16	112	0.19	119	0.19	173	0.20	213	0.21	253	0.24	237	0.24
UK	648	0.41	885	0.39	1,114	0.45	1,465	0.46	2,157	0.52	1,852	0.35	2,195	0.44
USA	3,242	0.28	4,360	0.26	4,682	0.25	5,663	0.27	4,684	0.20	7,138	0.27	5,783	0.20
CAD Countries' Total	8,616	0.33	13,953	0.33	15,733	0.33	19,992	0.35	22,820	0.35	27,264	0.38	25,635	0.35

Service charges excluded
Note: 1978 and preceding years' service charges excluded
Source: OECD

Table 8.13 – *Continued*

Low-income and Least-developed Countries	ADC total	Gifts	Loans	Liberality Element APD Loans	Liberality Element Total ADC
		$ M		%	
Uganda	0.4	0.4	–	–	100.0
Yemen Arab Repub.	158.9	134.1	24.8	47.6	91.8
Yemen Dem. Repub.	27.7	6.8	21.0	55.0	66.0
Zambia	2.0	2.0	–	–	100.0
Total	1,207.1	310.6	896.5	50.7	63.4
Middle Income Countries					
Bahrain	125.8	125.8	–	–	100.0
Cameroon	25.9	–	25.9	39.4	39.4
Congo	44.7	–	44.7	45.4	45.4
Grenada	2.5	–	2.5	38.4	38.4
Jordan	779.2	674.2	105.0	46.5	92.8
Lebanon	417.5	417.5	–	–	100.0
Malaysia	0.0	0.0	–	–	100.0
Malta	5.4	–	5.4	32.4	32.4
Morocco	267.2	267.2	–	–	100.0
Nicaragua	100.0	–	100.0	59.8	59.8
Oman	36.8	22.4	14.4	32.2	73.5
Seychelles	6.1	1.1	5.0	59.8	67.1
Syria	432.9	432.9	–	–	100.0
Thailand	76.9	–	76.9	45.2	45.2
Tunisia	109.2	0.0	109.1	45.0	45.0
Turkey	205.9	–	205.9	64.4	64.4
Zimbabwe	35.0	6.3	28.7	37.8	48.9
Total	2,670.9	1,947.4	723.6	52.1	87.0
Countries in the process of industrialisation					
Total	–	–	–	–	–
OPEC Countries					
Iran	1.0	1.0	–	–	100.0
United Arab Emirates	0.1	0.1	–	–	100.0
Total	1.1	1.1	–	–	100.0
Not valued separately/Not specified					
Africa South of the Sahara (not valued separately)	57.7	57.7	–	–	100.0
Africa	3.0	3.0	–	–	100.0
America	4.0	4.0	–	–	100.0
Asia	0.0	0.0	–	–	100.0
Arab Countries	65.0	65.0	–	–	100.0
Developing countries	3,574.8	898.7	2,676.1	53.1	64.9
Total	7,583.6	3,287.5	4,296.1	52.4	73.0
Total 1980	8,800.6	4,814.9	3,985.5	49.2	77.0
Total 1979	5,929.3	2,156.2	3,773.1	50.2	68.3
Total 1978	10,784.7	6,105.9	4,678.8	51.9	79.1

Source: OECD

9 ARAB DEVELOPMENT AGENCIES AND SOUTH-SOUTH CO-OPERATION

Abel Kader Sid Ahmed

Substantial oil price readjustments in 1973–4 and in 1979–80 were responsible for the considerable development of Arab funding of aid to other developing countries. 1961 had already seen the creation of the Kuwait Fund for Arab Economic Development (KFAED). In 1979, it was the Abu Dhabi Fund for Arab Economic Development (ADFAED). Meanwhile, the Arab Fund for Economic and Social Development (AFESD) had been started in Kuwait. Then in 1973, the movement gathered impetus with the creation in Khartoum of the Arab Bank for Economic Development in Africa (BADEA). 1974 was the year that saw the establishment of the Arab-African Technical Assistance Fund (AATAF) in Cairo, the Iraqi Fund for External Development (IFED) and, lastly, the Islamic Development Bank (IDB) in Jeddah.

The second wave of oil price readjustments in 1979–80 saw the transformation of the OPEC Special Fund, created in 1976, into the Agency for International Development, while a combined Algerian and Venezuelan proposal for a Development and Co-operation Agency and an Iraqi proposal for an Energy and Development Fund were examined by the OPEC Long-term Strategy Committee. Beyond the considerable extension of financial assistance, the major feature of the last decade has been the creation or extension of Arab aid institutions aimed at its more efficient channelling. This financial aid has been coupled with increasing activity from traditional Arab — or joint — financial institutions (a most significant example of this being the creation of ARLABANK in Lima, Peru), or with Islamic finance, where the role of Saudi Arabia is predominant. So that any evaluation of the input of the Arab Funds in the development of South-South co-operation must necessarily take into account these three levels of activity. To consider only the Arab Funds would give a totally erroneous idea of the Arab contribution to South-South development. The OPEC Fund, although not Arab, has been included in the analysis since the greater part of its resources come from the Arab world. The same holds true of the Islamic institutions. Finally, the analysis would be incomplete if one omitted the bi-lateral role played by countries such as Libya and Algeria. The fact that assistance from these countries is not institutionalised (there are no Funds as such) should not obscure the importance of their impact in the context of South-South co-operation. We shall therefore examine:

1. The size and importance of institutionalised Arab financial aid, the institutions concerned, their objectives, their resources and their *modus operandi.*
2. The complementary role of other Arab and Islamic financial institutions.
3. How this financial aid reinforces South-South co-operation.
4. Possible problems resulting from this aid, and its prospects.

The Extent of Arab Financial Assistance

Arab Funds

Table 9.1 lists all Arab development aid institutions, both national and regional. For reasons already explained, Islamic institutions and the OPEC Fund are included. The table also shows the resources, type of operation and eligibility criteria involved.

One can see that with time this aid has become increasingly multilateral (OPEC Special Fund, Islamic Fund) and that the national Funds that had previously only been concerned with Arab countries (KFAED, SDF, ADFAED, IFED) are now also involved in the 'international' context.

Soon after 1973, the main recipients of Arab aid were Arab countries, notably Egypt, the Sudan, Syria, Tunisia and Bahrain. These countries were either at the forefront of Arab world politics or were already sufficiently developed to absorb capital surpluses (Egypt, Syria, Tunisia) or offered great agricultural potential (the Sudan, Syria). The geographic and ethnic links of Bahrain with the other Gulf states made it an obvious beneficiary.

In the second stage, which began in 1975–6, Arab financial aid extended to Muslim countries in Asia (Pakistan, Bangladesh, Turkey, Malaysia) and in Africa (the Sahel region, Guinea, the Comores, etc.)

Finally, with the 1979–80 oil price readjustments, Arab financial aid reached global dimensions. The OPEC Special Fund had showed the way, as witnessed by the fact that only four years after its creation it had serviced more than 60 recipient countries. Other countries such as Libya and Algeria who advocated a 'Third World policy' for their aid programmes, were already involved with a wide range of countries including Portuguese speaking Africa, Vietnam, and Central America. To arrive at a complete picture of Arab financial aid the Libyan, Algerian and Qatar Funds must be added to those listed in Table 9.1.

Table 9.1, gives examples of the loans available from different Funds and their rules of application, and make it clear that Arab financial institutions have the following aims:

1. To ensure the beneficiary's participation and interest in the project, as these will condition its success. Thus projects can only be financed to a maximum of 50 per cent of the cost.
2. To obtain the widest possible spread of the Fund's services so as to concern a maximum number of developing countries and to reduce the loan's risks. Hence the rule that no loan can exceed more than a given proportion of the Fund's capital, or again, the rule that loans to a given country cannot aggregate more than 10 per cent of the Fund's capital.
3. To avoid the perverse fluctuations of key currencies by paying out and collecting the loans in local national currencies.
4. To reconstitute the Fund's capital so as to perpetuate its action. This effects a proportional reduction of admissable donations, the only exception being OPEC's Special Fund which now faces the problem of reconstituting its resources. It is this concern with efficiency which explains the importance given to the economic and feasibility studies of a project by the different Funds.
5. To allow for eventual increase of their resources. Thus while their freed capital is often smaller than their authorised capital, the Funds are generally entitled to issue shares in order to increase available finance. Certain institutions such as the Islamic Bank (Taïf Summit of 1981), have freed, or are on the point of freeing, their entire capital.
6. To act in unison with the great international institutions. In this way the Selinge barrage in Mali is co-financed by various Funds (ADFAED, BADEA, SFD and KFAED), with the added involvement of international and regional financial institutions. Similarily, one finds both the ADFAED and the BADEA involved in the financing of the Douala-Yaoundé road.

7. To ensure that the projects being financed do not conflict with the vital interests of the Arab World, the preoccupation here being to avoid any industrial or infrastructural duplication which would hinder regional integration.

The Funds' Operational Means

In most cases financing is concerned with concessional loans. Certain institutions confine their intervention to equity participation (IDB). However, this form of equity acquisition is not allowed in the case of the Kuwait Fund (KFAED). Owing to lack of experience on the one hand, and to the delicate problems of sovereignty on the other, direct investments have until now been limited. Egypt, Pakistan and Tunisia have tried to encourage them.

The element of *gift* is relatively important if one takes into consideration the substantial gap between the amount loaned and its projected return from repayment of the principal and interest. This element has increased all the more in recent years when international interest rates have soared while there has been practically no increase in the rates charged by Arab Funds. Lastly, Arab financial aid is not tied to the purchase of products or services generated in the area, which considerably reinforces its quality.

Certain institutions such as the OPEC Special Fund were the first to combine loans with balance of payment assistance for given projects. In this way, the Fund managed to ensure that each beneficiary should apportion local currency finances to meet the local costs of development projects. In this way the OSF was able to get round the bottleneck of the insistance by international financial institutions that they could finance only the strong currency costs of a project.

At first limited to project aids, Arab assistance has since developed to encompass OSF-linked programmes. For one must remember that project assistance entails the freezing of funds for a given project. This can have a very restrictive effect on countries with rigid planning systems where the project's timing is crucial.

The Objectives of Arab Financial Assistance

It is very difficult to assign precise objectives to Arab assistance programmes, as there are different needs and priorities in each of the countries concerned. These are geographical, political, cultural, religious, economic, ideological, etc.

In the case of non-oil exporting Arab countries, because of multiple links of all kinds, and owing to strict security considerations in Middle Eastern countries, the assistance flows naturally. The endemic economic underdevelopment, and political and social instability in the area, all constitute a grave danger for the small pockets of wealth. By stimulating development, financial assistance reduces the sources of tension and thus contributes to the security of the donating countries.

Apart from the security aspect, since they are for the most part sparsely populated, Arab OPEC countries are obliged to co-operate with countries that have abundant human resources. So that millions of unqualified Yemeni labourers, hundreds of thousands of Egyptian peasants or white-collar workers from Palestine, Egypt, Lebanon, Jordan and Tunisia are in fact the people who condition the development of the Gulf states.

Then there is the food threat which is brandished by Western powers and forces the oil producing countries, which are for the most part desert-like, to invest in developing Arab agricultural potential (Syria, the Sudan, Morocco, Somalia, etc.).

By deepening the divide in life conditions in these two categories of Arab country, the successive readjustments to oil prices have provided a humanitarian basis for the assistance, in so far as there exists an implied standard of social equality in the community.

The above considerations are also true of the aid to Muslim countries where the political element takes on much greater importance. Certain traditional countries such as Saudi Arabia try to channel the forceful Islamic tide in their own direction. In this context, the Taïf Action Programme and the Mecca Declaration of early 1981 constitute a vital turning point in the policy.

The financial assistance policy in favour of non-Muslim developing countries is based on the motivation and struggle for a New International Economic Order and a greater solidarity among developing countries in favour of OPEC members. These considerations play a considerable role in the policies of countries such as Algeria, Libya and Iraq, which are much more open to the principle of non-alignment. This was well demonstrated by the role played by Algeria and Venezuela in the creation of an OPEC Co-operation Agency for the Third World. This project coupled traditional assistance to a balance of payment aid programme more appropriate to Latin

American and South-east Asian semi-industrialised countries, the idea being to mobilise the whole Third World, and not just the poorest developing countries, under the banner of the New International Economic Order project.

Lastly, and at the risk of provoking a smile, it is undeniable that the solidarity linking the Arab countries to the rest of the Third World stems from a common history. Both kinds of country have been through the colonial traumas of poverty, spoliation and underdevelopment.

The Impact of Arab Financial Aid on South-South Co-operation

In order to make a true assessment of the impact of Arab financial aid on South-South co-operation one must also take into account the actions of other institutions such as:

a. *Arab commercial and merchant banks:* Arab Banking Corporation (ABC) or the Gulf Bank, with their affiliated banks in the Third World (ARLABANK in Peru, for example);
b. *The Islamic banks* (the most recent of which is the Dar al Maal in Geneva) which are present throughout the Muslim world;
c. *Inter-Arab institutions* such as the Arab Insurance and Reinsurance Company, the Arab Engineering Company, The Affiliates of Organisations of Arab Oil Exporting countries (OPAEC), etc.

By financing commercial loans, or guaranteeing certain investments, these organisations are opening up new patterns of exchange between Southern countries. Already, South-South co-operation, and in particular co-operation between Arab countries and other developing countries, has become a reality. Examples of contracts passed between Arab countries and other developing countries from 1975 to 1982 underline the increasingly important role of the newly-industrialised countries in developing the area. Since 1974, Brazil, India, Pakistan, Turkey, Yugoslavia, the Philippines, Taiwan, and South Korea, have contracted for billions of dollars in the Arab world. While construction and public works are their main area of expertise, the building of electric power stations, petrochemical complexes, pumping stations and irrigation works are also in undeniable evidence. Hundreds of thousands of technicians and management staff from Korea, India, Brazil and even Turkey are busy working in Arab countries.

New trade patterns have emerged in the area of agricultural and food products. Tea from Sri Lanka, products from Argentina, meat from Somalia and various goods from Jordan can now be seen in market places in Libya and the Gulf states. In 1981 for example, Jordan doubled its exports to the Gulf states and Iraq (food and manufactured goods reached $226.7 million in 1981 against $132.8 million in 1980). In Turkey, the first eight months of 1982 saw exports to the Middle East and North Africa increase 60 per cent over 1981 to reach $1.6 billion. This represents 46 per cent of total Turkish exports in the first eight months of 1982, as against 34 per cent in the same period the previous year. As a result, Arab countries are tending to replace OECD countries as Turkey's trading partners.

Brazil's exports to Arab oil-exporting countries almost tripled between 1979 and 1981, moving from $587.8 million to $1,543.8 million.

With regard to manpower, Arab oil exporting countries are increasingly calling on technicians and managers from the Third World. The sums repatriated by foreigners working in Arab countries are estimated at some $20 billion. Transfers by foreign workers to their families have become the main source of revenue for countries such as the two Yemens, Egypt, Jordan, and Pakistan, and one of the main sources of countries such as Lebanon, Tunisia, Sri Lanka, India, Bangladesh, Djibouti, the Sudan and the Philippines. It is true that one must counterbalance this income with the economic and social loss to the countries resulting from the departure of their most qualified and dynamic citizens. Nonetheless, in present world financial and economic circumstances, the net result is a bonus to their home economies.

Lastly, at the inter-Arab level, the fact that there exist a large number of Pan-Arab institutions and companies working in all areas concerned with collective autonomy at a regional level offers attractive and growing job prospects to managers who could not be usefully employed in their own countries. In this way, there are a large number of Iraqi and Algerian technicians who enable other Arab countries to profit from their oil exploration expertise within the framework of OAPEC and Arab engineering company-initiated projects.

Without doubt, OPEC's actions have initiated the emergence of financial, economic and human exchanges in South-South relations on a vast scale. The movement could be more efficient if the necessary institutional and co-operative mechanisms existed in the Third World. Understanding these objective limitations to South-South co-operative development, the Arab oil exporting countries assumed a determinant role in the adoption of the May 1981 Caracas Action Programme. With this, the concept of co-operation within the Third World is deliberately projected on a planetary level and reflects the 77 members' determination to begin restructuring the world economy without waiting for the industrialised countries. The starting point is as follows:

At their own level, developing countries have elaborated the techniques and qualifications that they need. The complementary nature of natural resources, financial expertise and capital are self-evident. The Caracas conference served to pinpoint the main sectors of imbalance (capacity surpluses and deficiencies) in developing countries: energy, technology, industrialisation, trade and raw materials. These are all capacities that can be exchanged among developing countries on the basis of mutual advantage. The conference further decided that such countries will concede preferential treatment to each other in the instance of most transfers; the constitution of groups of experts to determine the details in specific areas; the establishment of an inter-governmental co-ordination committee to decide the concrete orientations required, and to ensure their application and survival. A few months before, the Islamic Summit at Taïf had adopted a number of fundamental measures that constituted a turning point in Islamic co-operation, and were forerunners of the Caracas programme. The summit approved the 'plan of action for the reinforcement of Economic Co-operation between member states' which had been elaborated at the 1980 Ankara Conference. This defined the main lines of co-operation in the fields of agricultural and food policies, trade, industry, transport, finance, energy, science, technology, manpower, population, public health and technical co-operation.

Apart from creating a $3 billion Fund for economic development projects in the Islamic world (the Gulf states subscribing $2.3 billion in the following proportions: Saudi Arabia $1 billion, Kuwait and the United Arab Emirates $500 million each, and Qatar $300 million) the pariticipants above adopted the *General Agreement on Promotion, Protection and Guarantee of Investments* in member states. Lastly, an 'Islamic Centre for the Development of Exchanges between Muslim Countries will be created in Tangiers, as well as a ship-owners' Union in Jeddah.

The so-called Mecca declaration which concluded the summit puts Islamic action in line with the demand for a New International Economic Order. The declaration calls for

> the establishment of international economic relations based on equity, interdependance and balance of interests to bridge the abyss separating industrial from developing countries, that is, a New International Economic Order founded on justice and solidarity.

In another context, the Algero-Venezuelan proposal for the creation of a co-operation agency with a capital of $20 billion was proof of the oil exporting countries' desire to establish South-South co-operation on a concrete basis.

Future Prospects for South-South Co-operation

It seems unlikely that the considerable effort made by Arab oil exporting countries (close on $50 billion allocated to other developing countries since 1973) can be maintained over a long period.

Already, OPEC countries' financial surpluses have undergone a severe downturn, which has resulted in an important current account deficit in 1982 for the OPEC countries as a whole. The persistent world economic depression does not allow at present for a substantial demand for OPEC oil. Certain client countries' reinforced absorption capacity could also further reduce the financial surpluses which are in any case by nature of a temporary character.

Thus one can see that Arab countries' concessional aid to the Third World has every chance of diminishing just at a time when the industrialed countries seem ill-disposed to increase their aid.

Sooner or later assistance from the Arab world will have to be replaced by trade investments. One should seek means of preserving and increasing OPEC's assets while ensuring the development of recipient countries. Host countries should promote the appropriate structures (arbitration, investment-orientated economic policies, etc.). Secondary financial markets such as that created by Kuwait should then stimulate and make available the appropriate financial instruments which are a necessary precondition of the development of trade and co-operation in South-South relations.

References

Ibrahim Shihata, 'The OPEC Fund for International Development', *Third World Quarterly*, vol. 3, no. 2, (April 1981) pp. 251–68

Ragaei El Mallakh and Mihsen Kadhim, 'Arab Institutionalised Development Aid: an Evaluation', *The Middle East Journal* (Autumn 1976) pp. 471–85

Ragaei El Mallakh and Jacob K. Atta, *The Absorptive Capacity of Kuwait: Domestic and International Perspectives*, Lexington Book Co. (1981), ch. 9

Soliman Demir, *Arab Development Funds in the Middle East*, (Pergamon, 1979)

Ragaei El Mallakh, *The Economic Development of the United Arab Emirates* (Croom-Helm, 1981) ch. 7

Mahmoud Fouad, 'Petrodollars and Economic Development in the Middle East', *The Middle East Journal*, vol. 32 no. 3 (Summer 1978) pp. 307–23

Abdelkader Sid Ahmed, *Développement sans croissance: l'expérience des économies pétrolières du Tiers-monde* (Publisud, Paris, 1983)

Abdelatif Y. Al Hamad, 'Building up Development-oriented Institutions in the Arab World', KFAED, Kuwait (October 1972)

J. Nicholas Robinson, 'The Role of Oil Funds Recycling in International Payments and Adjustment Problems', *OPEC Review*, vol. IV no. 2 (Summer 1980) pp. 98–110

Ibrahim F.I. Shihata, 'The OPEC Fund for International Development: the First Five Years', *OPEC Review*, vol. V no. 3 (Autumn 1981) pp. 1–9

—— 'The Working Relationship between the OPEC Special Fund and other Development Finance Institutions', *OPEC Review*, vol. II no. 3 (June 1978) pp. 5–15

Abdelkader Sid Ahmed, *Mobilisation of Domestic Resources: Development and the Members of the Organisation of Petroleum Exporting Countries*, report for the UNCTAD secretariat, Doc. T D/B/C.3/145 (October 1978)

—— 'The role of the New Opec Development Agency' (Oxford, 1981)

—— 'La finance Islamique et le développement', *Revue Tiers-monde*, Paris (January 1983)

United Nations Economic Commission for Western Asia, *Resouce Transfers and Financial Co-operation in Western Asia*, Doc. 81–4327 (Beirut, August 1981)

Jawad Hashim, 'An Understanding of the Importance of Arab/Islamic Funds Available for Development Projects and Economic Support', *OAPEC Bulletin* (April 1979) pp. 29–35

John Waterbury and Ragaei El Mallakh, *The Middle East in the Coming Decade: from Wellhead to Well-being* 1980s Project Council on Foreign Relations (McGraw Hill, 1978)

John Whelan, 'Najadi looks to Arab-Asian Co-operation', *Middle East Economic Digest* vol. 26 no. 19 (7 May 1982) p. 4

—— 'Indonesia Pushes Middle East Efforts', *Middle East Economic Digest*, vol. 26 no. 23 (4 June 1982) p. 6

Gavin Sheeve, 'Political Tensions Cloud Arab-African Co-operation', *Middle East Economic Digest* (4 June 1982) pp. 24–6

Dunstan M. Wai (ed.), *Interdependance in a World of Unequals: African-Arab OECD Co-operation for Development*, Western Special Studies in Social, Economic and Political Development (Boulder 1982)

—— 'Iraqi Fund President gives Views on OPEC and the Third World', *OPEC Bulletin* (September 1980) pp. 14–20

Final Report on the High-level Conference on Economic Co-operation among Developing Countries, Caracas, Doc. Caracas/G.77/FR. (May 1981)

Table 9.1: Arab Funds and Developing Finance Institutions Linked to Arab Oil Exporting Countries

Institution	HQ and Year of Creation	Capital $M	Types of Operation	Number and Amount Loaned, Early 1982	Loan Terms and Gift Element	Vocation	Conditions/Eligibility
KFAED	Kuwait December 1961	$3,630	Technical Assistance, Project Loans, Guarantees. 60% of commitments are co-financed	Total committed $3,400	0.5 to 7%, i.e. an average rate of 3.2% plus 0.5% annual commission on part of loan in use. Repayment from 10 to 50 years. Grace period 4–5 years. Gift element of up to 60%	Infrastructure Agriculture Industry Energy	The Dinar is the unit of account. Loans cannot exceed 50% of total project cost or 10% of Fund capital. Projects must not conflict with Arab or Kuwaiti interests. All developing countries are eligible.
SFD	Riyadh September 1974	$2,900 then $4,400 then $7,400 in 1981	Project Loans		2 to 4% over an average 20 years	Infrastructure Agriculture Industry Energy Education Health	Saudi Riyal is the unit of account. Loans cannot exceed 50% of total project cost or 5% of Fund capital. Loans to a given country cannot exceed 10% of Fund capital.
IFED	Baghdad July 1974	$169 then $676 in 1980	Technical Assistance, Project Aid	Approx. 40 commitments $1.5 billion	Interest-free	Health Education	All developing countries that adhere to non-alignment
AFESD	Kuwait May 1980	$1,400 then $2,800 in 1981	Technical Assistance, Project aid	95 projects for a total $1,300	4 to 6% interest repayment 18 to 20 years, grace period 4–5 years, Gift Element 25–45%	Industry Infrastructure	Private and public Arab institutions only; the Fund does not take equity stakes.
IDB	Jeddah, December 1973, operational July 1975	$2,227 of which $899.5 subscribed; rest to be subscribed as per Taïf Summit 1981 decision	Loans, Equity stakes, Leasing, Technical Assistance, Financing inter-Moslem country Trade	commitments $1,416 in November 1980	Interest-free but bank participation in company's profit	All operations contributing to the collective autonomy of Islamic countries	Limited to Moslem countries or the Islamic community in non-Moslem countries

BADEA	Khartoum November 1979	$231 then $392 in 1975	Medium and small project finance in co-operation with other regional & international finance institutions		2 to 7% repayment over 11–25 years		restricted to non-Arab African countries
AATAF	Arab League Tunis, January 1974	$25	Loans, Technological know-how		1% Interest, grace period 3 years before repayment	Balance of payments finance	" " " "
AFOAF	BADEA, March 1974	$200	Oil Import Loans		1% Interest, repayment 15 years, grace period 10 years, Gift element 71%.	Balance of payments finance	Aid distributed among countries according to their previous level of oil imports
SFANOC	AFESD June 1974	$80	Oil Import Loans		Interest-free repayment 10 years after grace period of 10 years, Gift Element 80%	Balance of payments finance	Aid distributed according to previous level oil imports
OSF transformed into OFID in 1980	Vienna 1976	approx. $4,000	Project and programme Loans	Over 300 loans of which some 40 gifts to approx. 90 countries	0–7% interest, repayment 10–20 years, average grace period 4 years	Balance of payments finance, Health, Energy, Agriculture Transport, Communications, Industry, Education	Developing countries
AMF	Abu Dhabi 1976	$975	Balance of payments finance		Short and medium-term loans up to 7 years, 5–6% over 3 years, interest calculated on a number of	Reinforcement of inter-Arab country co-operation and	Reserved for Arab countries. Loans, over 12 months cannot exceed double the country's subscription

Table 9.1 — *Continued*

Institution	HQ and Year of Creation	Capital $M	Types of Operation	Number and Amount Loaned, Early 1982	Loan Terms and Gift Element	Vocation	Conditions/Eligibility
					elements	regional development.	
-IDF	Jeddah 1981	$3,000				Infrastructure, Industry and any stimulus to development	Islamic countries and communities
ADFAED	Abu Dhabi July 1971	$542 increased $1,084 in 1979	Projects, equity stakes, other forms of assistance		3–5% interest, 0.5% service charge, repayment period 11–19 years, Grace period 2–4 years, Gift Element, 29–48%	Infrastructure, Industry, Tourism, Agriculture, all stimuli to Arab economic development	Loans cannot exceed 50% of total project cost or 10% of Fund capital. Generally reserved for Project's currency needs. Under certain conditions 50% limit can be waived.

Table 9.2: OPEC Special Fund, Some Examples of Loans

Project	Date	Country	Amount ($ M)	Maturity	Grace Period
Textile complex at Kandahar	1977	Afghanistan	3.75	20	5
Sedawgyi Dam	1977	Burma	2.25	na	na
Talkha Fertilizer Project	1977	Egypt	14.45	na	na
Grain Silos	1977	El Salvador	1.75	"	"
Palm Oil Refinery at Tamatave	1978	Madagascar	3.10	"	"
Hydroelectric Project at Kulekhani	1977	Nepal	3.33	"	"
" " Samanalawewa	1978	Sri Lanka	1.56	na	na
Ashugarij Fertilizer Project	1978	Bangladesh	7.00	20	5
Agricultural Fields at Mamdi	1978	Chad	2.40	20	5
Airport at Yundun	1979	Gambia	2.00	"	"
Sugar Project at Juba	1979	Somalia	5.00	"	"
International Centre of Insect Pysiology and Ecology	1980	Kenya	4.00	na	na
Plan Assistance	1980	Guinea Bissau	0.006	20	5
Balance of Payments Assistance	April			10 years	3
	1980	Cape Verde Islands	1.50		
High Tension Lines	"	Tanzania	5.00	20	4
Balance of Payments Assistance	"	Seychelles	0.50	10	3
" " "	May	Jamaica	7.00		
	1980			10	3
" " "	"	Guyana	5.00	10	3
Interconnection Project	May 1980	Bangladesh	10.00	20	5
Balance of Payments Assistance	"	Madagascar	5.00	10	3
" "	"	Djibouti	1.50	"	"

Table 9.2 — *Continued*

Project	Date	Country	Amount ($ M)	Maturity	Grace Period
Balance of Payments Assistance	September	Rwanda	3.0	"	"
" "	October	Maldives	1.0	"	"
SOTEXKA Textile Project	"	Senegal	5	20	4
Thermal Power Station Project	"	India	20	20	4
Ocean Railway	"	Congo	8	20	4
Drinking Water Project	October	South Yemen	4	20	5
Thermal Power Station	"	Thailand	8	20	4
Road Project	"	Tunisia	6	"	"
Gas Project	"	Bangladesh	21	20	5
Ventiane plain project	"	Laos	1.5	15	5
Thermal Power Station	"	Liberia	5	20	4
Balance of Payments Assistance	November	Nicaragua	10	10	3
" "	"	Sierra Leone	1.0	10	3
Rural Development	"	Haiti		20	5
Hydroelectric Project	March 1981	Mauritius	2	20	5
Development Offshore Petroleum Fields	"	India	30	20	5
Rural Development	"	Philippines	7.5	"	"
Fertilizer Project	April	Syria	10	"	"
	"	Mali	10	10	3
" "	"	Sri Lanka	9	"	"
Hydroelectric Project	May	Solomon Islands	1.5	20	5
Balance of Payments Assistance	May	Samoa	1.5	10	3
" "	"	Guinea Bissau	1.5	"	"
" "	July	Grenada	2	"	"
Road Project	"	Benin	6	20	5
Balance of Payments Assistance	"	Dominican Republic	10	10	3

" "	"	Bangladesh	25	"	"
" "	"	Jamaica	10	"	"
Road Project	"	Togo			
Industrial Sector Finance	October	Morocco	15	20	5
Stock Holding	"	Paraguay	10	20	5
Balance of Payments Assistance	"	Turkey	25	10	3
Hydroelectric Project	"	Costa Rica	13.4	20	5
" "	"	Laos	4	20	5
Balance of Payments Assistance	"	Tonga	1		
				10	3
Hydroelectric Project	"	Nepal	7	20	5
Balance of Payments Assistance	"	Barbados	2	10	3
Feasibility Study on Charcoal Exploitation	January 1982	Mozambique	2.3	20	5
Rural Development	"	Burma	15	15	5
Technical Education Project	January 1982	Papua New Guinea	4	20	5
Balance of Payments Assistance	April 82	Senegal	10	10	3
Rural Electrification	"	Philippines	20	20	5
Thermal Power Station Project	May 82	India	30	"	"
Gabarone Airport	"	Botswana	3	"	"
Electrification Project at Mukalla	July 82	South Yemen	7.5	"	"
Thermal Power Station at Ashuganj	"	Bangladesh	30	"	"
Thermal Power Station at Boulaos	"	Djibouti	2.5	"	"
Irrigation Project at Bura	"	Kenya	12	"	"
Balance of Payments Assistance	"	Somalia	9	10	3
Road Network Maintenance	"	Central African Republic	5.1	20	5

Table 9.3: The Arab Development Funds

1.	KFAED	: Kuwait Fund for Arab Economic Development
2.	SFD	: Saudi Development Fund
3.	IFED	: Iraqi Fund for External Development
4.	AFESD	: Arab Fund for Economic and Social Development
5.	IDB	: Islamic Development Bank
6.	BADEA	: Arab Bank for Economic Development of Africa
7.	AATAF	: Arab-African Technical Assistance Fund
8.	AFOAF	: Arab-African Petroleum Assistance Fund
9.	SFANOC	: Special Fund for Non-petroleum-exporting Arab Countries
10.	OSF	: OPEC Special Fund
11.	AMF	: Arab Monetary Fund
12.	IDF	: Islamic Development Fund
13.	ADFAED	: Abu Dhabi Fund for Arab Economic Development

Sources: Reports of the various Funds, *Middle East Economic Survey, Middle East Economic Digest, Banker, Euromoney, OPEC Bulletin*.

Table 9.4: Abu Dhabi: Loans and Shares Granted and Taken up from BADEA: Some Examples

Period	Country	Amount (in DH)	Date	Interest %	Maturity	Grace period
King Talal Dam	Jordan	21.5	1974	3	18	3.5
Thermal Power Station at Sitra	Bahrain	40.0	"	3.5	16	1.5
Railways	Tunisia	13.5	"	3.5	14.5	3
Hotel Omar Khayam	Egypt	10.0	"	4	19	4.75
Drinking Water (Sanaa)	North Yemen	4.0	"	3.5	12	3.75
El Azrak Road	Jordan	5.0	1975	3	18	3.5
Abuokir Power Station	Egypt	13.0	1975	3.5	20.5	6
Rural Development	North Yemen	40.0	"	3	22.5	8
Commercial Centre	Morocco	40.0	1976	3	17	2.5
Fisheries	Burundi	4.0	"	2.5	21	6.5
Selingue Dam	Mali	16.0	"	3.5	20	5
Yandum Airport	Gambia	5.2	1977	3.5	15	3
Machine Tools	Bangladesh	40.0	"	4.5	13.25	3.75
Power Station at Bandung	Indonesia	57.0	"	4	20	5
Electric Power Station at Roga	Madagascar	16.0	1979	3.4	14.5	5
Airport Reconstruction at Anjouan	Comoro Islands	4.0	"	2	18.25	4
Electric Power Station at Bralin	Seychelles	0.8	"	4.5	11.5	2
Lesotho Airport, Maseru	Lesotho	3.0	1978	2	14.5	5
El-Guelb Mines	Mauritania	80.0	1979	4.5	16.25	5
Fish Refrigeration Project	Cape Verde Islands	1.2	1980	4	15	3

Construction of International Airport at Khartoum	Sudan	103.0	"	3	26	6
Hydroelectric Project at Anou Araren (Phase 2)	Niger	4.05	1981	na	na	na
Douala-Yaoundé Road	Cameroon	4.30	"			
Savare-Gao Road	Mali	8.10	"			

Table 9.5: Arab Bank Loans for Economic Development in Africa: Some Examples

Project	Country	Amount ($ M)	Date Granted		Maturity	Interest %
Cement Works	Benin	8.0	November 1975		25	6
Harbour Facilities	Cameroon	10.0	"		"	4
Cacao Project	Ghana	25.0	"		"	"
Road	Madagascar	5.0	"		"	3
Stock Breeding Project	Senegal	1.0	"		"	2
Railway	Upper Volta	10.0	"		"	"
Drinking Water	Zaire	10.0	"		"	4
Cement Works	Ghana, Ivory Coast, Togo	10.0	"		15	6
Water Supply	Burundi	4.0	June 1976		25	2
Rural Development	Gambia	3.3	March 1976		25	2
Selingué Dam	Mali	15.0	"		25	2
Electric Power Station	Mauritius	10.0	June 1976		15	4
Electric Power Station	Sierra Leone	5.0	March 1976		15	4
Railway	Zambia	10.0	June 1976		25	4
Paper Pulp Project	Cameroon	10.6	November 1977		11	7
Feasibility Studies	Comoro Islands	0.1	October 1977		gift	
Kyong Dam	Ghana	10.0	"		17	6
Construction Materials	Tanzania	10.0	"		15	7
Duty Free Zone	Liberia	7.1	July 1978		na	na
Cacao Project	Sao Tomé	5.0	"		"	"
Textile Project	Uganda	4.7	"		15	4
Installation of a Wave Circuit	Comoro Islands	1.57	1980	2	20	5
Construction of a Road (556 Kms)	Mali	10.0	"	4	20	5
Installation of two 2 MW Power Stations	Seychelles	2.20	"	5	12	2
Stabilisation of Frontier resources	Mozambique	10.0	"	6	13	3
International Airport at Maseru	Lesotho	6.00	"	4	17.5	3
Reconstruction of Benguela Railway	Angola	10.0	"	4	15	5.5
Hydroelectric Project	Mauritius	10.0	"	4	na	na
Construction of Gabelone Airport	Botswana	7.25	1980	5	15	3
Douala-Yaoundé Road	Cameroon	9.00	1981	na	na	na

Table 9.5 — *Continued*

Project	Country	Amount ($ M)	Date Granted	Maturity	Interest %
Stock Breeding Project	Senegal	0.05	1981		
Chemical Industries	"	10.0	"		
Brazzaville Airport	Congo	10.0	"		
Cotonou Port	Benin	2.70	"		
Sugar Complex	Burundi	10.0	"		
Fisheries Replacement	Angola	10.0	"		
Railway Modernisation	Zaire	10.0	"		
Forestry Development at Managaro	Madagascar	8.00	1981		

Table 9.6: Loans Granted by the Saudi Development Fund

Project	Country	Amount (Millions of Riyals)	Date	Maturity	Interest
Electric Power Station	Bahrain	75.0	January 1978	20	3
Suez Canal	Egypt	175.0	May 1975	18	3.5
Irrigation Project	Sudan	98.0	June 1975	20	3
Electric Power Station	Yemen	17.5	November 1975	15	2
Kabangsaan Project	Malaysia	56.0	July 1975	17	3
Telecommunications	Egypt	80.5	January 1976	18	3.5
Arrangement of the Port of Tartous	Syria	90.0	August 1976	20	3
Arrangement of the Port of Lattaquié	Syria	85.0	" "	20	3
Road	North Yemen	17.5	" "	30	0
Railway	Congo	88.3	July 1976	20	4
Division of the Port of Akaba	Jordan	81.0	October 1977	20	0
Road	Oman	263.9	July 1977	20	2
Sugar Project	Somalia	254.0	November 1977	20	3
Satellite Communications	Sudan	35.3	July 1977	20	2
Technical School	Tunisia	37.0	November 1977	20	3
Power Station	South Yemen	70.0	June 1977	20	2
Power Station	India	353.0	" "	20	4
Road	Indonesia	176.5	May 1977	20	3
Selingué Dam	Mali	52.95	February 1977	20	2
Drinking Water, Amman	Jordan	70.0	June 1978	20	2
Siti Saad Dam	Tunisia	245.0	March 1978	20	—
Railway	Gabon	70.6	" "	20	—
Power Station	Liberia	68.0	June 1978	20	2
Stock Breeding	Mali	46.85	February 1978	20	2
Road	Senegal	125.6	January 1978	20	3
Telecommunications	Taiwan	105.0	March 1978	20	5
Railway	Jordan	38.50	1980	na	3
National University	Somalia	35.30	"	na	2

Power Station at Hodeida	North Yemen	53.60	"	na	2
Stocking and Value Stabilisation of Agricultural Products	" "	36.85	"	na	2
Railway	Zaire	116.0	"	na	3
Financing four Supplementary Generators for Tarbala Dam	Pakistan	200.1	"	na	3
Preparatory Studies for the Technical Institute	Gabon	9.00	"	na	3
Development of the Anambé Basin	Senegal	5.04	1981		
Road Projects	Comores Islands	6.30	"		
Thika-Carissa Road	Kenya	24.81	"		
Congo-Ocean Railway	Congo	22.98	"		
Gitega-Ghofi Road	Burundi	7.32	"		
Nitrogenous Fertiliser Complex at Chittagong	Bangladesh	$86	1982		
Development Projects including Refinery at Malacca	Malaysia	$300	1982		

Table 9.7: Loans Granted by the Arab Fund for Economic and Social Development (AFESD)

Project	Country	Amount ($ M)	Date	Maturity	Interest
Division of the Port of Arzew	Algeria	6.0	April 1974	20	6
Road	Sudan	8.0	" "	20	4
Petroleum Reserves	Syria	2.0	February 1974	25	5
Drinking Water System Cairo	Egypt	9.7	December 1975	20	6
Electric Power Station	Jordan	6.0	April 1976	20	6
Electric Power Station	Mauritania	5.2	" "	25	4
Project Irrigation	Morocco	8.7	" 1977	15	5
Small Industries	Tunisia	6.4	" "	15	6
Electric Power Station	Yemen	8.7	1977	3	3
Aerial Security and Navigation Skills	Algeria	2.0DK	1980 (6)	12	2.5
Pump Installation on the Gharb Plain	Morocco	5.0DK	1980 (6)	20	5
Pilot Programme against Sleeping Sickness	Somalia	1.6DK	1980 (4)	15	5
Kassala-Gedaref Road	Sudan	5.2DK	1980 (4)	15	3

Table 9.7 — *Continued*

Project	Country	Amount ($ M)	Date	Maturity	Interest
Installation of an Irrigation Reservoir Wadi Tuban (Aden)	South Yemen	1.9DK	1980 4	20	3
Agricultural Project, Houz al-Awsat	Morocco	5.3	1982 —	—	—
Road Projects	Mauritania	5.3	1982 —	—	—
Electro-mechanical Equipment					
Thermal Power Station at Nouadhibou	Mauritania	0.695	1982 —	—	—

Table 9.8: Project Loans Granted by KFAED: Some Examples

Project	Country	Amount (K Dinars)	Date	%	Maturity	Grace Period
Sudanese Railways	Sudan	7.00	3/1962	4	15.7	3.7
La Goulette Electricity	Tunisia	3.80	12/1963	4	15.5	3.5
Expansion of Suez Canal	Egypt	9.80	7/1964	4	16	3.0
Agricultural Project, TADLA	Morocco	2.70	5/1966	3	19	4.0
Petroleum Pipeline	Algeria	2.50	5/1967	4	11.8	0.0
Grain Silos	Syria	7.00	8/1969	3.5	15.5	3.5
Um Qasr Cement Works	Iraq	3.76	8/1971	4	13.1	2.1
River Zarka Project	Jordan	4.60	3/1972	3	24.5	4.5
Irrigation Rahad	Sudan	3.30	4/1973	3	30	4.5
Petroleum Refinery	Syria	2.00	3/1974	1	24	4.5
Abyan Project	South Yemen	4.20	5/1974	0.5	49	9.4
Phosphoric Acid	Morocco	2.40	11/1974	4	14	3.7
Road	Mauritania	1.15	4/1975	0.5	25	4.7
Tea Plantation	Rwanda	1.00	6/1975	3	27	6.6
Stock Breeding	Uganda	5.75	6/1975	2.5	25	4.5
Rural Electrification	Bangladesh	6.40	6/1975	2	32	6.8
United Textiles	Tanzania	4.50	7/1975	4	22	4.6
Thermal Power Station	Somalia	6.20	7/1975	1.5	29.1	4.1
United Urea	Sri Lanka	7.50	9/1975	4	19	4.1
Aboukir Power Station	Egypt	10.00	10/1975	4	20	5
Hydroelectric Project, Kulekhani	Nepal	5.00	1/1976	3	31.6	6.6
Road, Taiz KM	Yemen	1.50	1/1976	1.5	39	9.1
Hydro-electric Project, Kalinadi	India	15.00	1/1976	4	25	5
Guddu-Karachi Line	Pakistan	13.00	1976	4	20	5
Electricity Project	Thailand	1.00	1976	3.5	25	5
Telecommunications	Guinea	2.70	1976	4.0	17	3
Roads	Comores Islands	1.80	1976	1	40	10
Airport Extension	Maldives	1.50	1976	1	20	6
Plantation of Coffee	Burundi	0.36	1976	3.0	26	7

Stock Fattening Project	Egypt	3.20	1976	na	na	na
Dam	Mali	5.00	1976	2.5	26	6
Stock Breeding	Senegal	1.20	1976	3.0	26	5
Feasibility Studies	Sudan	0.90	8/1976	1.5	39	9
Railway	Congo	4.00	12/1976	4.0	17	3.7
Electrification	Philippines	3.50	3/1977	4.0	19	3.4
Hydroelectricity	Ghana	8.97	4/1977	4.0	20	5.0
Sugar Factory, Baghland	Afghanistan	8.85	6/1977	3.5	23	4
Limassol Road	Cyprus	1.13	6/1977	5.0	15	32
Palm Oil Complex	Malaysia	2.30	6/1977	5.0	23	6.8
Urban Housing Zones	Bahrain	6.16	1980	4	17	3
Dairy	Djibouti	1.50	1980	1.5	20	5
Road Construction	Oman	2.00	1980	4	18	4
Construction of New Riyan Airport	South Yemen	4.00	1980	1.5	20	6
Construction of two Dams	Cyprus	2.50	1980	1.5	18	6
Wharf Construction	Gambia	1.40	1980	2	20	3
Central Extension, Treggam	Malaysia	1.50	1980	5.5	20	6
Purchase of Ships	Maldives	1.50	1980	3.5	10	3
Construction Hombori-Gao Road	Mali	4.20	1980	2	25	5
Installation of two Electricity Units	Mauritania	1.50	1980	4	18	4
Construction of Thermal Power Station using charcoal at Ano-Anaren	Niger	3.00	1980	4	20	4
Urea Project	Sri Lanka	0.57	1980	4	15	—
Paper Pulp complex at Mufindi	Tanzania	5.00	"	4	24	6
Irrigation Project at Wadi Rima II	North Yemen	2.00	"	2.5	36	6
Bangui-Bassembelé Road	Central African Republic	1.52	1981	na	na	na
Port at Dar-es-Salaam	Tanzania	28.40	"	"	"	"
Hydro-electric Project at Kpong	Ghana	14.20	"	"	"	"
Douala-Yaoundé Road	Cameroon	21.30	"	"	"	"
Railways	Zimbabwe	28.24	"	"	"	"
Lake Nyanza Road	Burundi	7.98	"	"	"	"
Kigali Airport	Rwanda	4.26	1981			
Extension of Thermal Power Station at Mogadishu	Somalia	$36.9	1982			
Financing Irrigation Project, Mogamba	Somalia	$40	"			
Electrical Project, Al-Mukha	North Yemen	$35	"	2.5	20	5

Table 9.9: Islamic Development Bank: Some Examples of Aid, 1976–82

Project	Country	Amount (million $)	Date	Maturity
Central Electricity	Cameroon	7.0	October 1976	25
Harbour Installations	Algeria	12.7	February 1977	na
University	Mauritania	0.8	December 1977	30
Fisheries	Tunisia	7.0	June 1977	30
Development Studies	Malaysia	1.8	February 1978	na
Central Electricity	Syria	6.5	January 1978	na
United Tractors	Turkey	12.0	February 1978	na
Ore Production	Jordan	6.45	1979	na
Petroleum Purchase	Senegal	15.0	1980	na
Mineral Exploration Centre	Upper Volta	4.2	1980	na
Palm Oil Purchases from Malaysia	North Yemen	5.0	1980	"
Main Water Supply to Hodeida	North Yemen	9.75	1980	"
Financing of Imports of Bangladeshi Jute Products	Sudan	17.0	1980	"
Balance of Payments Assistance	Gambia	3.9	1980	"
Gold Mining, Poura	Upper Volta	4.2	1981	"
Participation in the Development Bank of Niger	Niger	2.6	"	"
Financing Overseas Trade	Comores Islands	20.0	"	"
" " "	Senegal	15.0	"	"
" " "	Guinea-Bissau	5.0	"	"
" " "	Guinea	5.0	"	"
Douala-Yaoundé Road	Cameroon	6.0	"	"
Exports from Magnesite Mines, Kutahaya	Turkey	21.5	1982	

Table 9.10: Arab Petroleum Exporting Countries and South-South Co-operation: Some Examples, 1977–82

Date	Value ($ M)	Aim	Companies	Countries
April 1977	150	Electrification of the Assir Province	Hyundai	Saudi Arabia South Korea
May 1977	150	Delivery of 5.3 million tonnes of Brazilian Iron Ore over 5 years	–	Iraq Brazil
" "	120	Agreement on Delivery of Tea over 5 years, Payment in Advance	–	Libya Sri Lanka

September 1977	1,143	Completion of 7 projects in Turkey; joint venture 51% Turkish 49% Libyan	—	Libya Turkey
January 1978	700	Expertise from the Saudi Telephone Network	Dong Ah	Saudi Arabia South Korea
April 1978	300	Fattening Complex (1600 t/j ammoniac). Association TFC-SABIC with Taiwan 60% production	Taiwan Fertiliser Co.	Taiwan Saudi Arabia
June 1978	338	Construction of 200 houses in Jeddah	Hyundai	South Korea Saudi Arabia
October 1978	1,200	Construction of a 550-km	Mendez-Junior	Brazil Iraq
November 1978	na	Railway Providing 10,000 tonnes of Urea to Bangladesh		Iraq Bangladesh
" "	300	Construction of an Ammoniac/Urea Complex at Lasbela in Pakistan, Joint Venture	Pakistan Arab Fertiliser Co.	United Arab Emirates Pakistan
March 1979	310.0	Construction of First Stage of the International Highway Iraq-Kuwait Jordan-Syria		Yugoslavia Iraq
April 1980	27	Providing High Tension Cables to Kuwait	Kolon Electric Machinery	South Korean Kuwait
June 1980	300	Construction of an Export Terminal in Libya	Hyundai	Libya South Korea
October 1980	13.1	Provision and Installation of Steel Containers	Gulf Indian Contracting Co.	India Kuwait
November 1980	2	Provision by Brazil of 115 Generators	Hoos Maquinas Motores	Iraq Brazil
December 1980	282	Port Construction	Sezai-Turkes Feyzi Akkaya	Libya Turkey
January 1981	7.5	Delivery of 200 School Buses	Tata et Ruby	India Kuwait
" "	129	Road Construction	Kozanoglu	Kuwait Turkey
February 1981	170	Water Supply to 39 Villages	ICC	South Korea Saudi Arabia
March 1981	73.2	Road Construction	Taehwa	South Korea Oman
June 1981	20	Provision of a Marine Platform	Far-east Levingston Shipbuilding	United Arab Emirates Singapore
July 1981	570	Construction of Euphrates Project in Iraq	Hidrogradnja	Iraq Yugoslavia
September 1981	18	Maintenance Equipment	Singapore Slipway Engineering Co.	United Arab Emirates Singapore
October 1981	60	Railway Line Construction	Mendez-Junior	Iraq Brazil
October 1981	56.7	Provison of High Tension line Equipment	Energoinvest	Yugoslavia Iraq
" "	65.5	Provision of Hydro-mechanical	Metalna	Iraq Yugoslavia
November 1981	na	Provision of 1.5 million tonnes per year of Indian Iron Ore	Kudermukh	Bahrain India

Table 9.10 — *Continued*

Date	Value ($ M)	Aim	Companies	Countries
" "	50	Sale of 15,000 Honda Cars to Algeria	Honda	Algeria Japan
" "	300	Construction of 2 Dams	Hidroelectrica	Algeria Yugoslavia
" "	na	Sale of wood		Mozambique
December 1981	3	Management of Nitric Acid and Ammonia complex, SONATRACH	RCA Company (Bombay)	India Algeria
January 1982	230	Construction of Separation Unit for Gas and Offshore Petroleum	Hyundai	South Korea Saudi Arabia
January 1982	164	Construction and setting up of 100-bed Hospital	Kug Dong Construction Co.	Saudi Arabia South Korea
" "	114	Construction of four Petroleum Platforms	Verolme Estaleiros Reunidos do Brazil	Brazil Saudi Arabia
January 1982	3	Bicycle Sales	Hyundai	Iraq South Korea
" "	38	Extension of Sugar Cane Plantations	NPCC India	Iraq India
February 1982	6.8	Sale of 40,000 refrigerators to Algeria	Arcelik	Turkey Algeria
" "	21.3	Construction of the Queen Alia Hospital	Sam Whan Corp. South Korea	Jordan South Korea
" "	395	Housing Project, Riyadh	Daelim industrial Co.	South Korea Saudi Arabia
" "	155	Construction of the Ministry of Foreign Affairs	Miryung Construction	South Korea Saudi Arabia
" "	140	Housing Complexes	Ozdemir Insaat	Turkey Libya
1st trimester, 1982	Provision by Kuwait of Capital operat-ting costs of Project (1,500 M)	Mixed Fertilisers (Phosphates and Phosphoric Acid, 350,000 tonnes and 100,000 tonnes respectively)	—	Turkey and Tunisia Delivery of Tunisian Phosphates
March 1982	19	First Stage of Nahar-Saad Irrigation Project	Baytur	Turkey Iraq
Beginning of 1982	130	Construction of 160 km Bajiil-Maabar Road	Sam Whan Corp.	North Yemen South Korea
March 1982	106	Housing Construction at Yaubo (Saudi Arabia)	Nurol Construction Trading Co.	Turkey Saudi Arabia
" "	316	Construction 5,000 Houses at Najran	Joannou-Pareske-vides Midmac Arabia (Libya) and National Construction Co. (Pakistan)	Cyprus Libya Pakistan and Saudi Arabia

March 1982	124	Housing Construction at Arar	Kolon Construction Co.	Saudi Arabia South Korea
" "	150	Construction of 576 Houses at Tabuk	Indian Overseas Construction Consortium and Fiafi Trading Co. (Saudi Arabia)	India Saudi Arabia
" "	39.5	Sale of 5,000 Turkish Tractors,	Turk Tractor	Turkey Iran
April 1982	na	Cement Works Feasibility Study, Djibouti	Associated Cement Co. (India)	Djibouti India
April 1982	na	Harbour Feasibility Studies	Daewoo Development Co. (South Korea)	Egypt South Korea
" "	na	Assembly of 5000 Jeeps	Mahinodra-Mahindra (India)	Iran India
" "	7.05	Water Supply	Enka Construction Co. (Turkey)	Turkey Iraq
" "	17.0	Water Treatment Plants	Hanbo General Construction Co. (South Korea)	South Korea Jordan
" "	44	Civil Engineering	Montinvest (Yugoslavia)	Iraq Yugoslavia
" "	132.4	Civil Engineering	Ivan Milutinovic (Yugoslavia)	Kuwait Yugoslavia
" "	39	Dam	Continental Construction (India)	India Libya
" "	54.5	Airport Facilities	Ret-Ser Engineering (Taiwan)	Saudi Arabia Taiwan
" "	384	Housing Construction	Joint venture Turkey Kutlutas and Enka	Turkey Saudi Arabia
" "	125.4	Commercial Buildings	Nam Kwang Construction Co. (South Korea)	South Korea Saudi Arabia
" "	485	Housing Construction	Soyak Insaat Ticaret and Mohamed Binladet	Turkey Saudi Arabia
May 1982	165	Construction of Sporting Complexes	Gammon Pakistan Co.	Saudi Arabia
" "	371	Housing Construction, Jeddah	Mohamed Binladen	Turkey Saudi Arabia
" "	45	Irrigation Project and Drainage, Abou Beshoot	Hanyang Co. (South Korea)	Iraq South Korea
" "	186	Water supply, Taïf	Dong Ah (South Korea)	South Korea Saudi Arabia
" "	3,000	Construction of 100,000 Houses in Algeria. Creation of an Algerian-Brazilian Company for Mineral Exploration in Africa.	Constructora Mendez-Junior	Algeria Brazil
June 1982	0.775	Construction of a Sulphuric Acid Plant in Bahrain	Sinion Carves	Bahrain India
" "	17.5	Creation of an Iraqi-Brazilian Bank	Rafidani Bank and Other Brazilian Banks	Iraq Brazil

Table 9.10 — *Continued*

Date	Value ($ M)	Aim	Companies	Countries
" "	208.575	Irrigation Project, Kizkouk	Hanyang	Iraq South Korea
" "	19.5	Pumping Station at Karbala Cement Works	Enka	Turkey Iraq
" "	225.2	Infrastructure of the Military City of King Khaled	Samwhan Corp.	Saudi Arabia South Korea
July 1982	45	Provision of 845 Trucks to Iraq	MIN Yugoslavia	Iraq Yugoslavia
" "	48	Housing Construction, Otas	—	Turkey Libya
August 1982	43.5	Rice Sales	—	Thailand Iran
" "	34	Provision of High Tension Wires	Hyundai	South Korea Saudi Arabia
" "	100	Creation of Commercial Bank of Tunisia, United Arab Emirates	—	Tunisia Abu Dhabi
" "	na	Ghana-Iran Agreement on Exchange of Petroleum and Information concerning its Use with Cocoa, Wood and Minerals	—	Ghana Iran

10 A NEW APPROACH TO NORTH-SOUTH CO-OPERATION

Georges Hoyos

It is always difficult to pinpoint the date that marks the start of a process such as the New International Economic Order. Nonetheless, even by specialist standards, it seems that 1964 marks its beginning. It was during that year, on the occasion of the first UNCTAD that the 'general and specific principles governing international trade relations and the trade policies suitable to development' were defined. However, for the initiated observer, it is clear that the debate on the fundamental issue only really began with the advent of what is now termed the 'first oil crisis'. One could even postulate that without this and the subsequent decisions engendered at the time by the OPEC countries, the North's understanding of Southern problems and of their mutual relationship, would be much the same in the 1980s as it was in the 1960s.

Yet while perception may have evolved, what of actual North-South relations themselves? What conclusions can we draw concerning co-operation between the two hemispheres?

A reminder of the major demands made by the South in their quest for New International Economic Order agreements to cover basic products; a 'fair and just' balance between the price of basic products and manufactured goods; internal adjustments of Northern state economies related to Third World production; compensation for deteriorating trade terms; extension of the generalised preference system; reform of the international monetary system, etc.

After five UNCTADs, two special sessions at the UN General Assembly, the Paris Conference on International Economic Co-operation and countless other top-level conferences and meetings, one has to admit that the results are far from commensurate with the efforts deployed. While in terms of actual achievement the Lomé convention seems to be the most innovative, there is still considerable ground to cover before arriving at a real New International Economic Order.

Yet the theory that the application of appropriate measures to developing countries would enable them to catch up with industrialised countries seems to have lost its last defendants. Today it seems clear to most observers that the global development of the Southern countries cannot be achieved without an economic transformation of the Northern states, a change in North-South relations, and an important transfer of technical and financial resources to the South. But how many tens of million unemployed will this entail in OECD countries before any significant steps are achieved in this direction? Quite naturally, the question remains unanswered.

In this context, it is total conjecture to try to examine the role that companies could play, at their level, in North-South co-operation. Yet it is a fundamental question because, while conferences and meetings on the topic of a NIEO are convened, the reality of economic life continues, just as business life goes on: projects are set up and investments are made. And, whatever their size, nationality or multi-nationality, it is companies that put co-operation into practice. Such is the reality.

In the economic system we live in, states cannot indulge in philanthropy, which remains the privilege of individuals or groups of individuals who set out with that vocation, and companies are for the most part in the business of ensuring their own profitability. There are no international laws or standards governing business practices, particularily in the area of technology transfers, precisely because governments are incapable of establishing them from a common accord. As a result, those involved in international business and economic relations, i.e., companies, follow their own logic and imperatives.

There are many consequences to this situation, ranging from Northern countries' inability to charge better prices to their Southern partners for fear of endangering their own profitability, to the deliberate decision by the Northern partners to under-pay for the products they buy from Southern production units.

Yet, on the spot, opportunities do exist to put North-South co-operation into practice. The SIPEM (*Société Internationale de Publications et d'Etudes Multimedia*) is trying an experiment in this area. Firstly, SIPEM wants to establish a North-South mass communication service through an association of partners who control multimedia production and distribution techniques. It has recently implemented this new and original concept in North-South co-operation, and I would like to describe the experiment's objectives in the context of traditional forms of North-South co-operation.

Traditional Forms of North-South Co-operation

Over the last twenty years the forms of North-South co-operation implemented by companies have evolved considerably. Until the early 1970s, the principal form it took was *direct investment*, essentially by creating subsidiary companies in which the Northern mother company held a majority, or 100 per cent, equity stake. This has gradually been replaced by other forms of co-operation, mostly at the prompting of the South which wishes to increase its control over the economic transactions that take place on its territory and also in answer to the North's preoccupation with reducing the risk element.

This type of co-operation took a variety of forms: There was the period of 'turnkey' contracts, whereby the industrialised partner was responsible solely for the construction, and no more, of factories or industrial complexes in developing countries. The weakness of this approach cleared the way for the 'product in hand' type of contract which supplemented the previous type with a performance guarantee. Not only did the factory have to be built according to the rules, but it had to be operational, staffed by trained and competent personnel, etc. Today, we have arrived at 'market in hand' contracts.

Another form of co-operation that developed was *sub-contracting* to the South, whereby Northern businesses, often multinationals, placed orders with production units in developing countries.

Licence agreements are another form of co-operation enabling the Southern country to acquire and exploit locally a given technical expertise against a remuneration that can take different forms.

There are also the famous *joint ventures* in which two or more partners, whether public or private companies, pool resources for a given project (they can span capital, technology, and infrastructure). The details of implementation of such contracts can vary considerably, but it is noteworthy that in this type of project the majority equity stake is increasingly controlled by the South.

In certain cases one also finds simple *management contracts* under which the Northern company will ensure the management and contractually varying responsibilities of an existing and performing business in a developing country.

Finally, there are *temporary partnerships* between North and South, involving company co-operation in the performance of a project in a third market.

One cannot give an automatic value scale for these different types of collaboration. Depending on the technique and specific nature of a project (sector, degree of integration in the local economy, price, particularities of repatriation of profits, etc.) direct investment (100 per cent foreign shareholding) can turn out to be the most beneficial form of co-operation for the host country. In reality, the essential issue in this area is the partners' ability to negotiate and to define, in the final analysis, the mutual costs and benefits of the operation.

One must also underline the essential role of the government authorities in defining different forms of co-operation. Thus, liberal investment policies and legislation, tariff regulations, 'free export zones', etc., are all elements that will guide companies into adopting this or that form of co-operation.

Having said that, the different forms we have reviewed have two major characteristics:

1. The form and details of the co-operation are defined once and for all between partners that usually have unequal powers of negotiation, with the further corollary that the reciprocal benefits are also very often just as unequally balanced.
2. The limitation of the object of co-operation (in terms of duration, geographical area, etc.) within a restrictive contract also defines in detail the terms, obligations and involvement of each partner.

The direct result is a fragmentary, uneven and short-term form of co-operation, totally out of proportion with the vastness of the needs which, on the contrary, usually call for a global and long-term action which will guarantee the ultimate interests of the Southern partner.

It is precisely to tackle this more ambitious, fundamental issue that several companies have grouped together in an international North-South structure aimed at achieving co-operation in the service of Communication. I refer to SIPEM.

SIPEM: a New Approach

The terms of the draft agreement between members of the group are the best illustration of this novel form of co-operation:

Seeing the essential role of media, in particular books, in achieving development through transfer of know-how;

Seeing the vast needs in the areas of education, science and culture;

Seeing the interest of developing knowledge of the numerous cultures and in order to develop inter-cultural relations;

Seeing the necessity of encouraging collaboration between publishers in order to better service the needs of the populations in the above-mentioned areas . . .

The undersigned

have decided to pool together their know-how and resources in a collaboration aimed at satisfying these needs.

This collaboration will concern all media used in general education of populations at whatever level of teaching scientific, cultural or literary subjects from primary to university classes.

A further aim of this collaboration will be to promote the languages of the Southern countries.

It shall include all forms and applications judged necessary to achieve the above objectives.

The undersigned will be particularly concerned with the design, production, publishing and distribution in all relevant areas of products that will answer the realities and diversity of needs and different languages in the countries concerned . . .

It is in this frame of mind that the undersigned agree and decide to create a joint company.

As this draft emphasises, the Northern and Southern companies' motivation in undertaking a joint action, and creating together a new company to that end, is the recognition of the needs in these areas of culture, education and science, and the understanding that the needs will best be answered through a concerted effort. Thus the driving force behind the association is not a given project designed to satisfy its executors, but more the existence of needs and the absolute necessity to co-operate in order to satisfy them. The company's vocation is thus to define simultaneously the strategy and resources needed to be able to answer the needs we have described.

As such, SIPEM's first originality is the fact that Northern and Southern partners come together with one objective, which is to co-operate for the development of their areas of expertise and competence.

The second characteristic is that the strategies and choice of project are defined by joint decision. No element of prior negotiation impedes the limits and consequent mutual benefits of a given co-operation agreement. On the contrary, the mutually favourable basis of the co-operation fosters total freedom as to the choice of the project and its immediate corollary benefits.

There is thus a notable difference between this and the more traditional forms of co-operation reviewed above: SIPEM has an in-built form of North-South co-operation:

1. Since the participants' motivation is by definition their co-operation, in particular between Northern and Southern partners, survival is linked to a mutually beneficial co-operation. Co-operation is therefore indispensable.
2. Whatever the project and however it is realised, a consequence of the company structure is that each of the partners shares in the profits.
3. The open financial management structure and the joint decision process offer the guarantee that the concerns of each partner will be taken into account.
4. Association with the group and its diversified members (in terms of experience, techniques, etc.) gives the Southern companies access to new markets and new technologies in the best conditions; the risks are limited by the association of members; technical transfer takes place under maximum control; the follow-up is ensured by the permanence of the relationship.
5. The input of the Southern members gives the Northern members an unparalleled knowledge of the real developmental needs and the market conditions pertaining to the economic, social and cultural context of the country, area or region concerned.

SIPEM has an external capacity for North-south co-operation:

1. Through its experience and in-built form of North-South co-operation, SIPEM can better promote and realise this co-operation with new partners.
2. The unique expertise of Southern SIPEM members allows for a better analysis of the developing countries' real needs, and

contributes to the definition of techniques and products as well as projects that are better adapted to development requirements.

3. SIPEM's available expertise and capacity, together with the accumulated experience of its members in their different areas of intervention, constitutes the guarantee of a satisfactory conclusion.
4. SIPEM's deliberate policy of acting in close partnership with all participating parties (states, regional, national or international institutions) and its readiness to include other public or private local structures in the execution of projects in hand, also constitute the guarantee that it will be well integrated into its environment.

Besides the novelty of approach to North-South co-operation as practised by SIPEM members, it is equally important to emphasise the importance of the area of intervention under consideration: the media.

Media Control: The Condition for Development

At a recent conference, Mr Amadou Mahtar M'Bow, Director General of UNESCO, quoted a phrase from the 1976 Policy Statement that concluded the fifth Conference of Non-aligned Countries in Colombo:

> That a new international order in the areas of mass communication and information is as important as a New International Economic Order.

These words are particularily relevant today, at a time when there is talk of 'barefooted microprocessors' which could revolutionise communications in the Third World, while at the same time literacy rates are stagnating in many parts of it. Every training or education project poses enormous problems, not only in terms of resources but also in those of cultural problems and teaching methods.

We have already evoked the quasi-unanimous conviction of development experts concerning the illusion of the 'catching-up' theory. But having said that, the question that must be answered concerns the type of development model that is suitable to each large community, taking into account political, cultural and economic development policies. It is precisely at this point that the greatest distortion lies, between the expectations that are fostered by imported educational and cultural models and the necessity of finding new and original development patterns. How can one develop alternative models and systems in a context where everything, the education you receive and the information at your disposal, suggests the following of a prefabricated model? So the very condition of development is the mastery by the Third World nations themselves of communication techniques, structures and networks, together with regained control over the contents and means of education.

SIPEM aims at the heart of this problem. Deliberately focused on training and educational needs, and through mastery of information techniques (be it pamphlets, software, radio or audio-visual programmes) it seeks to collaborate with all state, regional, national or international institutions concerned with the definition and execution of the strategies required in this area of need.

The Role of the Arab Development Funds

It is an understatement to say that development aid dispensed over the last two decades by the international community has fallen far short of the objectives purportedly pursued. It is certain that classical development assistance programmes cannot answer the challenge, as they are based on the concept that underdevelopment is a position that is defined in terms of laps on the track that has already been followed by industrial countries.

If one accepts that a New International Economic Order is the necessary condition of development of the Southern countries, the essential problem is to define new models for co-operation agreements which are really in line with the objectives to be pursued. In this context the role of the Arab Development Funds is vital.

The inevitable weight of the multi-lateral development assistance institutions impedes any fundamental readjustment of policies in the immediate future, even though certain of these agencies have made great efforts to adapt. As for bi-lateral agencies, the basis of their actions is generally dictated by short-term considerations, with the result that their policies are basically at the mercy of the economic war that is being waged by industrial countries operating in Third World markets.

The Arab Funds have two advantages. Firstly, their greater innovative capacity which results from their recent entry into the international arena. Secondly, being institutions that themselves originate from the developing world, they are in a better position to assess priorities while taking into account real difficulties in the field.

Thus their role is fundamental to the issue of development aid, the more so since financial efforts already begun and future available resources are not inconsiderable. Furthermore, owing to the very origin of their resources, they are naturally concerned with the whole problem of a NIEO; they can also boast a marked experience of North-South negotiations. They are particularily well-informed partners.

However, it is the choice of projects and the vectors of proposed aid which pose a problem for the Arab Funds in their financing capacity.

The choice of projects must be in line with the development strategy that is defined by and for each state or region, and must be made by the political authorities. Yet it is difficult to imagine a situation where the sponsors, that is, the Arab Funds, would not be involved at all!

The choice of vectors of the aid is equally crucial. There cannot be any project at all without the arms and the legs to carry it out. To achieve a strategy is often a question of finding the right contractor or vector. It is an aspect that has only too often been neglected by the decision-makers who, involved as they are in over-rigid tender procedures and with other constraints, have lost touch with the heart of the problem, which is development.

It is in this context that the new approach to North-South inter-company co-operation which I have briefly outlined takes on importance. For, apart from development plans, there is the whole political question of conceiving and putting into practice the various projects and specific actions without which there can be no start to the development process. We are only too aware in too many instances of the gap between objectives and execution on the ground. Only too often a project results not from a national political decision but from a series of interlinked considerations that have little to do with the central issue of development. Furthermore, at both ends of the line regarding design and execution, the companies specialising in international aid exercise considerable influence.

This is why the creation of true North-South companies to relay the co-operation corresponds to a real necessity: how to achieve the structural link between the designers and the contractors of development projects, and the objectives pursued. The influence of the financial sponsors in this process is essential. To a great extent it is the choices they make that will determine the evolution in this area.

11 THE AFRO-ARAB ALLIANCE: AN ECONOMIC STRATEGY FOR THE 1980s*

Bichara Khader

According to data compiled by the Arab aid agencies, Arab governments committed a total of nearly $7.5 billion for direct aid to non-Arab Africa in the period from 1975 to October 1982, mostly on concessional terms.[1] These financial data do not include sizeable Arab contributions to the IMF's oil and supplementary facilities and to international institutions which, in turn, assit African countries.

In view of the inherent characteristics of the economies of the donor countries of the Arab world, their expanding aid to Africa should not conceal the fact that concessional flows cannot, *in the long term*, represent a balanced relationship among developing countries. As a matter of fact 'the large liquid assets which enabled this relationship to grow can hardly be conceived of as a lasting phenomenon which will persist on the same impressive scale as is experienced at present.'[2]

Before embarking on a review of the principal areas of co-operation between the Arabs and the Africans, I would like to present some concise general considerations on the thorny problems of surpluses and their recycling.

Transient Surpluses

Arab aid to Africa has certainly been eased by the availability of surpluses in the Arab oil countries. The accumulation of net liquid assets by some Arab countries 'has generally been looked at as a "problem"' by current literature. There appears to have been somewhat less stress placed on the reasons behind the accumulation of surpluses. This marked tendency to ignore the core of the problem, led to misconceptions detrimental to the Arab image in the Third World.

Although depicted in biased literature as *nouveaux riches*[3] all the

* I am indebted to Mr Hamid Chabar for compiling some statistical data for this chapter.

Arab countries are 'at an early stage of development if judged by the relevant social and economic indicators and not by the false appearances of wealth'.[4]

As with the rest of the Third World countries, the seven Arab oil countries are all food-deficit ones, not one of them having a powerful industrial base, none of them having major exports other than oil, and only four of the seven Arab oil countries (Libya, Saudi Arabia, Kuwait and the Emirates) having surpluses.

The existence of these surpluses does not necessarily put these countries in the rank of the developed countries, 'whose wealth is based on recurrent production from an established industrial and/or agricultural base'. Surpluses are a salient phenomenon. Liquidity is not wealth. And as Shihata correctly points out: 'the transformation of a depletable natural resource into cash, which cannot be absorbed immediately in real new investments, may in fact make the country poorer rather than richer in the long run.'[5]

One might argue that 'these net liquid assets of Arab oil countries could have been avoided and could still be eliminated, under more restrictive oil production policies.'[6] But such argument ignores the very nature of oil: it is indispensable to the world economy. This means that any serious attempt on the part of Arab countries to diminish oil production will result in higher prices and serious supply problems, thus putting in jeopardy the interests of oil consumers and endangering the world community at large.

The real problem for the Arabs lies in bringing about a conversion of financial instruments or paper claims into real resources under present conditions. In other terms, the real challenge lies in the transformation of contingent liquidity into a renewable productive and diversified economic base.[7] This process must take into account the transient nature of oil surpluses, as depletable assets, and the necessity of utilising them for the benefit of the future generations.

A few other remarks should be made. First of all, it should be noted that Arab surpluses, in nominal value, have fluctuated considerably during the last ten years, with a sharp rise in 1974, a serious drop in 1978, and another rise in 1980. One estimate which takes into account the present cutbacks and the downward pressure on oil prices due to oil-glut on the world market, indicates that the thirteen countries of OPEC could well post a deficit of US$27 billion on their current account. Available data on Arab surpluses show a similar trend of gradual erosion of net assets. Some Arab oil countries, like Iraq and Algeria are becoming net borrowers on the capital market.

If current trends in the erosion of the Arab surpluses were to persist, then the whole strategy of Arab aid to the Third World in general and the African countries in particular, would be severely damaged.

Indeed, the prospects of Arab aid beyond the short-term will be influenced by many factors: the inflationary pressures which tend to erode net assets, the uncertain developments related to oil production and oil revenues, the increasing propensity to import and the possible increasing absorptive capacity of Arab economies (that is, the increasing ability to spend domestically on economic development). It is of the highest importance to keep this point in mind.

Recycling Arab Surpluses in Third World Economies

Transforming Assets

At the risk of repetition, we must reaffirm that Arab surpluses should be seen in their true perspective: as the monetary form of a depleting asset.[9]

It is therefore in the interest of the Arabs to transform these assets, through the promotion of South-South co-operation, into new real investments. This strategy would attain several objectives:

a. provide the Arabs with revenues in the post-oil era;
b. facilitate an international redistribution of income to the benefit of the poorer nations;
c. reinforce, more specifically, the Afro-Arab strategic alliance.

Recycling Arab money in investment projects in Third World countries should procure adequate returns both for the Arab investors and the host developing country. This should be the basis of a more balanced pattern of Third World solidarity.

Investing Arab funds in new real investments in the developing countries, where they have their greatest potential, would protect their real value while adding to the real wealth of the world and curbing inflation.

Enhancing Trade between Arab Countries and Developing Countries

Trade patterns between Arab countries and the world show a high degree of dependence on the AICs (advanced industrialised countries). If we look at the Arab countries' import pattern we discover that in 1982, the AICs accounted for more than 85 per cent of Arab imports. Among the industrial countries there was not a single country which did not increase its exports to Arab countries severalfold.

In contrast, the *non-oil exporting less developed countries* (NOLDCs) hardly benefited from the trade flows of Arab countries. The major NOLDC's exporters of manufactured goods (i.e. South Korea, Taiwan, Hong Kong, China, Singapore, India, Brazil, Argentina, Mexico, Malaysia) hardly improved their share of Arab imports.

And yet, many less developed countries (LDCs) are quite willing to respond to the challenge posed to their own economies by the oil prices rise and its subsequent exaggerated repercussion on industrial products imported from the AICs, and to seek to recoup their positions through intensive development of commercial contact with Arab countries. Some of them have taken some initiatives in this direction. Unfortunately, these were constrained by the limits imposed by their own economic structures but also, it should be acknowledged, by the fascination of the Arab oil countries for the most sophisticated technology of the West and its most expensive products for current consumption.

Faced with a situation where cost was not immediately seen as a constraint, 'LDCs promoting more appropriate technologies without the household brand names of the developed world' had much headway to make before they could persuade the Arab oil exporters to look at their wares'.[10]

We can expect a gradual change in this situation in the near future. Several reasons suggest a need for an increase in the import pattern between the Arab countries and Third World's exporters. The most relevant of them resides in the fact that Arab countries are becoming more and more reluctant to pay the price of astronomically inflated import costs as a result of their preference for Western technology and services.

Thus, a redirection of Arab trade towards the countries of the South is not only to be recommended, it is also the highest necessity. Any redirection of Arab countries' expenditures should aim, *inter alia*, for the following objectives: diversifying sources of supply; acquiring command over real goods and services; adding to the capacity of the LDCs; and ensuring fuller utilisation of their human and material resources. Such a new policy should be predicted on a mutuality of interest within the framework of South-South co-operation.

But in order to prevent this 'redirection of Arab trade' from remaining wishful thinking, it is of paramount importance to undertake a full-scale study to identify the composition of Arab imports and the factors inhibiting any enhancement in the share of the LDCs.

Labour Migration from Adjacent Developing Countries

Labour migration to the seven Arab OPEC countries accounted[11] for remittances to ten developing countries amounting to $5.5 billion in 1977 and more than $10 billion in 1982. Remittances to Jordan and North Yemen already constitute the main source of revenue of these two countries. Nigeria provided labour for millions of Africans from neighbouring countries. But social costs of international labour migration pose a real problem for the labour exporting countries, which may suffer from a shortage in their workforce and a dangerous brain-drain, with all its devastating effects on the productivity of the economic system. The host countries also cannot indefinitely exploit the foreign workers without ensuring a minimum of social security and basic rights.[12]

There is a host of other areas where Arab surpluses can be utilised in the Third World. Afro-Arab co-operation can act as a good example.

A New Approach to the Enhancement of Afro-Arab Co-operation

Afro-Arab alliance is based not only on political proclamations, or on speeches made at international gatherings. It is based on solid facts.

Almost 60 per cent of Arabs live in Africa. Table 11.1 illustrates this point:

Table 11.1: Population of the Arab World, 1982 (Millions)

Africa		The Middle East	
Morocco	20	Jordan	3
Mauritania	2	Lebanon	3
Algeria	19	Syria	9
Tunisia	6	Iraq	13
Libya	3	Kuwait	1.3
Egypt	43	Saudi Arabia	9
Sudan	18	UAE	0.8

Table 11.1 — *Continued*

Africa		The Middle East	
Somalia	3.7	Qatar	0.2
Djibouti	0.3	Bahrain	0.4
		North Yemen	6
		South Yemen	2
		Oman	0.8
Total	115.0	Total	48.5

Two-thirds of Arab lands lie in Africa:

Table 11.2: Distribution of Arab Lands (Thousands sq km)

Africa		The Middle East	
Morocco	712	Jordan	98
Mauritania	1,031	Lebanon	10
Algeria	2,382	Syria	185
Tunisia	164	Iraq	435
Libya	1,760	Kuwait	18
Egypt	1,001	Saudi Arabia	2,150
Sudan	2,506	UAE	84
Somalia	638	Qatar	11
Djibouti	22	Bahrain	1
		North Yemen	195
		South Yemen	333
		Oman	212

One in four Africans is Arab.

Table 11.3: African Population

Country	Area (sq km)	Population	Density (pop./km^2)	GNP (US$)
Angola	1,246,700	6.9M	5.5	440
Benin	112,622	3.47M	30.8	250
Botswana	582,000	840,000	1.42	620
Burundi	27,834	4.1M	148	180
Cameroon	475,000	8.3M	18	490
Central African Republic	622,984	2.3M	3.7	270
Comores	2,171	325–370,000	114	180
Congo	342,000	1.5M	4.4	580
Equatorial Guinea	28,051	250,000	8.9	
Ethiopia	1,237,000	31M	25	110
Gabon	267,687	1.3M	4.9	3,590
Gambia	11,295	580,000	51.3	230
Ghana	238,537	11.3–11.9M	49	380

Guinea	245,957	5.3M	21.3	260
Guinea Bissau and Cape Verde Islands	4,033	320,000	80	160
Ivory Coast	322,463	7.8–8.2M	24.8	950
Kenya	582,646	15.32M	24	380
Lesotho	30,355	1.3M	42.5	300
Liberia	111,369	1.8M	16.1	460
Madagascar	587,041	8.5	14.3	250
Malawi	118,484	5.562M	46	180
Mali	1,240,000	6.5M	5.2	130
Mauritius	2,045	970,000	485	830
Mozambique	783,030	11.7M	15	240
Namibia	823,620	1M	1.2	1,080
Niger	1,267,000	5.3M	4.2	240
Nigeria	923,768	80–85M	86	600
Rwanda	26,338	4.9M	186	190
São Tomé and Principe	964	0.85M	—	500
Senegal	196,192	5.5–5.9M	28	360
Seychelles	404	62–65,000	162.5	1,068
Sierra Leone	7,326	3.4M	463	230
South Africa	1,221,037	24.2M	19	1,580
Swaziland	17,363	541,000	31	590
Tanzania	945,000	18M	19	240
Tchad	1,284,000	4.4M	3.4	150
Togo	56,000	2.5M	44.6	320
Uganda	236,036	14M	59	290
Upper Volta	274,200	6.7M	24.8	160
Zaire	2,345,409	28M	11.9	240
Zambia	752,614	5.8M	7.7	510
Zimbabwe	391,109	7.3M	18.6	480

The Arabic language is the first language spoken in Africa.

Table 11.4: Principal languages of Africa (Millions of speakers)

	1980	2000
Arabic	110	190
Swahili	35	65
Hausa	30	52
Bantu	25	40
Berber	15	25
Yoruba	15	25
Lingala	13	22
Gala	12	20
Peul	10	17
Amharic	10	17
Kikongo	10	17
Total	260	490

Source: Mehdi El Mandjara, 'Horizon 2000: et dans 20 ans?', *Jeune Afrique* (January 1982) p. 49

Afro-Arab solidarity is, then, not a mere slogan, devoid of content. Thus, both Arabs and Africans look upon Arab foreign aid as the cornerstone that could enable them to join their efforts and collectively build an effective base for future economic, social and political progress.

Africans and Arabs: a Changing Relationship?

Arab aid to Africa has been minimised by the Western media and literature and Afro-Arab relationships have been denigrated. Doubt has been cast on its solidity and perspectives. In their study of Afro-Arab relations, Le Vine and Duke argued, in a polemical way, three related sets of propositions:

a. The era of Afro-Arab solidarity, widely hailed by statesmen and scholars alike, turns out to have been relatively short-lived, having run its course in little over ten years.
b. The principal factor in the deterioration of Afro-Arab relations has been a basic shift in the international status and mobility of Arab states. Led by their oil producing states, the Arabs have 'moved to a better part of town', leaving their former friends behind and taking on the behaviour of their new, rich neighbours.
c. The Arab shift has left erstwhile African friends much worse off than they were before the new era dawned, turning them into clients and/or dependants where they had been equals, and leaving them doubly vulnerable to political and economic changes in the international environment.[13]

This kind of argument is symptomatic of that presented in the Western media which continuously endeavours to depict Arabs as 'money lenders', 'rapacious merchants', 'immoral exploiters', 'warmongers', 'slave-traders' and so on and so forth.

The ultimate objective of this kind of denigration is to kill Afro-Arab co-operation at source by arguing that Arabs are ill-intentioned, and pay no attention to the plight of the Africans, merely imitating the West in a childish way, and in the final analysis, seeking to replace the old colonial powers in Africa.

To refute such arguments is time-consuming and to no avail. Suffice to say that Afro-Arab co-operation, in spite of its constraints and limits, is not doomed to failure, because the very future of millions of Arabs and Africans alike is at stake. That's why I shall concentrate my attention in the following section on the future prospects of Afro-Arab economic co-operation, as a good case study of South-South co-operation.

Future Prospects for South-South Co-operation and for Afro-Arab Economic Co-operation

The purpose of this section is to develop the logic of South-South co-operation in general and Afro-Arab co-operation in particular and to ascertain the viability of such co-operation.

South-South Co-operation: the New International Economic Order an Impossible Task

The very idea of South-South co-operation has been fostered by a sense of frustration at what the South feels is the Northern bias of international economic institutions and relations. And yet, the call for a New International Economic Order, somewhat paradoxically, has been largely a call for the North to help the South.[14] But as Nugent puts it: 'The South has alternatively begged, bargained with, preached to, threatened and cajoled the North, but always with the same negative result of non-response by the North'.[15]

Likewise the appeal to the North to 'help' the South has always been met with lip-service. Not only has the North turned a cold shoulder to the call of the South for specific reforms in the monetary system, in the terms of exchange, in the flexibility of financial institutions, in moderation of the prices of industrial products, in flow of technology and so on, but it has also begun to invoke increasing protectionist restrictions on trade with the South (textiles for example) — and retracted further from its prescribed Official Development Assistance (ODA) targets, as is shown by Table 11.5:

Table 11.5: OECD Official Development Assistance, 1980

	(% GNP)	$M
Italy	0.17	683
New Zealand	0.33	72
UK	0.35	1,851
Finland	0.23	110
Australia	0.48	667

Table 11.5 — *Continued*

	(% GNP)	in % $
Japan	0.32	3,353
Canada	0.43	1,075
Austria	0.23	178
USA	0.27	7,138
Holland	1.03	1,630
France	0.64	4,162
Belgium	0.50	595
Denmark	0.73	474
Sweden	0.79	962
Federal Republic of Germany	0.43	3,567
Switzerland	0.24	253
Total	0.38	27,256

Thus, in 1980, the ODA amounted to $27.3 billion at nominal prices, which constitutes an average of 0.38 per cent of the Gross National Product of that year for the OECD countries ($7.2 trillion at nominal prices).

Not surprisingly, the South's reaction to the increasingly bleak prospect of benefitting through greater co-operation with the North (increased ODA, increased flow of trade on more equal terms, opening up of the Northern markets to Southern industrial and agricultural products and so on) has been to turn further inward, without systematically calling for delinking from the North.

Gloomy Predictions for the Economic Development of the South: Ravaging Indebtedness

What adds to the anxiety of the Southern countries is the bleak future economic prospect. Almost every recent study of the economic prospects of the South in the 1980s concludes with gloomy predictions.

First of all, the South will have to deal with 'an inhospitable international environment in the 1980s.'[16] The world economy, which is crucial for its progress, is characterised by an uncertain outlook: faltering growth rates, high rates of inflation and increasingly protective measures against the exports of the South.

Another preoccupying factor one has to mention is the South's indebtedness. Although this is not a new phenomenon in the South, the magnitude of borrowing and the constraints it has placed on its economies threaten a serious crisis in international financial obligations, with adverse effects on the world economy.[17]

Table 11.6: Third World Indebtedness

	Debt (US$ M)		Debt per capita ($)	Debt (% GNP)		Debt service as % of exports, 1979
	1970	1979	1979	1970	1979	
1. Afghanistan	454	1,143	1,374	48.2	29.1	na
2. Algeria	937	15,330	842.31	18.5	49.1	25.6
3. Argentina	1,878	8,716	319.27	7.6	8.6	15.5
4. Bangladesh	na	2,842	31.79	na	29.6	8.4
5. Benin	41	186	54.71	16.0	19.2	5.1
6. Bolivia	477	1,835	339.81	46.4	38.7	29.6
7. Brazil	3,227	35,092	301.22	7.2	17.7	34.6
8. Burma	101	1,141	34.68	4.7	23.2	22.0
9. Burundi	7	103	25.75	3.1	12.9	3.1
10. Cameroon	131	1,634	199.27	12.1	32.9	9.5
11. Central African Republic	19	150	75.00	11.2	24.0	0.1
12. Chad	32	172	39.09	11.8	30.8	14.4
13. Chile	2,066	4,767	437.34	26.4	23.6	26.2
14. Colombia	1,249	3,426	131.26	18.1	12.6	12.5
15. Congo	143	799	532.67	54.5	75.8	7.3
16. Costa Rica	134	1,277	580.45	13.8	33.0	23.1
17. Dominican Republic	212	828	156.23	14.6	16.2	13.9
18. Ecuador	213	2,207	272.47	13.3	22.8	29.6
19. Egypt	1,644	11,409	293.29	23.8	60.4	15.8
20. El Salvador	88	397	90.23	8.6	11.5	3.2
21. Ethiopia	169	620	20.06	9.5	15.7	4.9
22. Ghana	489	977	86.46	22.6	9.6	4.2
23. Guatamala	106	482	70.88	5.7	7.0	2.2
24. Guinea	314	990	186.79	51.7	68.6	22.2
25. Haiti	40	209	42.65	10.3	18.0	2.9

	Debt (US$ M)		Debt per capita ($)	Debt (% GNP)		Debt service as % of exports 1979
	1970	1979	1979	1970	1979	
41. Madagascar	93	348	40.94	10.8	12.6	3.9
42. Malawi	121	423	72.93	38.7	33.1	9.4
43. Malaysia	390	3,004	229.31	10.0	15.4	4.7
44. Mali	238	545	80.15	88.1	44.2	8.5
45. Mauritania	27	590	368.75	16.8	120.9	32.4
46. Mexico	3,206	28,805	439.77	9.7	24.5	64.1
47. Morocco	711	6,227	319.33	18.6	40.3	21.8
48. Nepal	3	125	8.93	0.3	6.9	1.4
49. Nicaragua	155	1,101	423.46	20.6	62.9	8.1
50. Niger	32	234	45.00	8.7	14.4	3.6
51. Nigeria	478	3,744	45.33	6.4	5.0	1.5
52. Pakistan	3,059	7,998	100.35	30.5	38.5	12.0
53. Papua New Guinea	36	393	135.52	6.2	19.5	4.3
54. Paraguay	112	491	163.67	19.1	14.4	8.5
55. Peru	856	5,931	346.84	12.7	42.9	22.3
56. Philippines	633	5,180	110.92	9.2	17.3	12.6
57. Rwanda	2	124	25.31	0.9	13.0	0.6
58. Senegal	98	786	142.91	11.6	32.2	13.7
59. Sierra Leone	59	289	85.00	14.3	33.4	22.2
60. Singapore	152	1,323	551.25	7.9	14.8	1.3
61. Somalia	77	546	143.68	24.4	40.4	1.1
62. South Africa	1,089	7,399	259.61	6.3	13.9	10.6
63. Sri Lanka	317	1,086	74.9	16.1	32.4	6.5
64. Sudan	309	2,114	118.1	11.6	34.5	33.0
65. Syrian AR	232	2,283	265.47	13.6	24.9	16.5
66. Tanzania	248	1,153	64.06	19.4	25.3	7.4

Table 11.6 — *Continued*

	Debt (US$ M) 1970	Debt (US$ M) 1979	Debt per capita ($) 1979	Debt (% GNP) 1970	Debt (% GNP) 1979	Debt service as % of exports, 1979
26. Honduras	90	746	207.22	12.8	36.3	12.7
27. Hong Kong	2	405	8.100	0.1	2.2	na
28. India	7,935	15,641	23.73	14.8	12.3	9.5
29. Indonesia	2,443	13,326	93.25	27.1	28.3	13.4
30. Iran	2,193	7,372	199.24	20.8	na	na
31. Iraq	274	878	69.68	8.8	3.9	na
32. Israel	2,274	9,954	2,619.47	41.3	55.1	10.3
33. Ivory Coast	256	3,647	444.76	18.3	40.3	15.2
34. Jamaica	154	1,182	537.27	11.5	49.4	15.9
35. Jordan	118	1,047	337.74	na	38.1	5.3
36. Kenya	313	1,427	93.27	20.3	24.3	7.5
37. Korea Republic	1,797	14,964	388.73	20.9	24.5	13.5
38. Lebanon	64	93	34.44	4.2	na	na
39. Lesotho	8	52	40.00	9.2	11.1	0.6
40. Liberia	158	454	252.22	49.6	48.4	13.8

	Debt (US$ M) 1970	Debt (US$ M) 1979	Debt per capita ($) 1979	Debt (% GNP) 1970	Debt (% GNP) 1979	Debt service as % of exports 1979
67. Thailand	322	2,699	59.32	4.9	9.9	4.2
68. Togo	40	851	354.58	16.0	85.9	24.4
69. Trinidad & Tobago	101	422	351.67	12.5	10.5	2.3
70. Tunisia	545	3,057	493.06	38.5	43.5	11.8
71. Turkey	1,854	10,972	248.24	14.4	19.0	12.9
72. Uganda	128	245	19.14	9.8	2.6	7.4
73. Upper Volta	21	256	45.71	6.4	25.4	3.8
74. Uruguay	267	914	315.17	11.0	13.3	9.9
75. Venezuela	728	9,797	675.66	6.6	20.0	9.4
76. Yemen AR	na	466	81.75	na	11.9	1.8
77. Yemen SR	1	441	232.11	na	49.0	2.8
78. Zaire	311	3,780	137.45	17.1	51.8	9.1
79. Zambia	596	1,559	278.39	34.5	50.5	19.7

Source: World Bank, *World Development Report 1981*

Tables 11.6–11.10 are illustrative of the astronomical magnitude of the debts and their current interest cost.

Table 11.7: Total Debt of Developing Countries (Disbursed), at Year End, 1971–81, by Source of Lending

								$ billion
Source of Lending	1971	1975	1976	1977	1978	1979	1980 prelim.	1981 est.
1. DAC countries and capital markets	68.8	137.6	166.7	202.4	261.8	308.7	351.0	398
–ODA	24.7	34.3	36.5	41.4	49.0	53.1	57.0	61
–Total export credits	27.5	45.4	54.2	65.8	85.3	100.7	114.0	128
–Capital markets[1]	16.6	57.9	76.0	95.2	127.5	154.9	180.0	209
of which: bank loans	9.4	46.9	60.6	78.7	105.7	129.9	149.0	172
2. International organisations	10.0	21.8	26.7	33.5	40.2	47.9	56.0	65
of which: concessional	3.2	8.0	10.0	13.2	16.4	19.6	23.2	27
3. Centrally-planned economies	6.4	9.8	10.8	12.6	13.8	16.2	18.2	21
4. OPEC countries	0.4	6.4	8.4	10.8	13.2	15.2	18.5	23
5. Other LDCs	1.0	2.4	2.8	3.3	4.1	5.3	6.5	9
6. Unspecified and adjustments	–	1.1	1.5	2.0	3.5	4.0	6.0	8
Total	86.6	179.1	216.9	264.6	336.6	397.3	456.2	524
Annual nominal increase %	16	24	21	22	27	18	15	15

[1]Bank loans (other than export credits), bonds and other private lending.
Source: OECD, Development Co-operation Directorate, Doc. DCD 181.33, 22 September 1981

Table 11.8: Total Debt Disbursed at Year End and Total Annual Debt Service of Developing Countries during 1971–81, by Terms of Lending

								$ billion
	1971	1975	1976	1977	1978	1979	1980 prelim.	1981 est.
Debt								
1. Bi-lateral and multi-lateral ODA	32.4	52.2	59.7	70.4	84.3	94.8	106.4	118.0
2. Other multi-lateral lending	6.8	13.8	16.7	20.3	23.8	28.3	32.8	38.0
3. Total export credits	30.8	54.1	62.6	76.5	96.8	114.3	129.5	148.0
4. Other lending at market terms	16.6	59.0	77.9	97.4	131.7	159.9	187.5	220.0
Total Debt	86.6	179.1	216.9	264.6	336.6	397.3	456.2	524.0

Table 11.8 — *Continued*

	1971	1975	1976	1977	1978	1979	1980 prelim.	1981 est.
								$ billion
Debt Service								
1. Bi-lateral and Multi-lateral ODA	1.8	2.8	3.0	3.4	4.0	4.4	5.1	5.9
2. Other multi-lateral lending	0.6	1.2	1.5	1.9	2.4	3.0	3.9	5.0
3. Total export credits	5.8	12.0	14.6	18.3	23.0	28.1	34.3	41.9
4. Other lending at market terms	2.7	10.2	13.1	17.4	27.5	38.1	47.9	58.9
Total Debt Service	10.9	26.2	32.2	41.0	56.9	73.6	91.2	111.7

Source: OECD, Development Co-operation Directorate, Doc. 181.33, 22 September 1981

Looking more closely at African indebtedness, we find that African countries share the same lot as other Southern countries, although less acutely.

Table 11.9: African Indebtedness, 1980

			Debt Service (%)		Internal reserves	
	$ M	% GNP	of GNP	of Exports of Goods and Services	$ M	in Months of Imports
Chad	159	31.7	3.1	—	11	—
Ethiopia	728	17.8	1.1	7.6	263	3.6
Mali	621	43.8	0.8	3.6	26	0.4
Burundi	137	15.6	0.6	—	105	—
Rwanda	158	15.1	0.2	1.1	186	5.8
Upper Volta	323	24.2	1.2	—	73	—
Zaire	4,190	78.5	5.8		381	
Malawi	122	42.6	4.5	18.4	75	1.6
Mozambique	—	—	—	—	—	—
Sierra Leone	344	34.2	4.2	18.4	31	1.3
Tanzania	1,360	27.6	1	7.3	20	0.2
Guinea	1,074	68.6	6.1			
Central African Republic	155	21.3	1.0	4.5	61	2.5
Uganda	669	4.8	0.3	11.9	17	0.5
Benin	262	23.4	0.6		14	
Niger	399	22.1	2.2	2.3	132	2.1
Madagascar	1,035	31.6	1.8	7.4	5	0.1
Togo	907	86.7	14.4		84	
Ghana	1,745	25.5	2.6	8.8	539	2.1
Lesotho	71	11.1	0.8			
Senegal	906	34.9	6.9		25	
Angola	—	—	—		—	—
Liberia	537	52.8	4.2		4	

Zambia	1,815	51.2	9.5	24.4	207	1.3
Zimbabwe	698	13.8	0.9	2.6	373	2.4
Cameroon	2,002	34	3.1	7.7	206	0.9
Congo	898	77.4	6.1	9.3	91	0.9
Nigeria	4,997	5.5	0.5	1.9	10,642	5.8
Ivory Coast	4,265	41.9	8.2	23.9	43	0.4
South Africa					7,888	3.7

The Arab countries are not sheltered from the ravages of foreign debts. Apart from the four surplus countries, Kuwait, the United Arab Emirates, Libya and Saudi Arabia, all the other Arab states spend a considerable share of their meagre resources and debt service as indicated in Table 11.10:

Table 11.10: Arab Indebtedness, 1980

			Debt Service (%)		Internal reserves	
	$ M	% GNP	of GNP	of Exports	$ M	in Months of Imports
Somalia	698	45.3	0.5	3.5	27	0.6
Sudan	3,097	37.2	1.8	14.4	48	0.4
Dem. Yemen	499	58.6	1.5	1.5	257	5.6
Arab Republic of Yemen	836	27.1	0.6	1.1	1,289	6.8
Mauritania	714	139.7	5.9	32.9	146	3.2
Egypt	13,054	51.7	6.9	18.9	2,478	3.0
Morocco	7,098	38.6	6.5	27.5	811	1.7
Tunisia	2,955	33.9	4.7	12.2	703	2.2
Syria	2,493	20.1	3.2	14.5	826	2.0
Jordan	1,266	37.4	3.9	5.4	1,744	6.1
Lebanon	194				7,023	
Algeria	15,073	35.7	9.5	24.9	7,050	5.7
Libya					14,906	10.2
Saudi Arabia					26,131	4.8
Kuwait					5,426	6.1
UAE					2,357	

The volume of South's indebtedness indicates the tremendous risks to the world economy. In spite of cautious optimism about the ability of developing countries to ward off the prospects of defaults, these cannot be ignored. Paradoxically, the Southern countries have been able, in spite of their increased indebtedness and the deterioration of their terms of trade, to maintain an average growth rate of 2.7 per cent throughout the 1970s. This fact should not overshadow the following factors which, if they remain unchecked, may lead to a catastrophe:

a. *The rapid population growth and the unprecedented shift of people to urban areas.* In the absence of a vast campaign discouraging excessive births and emigration to the urban areas, by the year 2000 the total population of developing countries will reach some 4.9 billion, with 25 per cent living in urban areas.

b. *Spending on arms.* The Brandt Commission estimated current global military spending at US$450 billion a year[18] of which about $14 billion in foreign exchange was spent by developing countries. This figure seems to us far below reality.[19]

c. *Food deficit.* Although world food production has more than doubled over the past twenty-five years, the Southern countries have moved from the food-surplus position, which they held prior to the Second World War to one of serious deficit. Imports of cereals by the Southern countries have increased from relatively low levels in the 1950s to 20 million tons in 1960–1, and to nearly 80 million tons in the year 1978–9 and it is estimated that they will reach 145 million tons by 1990.[20] The Middle East is a good case in point.

The Arab world is not normally identified with hunger and mass starvation. Middle Eastern countries have the distinction, nevertheless, of forming 'the world's most rapidly growing food deficit area'.[21] Between 1973 and 1980, the value of agricultural imports rose from about US$4 billion to more than US$20 billion.[22] Nearly 60 per cent of the region's wheat requirements now come from non-domestic sources, as do between 20 and 25 per cent of its meat supplies. The cost to national treasuries has been enormous and is growing. Economically hard-pressed Egypt spent US$2 billion on food imports in 1978. The oil exporting countries are forced to divert an ever-larger proportion of their revenues to agricultural imports. Algeria devoted more than $1 billion to food imports in 1979. In 1980, Iraq budgeted $1.4 billion. Predictably, the costs for Saudi Arabia topped those of the others; its food bill in 1980 represented US$4.5 billion.

d. *Energy gap.* The Southern countries import the bulk of their energy needs. In 1978, their total imports represented 4.38 million barrels per day.[23]

Total oil demand in developing countries has amounted to 9.2 mb/d in 1980 and is projected by the World Bank to increase to about 15.4 mb/d in 1990. The incremental demand might be met by

Figure 11.1: Net Imports of Crude Oil and Refined Products of non-OPEC Developing Countries, 1978

(Total: 4.38 million barrels per day)

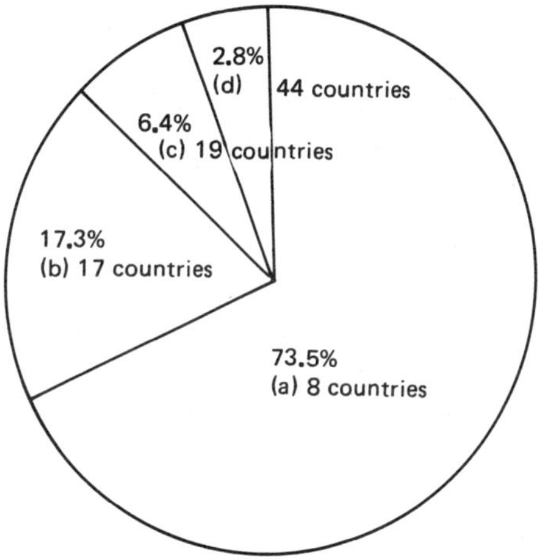

(a) Countries with net imports of more than 100,000 barrels per day or 73.5 per cent of the total
(b) Countries with net imports between 20,000 and 100,000 barrels per day or 17.3 per cent of the total
(c) Countries with net imports between 10,000 and 20,000 barrels per day or 6.4 per cent of the total
(d) Countries with net imports of less than 10,000 barrels per day or 2.8 per cent of the total

Note: Excludes non-OPEC developing countries which are net exporters of crude oil and refined products
Source: OPEC Secretariat, from I. Shihata, p. 260

exploitation of the developing countries' own potential alternative sources of energy, provided that adequate financing is forthcoming.

Collective Self-reliance in the South

These major problems facing the countries of the South constitute a serious challenge. The gloomy prospects should not conceal the fact that there are immense opportunities in developing nations for high priority, economically sound investments which at present lack the required capital and the necessary political will of dedicated and serious politicians and leaders.

The concept of collective self-reliance of the South, although challenging, has unfortunately remained an empty slogan devoid of practical content. It has seldom been articulated into practical and workable forms of co-operation among Southern countries. As an example, the percentage of intra-Southern regional trade is insignificant compared with the percentage of trade flow between the South and the North. Another example is provided by the recycling strategy of the capital-surplus oil exporters. Essentially, as Fehmy Saddy points out, 'what this strategy accomplished was the transformation of OPEC's surpluses into debts to developing countries through the Western banking system which reaped the benefits'.[25] In spite of the simplistic formulation of this statement, there is some truth in it.

And yet, South-South co-operation constitutes the most promising vehicle for achieving the industrialisation targets of developing countries set in Lima in 1975 (25 per cent of the world manufacturing value added by the year 2000) — catering for the basic needs of the population and bridging the widening energy gap. Co-operation among Arab countries, tropical Africa and Asia seems particularly important in view of the fact that these three regions are by far the least developed industrially. As shown in Table 11.11, as recently as 1979, these three regions, which together have populations of more than 1.4 billion, or some two-thirds of the population of developing countries outside China, and over 43 per cent of world population, have less than one-quarter of the manufacturing value-added, at 1975 prices, or less than 2.5 per cent of the world's manufacturing.

Table 11.11: Shares of the Arab, Tropical Africa and South Asia Regions in Manufacturing Value Added (at 1975 Prices) of the South, and of the South in the world (excluding China), 1979

Industry	Share of South World	Share of Arab North Africa, Middle East in South	Share of Tropical Africa in South	Share of South Asia in South	Share of Three Regions Total in
Food Processing	16.21	9.76	7.89	8.60	26.25
Basic Products	9.99	9.49	5.99	10.76	26.24
Light Industry	9.89	9.99	3.21	10.57	23.77
Coal and Petroleum Products	31.59	38.79	1.92	2.29	42.98

Capital Goods	5.41	5.25	1.44	8.61	15.30
Total Manufacturing	9.00	11.40	4.48	9.10	24.98
Population	64.20	8.44	14.87	44.19	66.50

Source: UNIDO data base, information supplied by the Statistical Office of the United Nations, with estimates by the UNIDO Secretariat

It is true that industrial production in the South over the period 1955–74 has expanded faster, at 6.9 per cent a year, compared with 5 per cent in the developed market countries. In the 1970s the South's comparative industrial performance has further improved, while world recession in recent years has slowed down industrial growth in the advanced countries (8.2 per cent compared with 4.5 per cent).

As a result of faster growth in the South, its share of total industrial output increased from 9.1 per cent in 1955 to 11.3 per cent in 1974, and to 12.3 per cent in 1977 (UNCTAD, 1978).

Table 11.12 shows the UNCTAD estimates of the growth rates necessary for the South's share of world industrial production in order to reach 25 per cent in the year 2000.

Table 11.12: Implication of Lima Target for Growth of World Manufacturing Output, 1972–2000.

	1960–72 (actual)	1972–2000	1975–80	1980–90	1990–2000
Developing Countries	6.6	9.6	11.0	10.3	9.3
Developed Market Economies	5.6	5.1	7.0	5.4	4.7
Socialist Countries (E. Europe)	9.0				
Total	6.3	5.8	7.4	6.1	5.6

Note: 'Developing countries' excludes Asian socialist countries, but includes Yugoslavia and Israel; 'Manufacturing output' referes to net value added
Source: UNCTAD (1978b)

Future Prospects for Afro-Arab Co-operation

Before conceiving a future outlook for the promotion of Afro-Arab co-operation within the framework of South-South co-operation, a rapid glance at the specific comparative advantages of the two regions and their respective endowment in human and natural resourccs is imperative.

Human Resources of Both Regions are Considerable

The Arab population was 166,500,000 in 1980. It is projected to be 272,700,000 in the year 2000 as is shown in Table 11.13:

Table 11.13: Arab Population

	Arab population, 1980	Projection, 2000
Morocco	20,000,000	34,000,000
Mauritania	2,000,000	3,000,000
Algeria	19,000,000	34,000,000
Tunisia	6,000,000	9,000,000
Libya	3,000,000	5,000,000
Egypt	42,000,000	62,000,000
Sudan	18,000,000	31,000,000
Somalia	3,700,000	6,000,000
Djibouti	0,300,000	0,540,000
Jordan	3,000,000	5,000,000
Palestine	4,000,000	7,200,000
Lebanon	3,000,000	5,000,000
Syria	9,000,000	15,000,000
Iraq	13,000,000	23,000,000
Kuwait	1,300,000	2,000,000
Saudi Arabia	9,000,000	15,000,000
UAE	0,800,000	1,440,000
Qatar	0,200,000	0,360,000
Bahrain	0,400,000	0,720,000
Oman	0,800,000	1,440,000
North Yemen	6,000,000	9,000,000
South Yemen	2,000,000	3,000,000
Total	166,500,000	272,700,000

The growth of the African population in the coming twenty years will follow the same trend, as indicated in Table 11.14:

Table 11.14: Population of Tropical Africa

	Population, 1980	Projection, 2000
Angola	6,700,000	11,000,000
Benin	3,300,000	6,000,000
Botswana	0,800,000	1,440,000
Burundi	9,000,000	18,000,000
Cameroon	8,100,000	13,000,000
Cape Verde	0,320,000	0,577,000
Central Africa	1,900,000	3,000,000
Congo	1,500,000	3,000,000
Ivory Coast	7,800,000	14,000,000
Ethiopia	31,000,000	52,000,000

Gabon	0,550,000	1,000,000
Ghana	11,000,000	21,000,000
Guinea	5,100,000	9,000,000
Guinea Bissau	0,570,000	1,020,000
Equatorial Guinea	0,377,000	0,668,000
Upper Volta	5,600,000	9,000,000
Kenya	14,700,000	32,000,000
Lesotho	1,300,000	2,000,000
Liberia	1,700,000	3,000,000
Madagascar	8,300,000	14,000,000
Malawi	5,700,000	11,000,000
Mali	6,300,000	11,000,000
Mauritius	0,900,000	1,625,000
Mozambique	9,900,000	17,000,000
Namibia	1,000,000	1,800,000
Niger	5,000,000	9,000,000
Nigeria	80,600,000	153,000,000
Uganda	12,400,000	23,000,000
Reunion	0,490,000	0,900,000
Rwanda	4,500,000	8,000,000
Senegal	5,400,000	9,000,000
Sierra Leone	3,300,000	6,000,000
Swaziland	0,550,000	1,000,000
Tanzania	16,900,000	32,000,000
Chad	4,300,000	7,000,000
Togo	2,400,000	4,000,000
Zaïre	26,800,000	47,000,000
Zimbabwe	6,900,000	13,000,000
Comores	0,400,000	0,720,000
Sychelles	0,100,000	0,180,000
Gambia	0,600,000	1,080,000
São Tomé and Principe	0,100,000	0,720,000
South Africa	27,700,000	49,000,000
Zambia	5,300,000	10,000,000
	340,257,000	631,730,000

The Arab world and Tropical Africa have great human resources. In the year 2000, these two regions will have almost 900,000,000 persons. If the brain-drain of highly qualified people to the North controlled, and if the rate of illiteracy is checked, this human resource can easily be transformed into a positive driving force for development.

Mineral Resources in the Arab world are Considerable

Of the thirteen countries forming OPEC, seven are Arab. This is not fortuitous. The Arab world contains 54 per cent of proven world oil reserves and contributes 32 per cent of world oil production.

Table 11.15: Arab Oil Reserves

Country	Reserves (million/barrels)	% of World Reserves
Abu Dhabi	30,000	4.67
Bahrain	250	0.03
Dubai	1,300	0.20
Iraq	32,100	5.00
Kuwait	66,200	10.31
Neutral Zone	6,480	1.01
Oman	2,500	0.39
Qatar	4,000	0.62
Saudi Arabia	165,700	25.82
Charkah (UAE)	16	0.00
Syria	2,080	0.32
Algeria	6,300	0.98
Egypt	3,200	0.49
Libya	24,300	3.78
Morocco	125	0.00
Tunisia	2,300	0.35
Total	346,726,125	53.97

Table 11.6: Arab Oil Production

Country	% of World Production
Abu Dhabi	2.41
Bahrain	0.09
Dubai	0.60
Iraq	4.16
Kuwait	3.16
Neutral Zone	0.70
Oman	0.53
Qatar	0.80
Saudi Arabia	13.00
Charkah (UAE)	0.04
Syria	0.28
Algeria	2.10
Egypt	0.81
Libya	3.41
Tunisia	0.16

Apart from its oil wealth, the Arab world accounts for 14 per cent of world gas reserves.

Table 11.17: Arab Natural Gas Reserves (Millions of cubic meters)

Country	Reserves	% of World Reserves
Abu Dhabi	20,000	0.79
Bahrain	7,000	0.27
Dubai	1,600	0.06
Iraq	27,800	1.11
Kuwait	31,300	1.25
Neutral Zone	5,000	0.19
Oman	2,000	0.07
Qatar	40,000	2.59
Saudi Arabia	93,900	3.75
Syria	1,500	0.06
Algeria	105,000	4.19
Egypt	3,000	0.11
Libya	24,200	0.96
Morocco	30	—
Tunisia	6,000	0.23
Total	368,330	15.63
World Total	2,502,010	100.00

Natural Resources in Africa are Considerable

At least seven African countries have oil, but it is extracted in negligible quantities. They are the Angola, Congo, Cameroon, the Ivory Coast, Gabon, Zaire and Nigeria.

But does Africa have enough other mineral and power resources to provide the essential foundations for industrial growth? It is the second largest continent in the world, after Asia, but it has never been adequately geologically surveyed. In recent years, new exploration and geological surveys have, however, opened up new sources of mineral and power wealth. Deposits of iron ore considered among the best in the world are being developed in Mauritania, Liberia, Sierra Leone, Guinea, Swaziland, Gabon and Angola. Phosphates for fertilisers are being produced in Togo, Senegal, Morocco, Algeria and Tunisia. Africa is known to have about 40 per cent of the world's potential hydro-electric power. The Inga Dam project in the Congo alone could produce as much hydro-electric power as is now available from all European Community countries.

So Africa has the mineral and power resources necessary for extensive modern industrial development. The economic task facing the continent is how to harness this potential to meet the need of the African peoples themselves.

Table 11.18: African Mineral Output (including Arab African states)

	Uses	African Output (% World Total)	
Metallic			
Antimony	Hardens metals	19% (1976)	
Bauxite	Raw material for aluminium	16% (1976)	14% (1980)
Chromite	For steel	36% (1976)	43% (1980)
Copper	Electric wire, brass	20% (1976)	16.2% "
Gold	Standard value	85% "	
Iron	Basic metal for steel	7% "	9.7% "
Manganese	For steel	38% "	
Tin concentrates	Rust-resistant	7% "	
Uranium	For nuclear energy	24% "	
Vanadium	Medicinal	39% "	
Non-metallic			
Asbestos	Unburnable, used for insulation, etc.	10% "	
Coal	Energy source	3% "	
Diamonds	Industrial cutting and precision tools, jewels	69% "	
Phosphate rock	Fertiliser	31% "	

Note: For 1977 figures, see UN statistics, 1977, for 1980 figures, see J. Beaujeu-Garnier, A. Gamblin and A. Delobez, *Images économiques du Monde*, 1981

The conditions under which African mineral resources are presently exploited are well known. A very few large foreign firms dominate modern export-oriented enclaves. All Zambia's major copper mines, producing about 90 per cent of its exports, for example, are affiliates of the Anglo-American Corporation and American Metal Climax. The rich uranium, copper and tin mines of Zaïre were primarily controlled by the Union Minière du Haut Katanga, owned by Belgian, British and American interests. Iron deposits in Mauritania, Sierra Leone, Liberia and Gabon are being exploited by large foreign combines which in most instances have at their command more capital and assets than any one of the individual African states.

The bulk of the profits, interests and dividends produced by the mines are still drained off by the large foreign firms through their direct control of the export and import trade and related shipping, banking and insurance interests.

Thus, while Africa as a whole is well endowed with most, if not all, the natural resources necessary for modern industrial development, African states have not been able, up until now, to process African materials, because of the domination of foreign interests and the

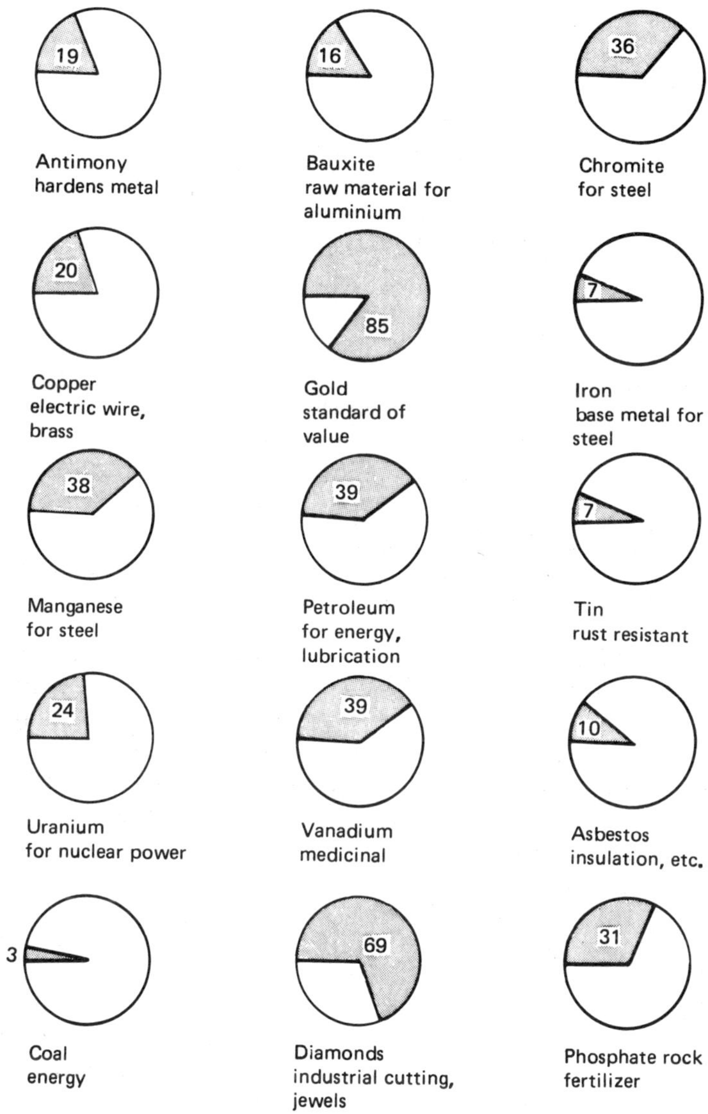

Figure 11.2: Africa's Share of World Output, 1976

Source: *UN Statistical Yearbook*, 1977, Ann Seidman, *An Economics Textbook for Africa*, 3rd edition, (Methuen, London, 1980), p. 40.

scarcity of the capital required to establish basic industries, together with the weak absorptive capacity of local markets.

Agricultural Potential but Food Deficit

Africa is the only area in the world where per capita food production has declined over the last twenty years. In the period 1950–75, according to the Brandt Report, while food production rose $2\frac{1}{2}$ per cent a year in developing countries generally, demand rose by 3 per cent. According to the *FAO Trade Yearbook* for 1977, no fewer than 35 African countries have a food trade surplus. A high proportion of them, nonetheless, were unable to feed themselves adequately and have had to become food importers. As Guy Arnold puts it: 'The discrepancy resulted from the fact that although they were large exporters of one or two food commodities such as tea or coffee, they were not producing enough food for home consumption.'[24]

Although suffering from an increasing food deficit, then, for many years Africa has had cash crops for export. Coffee (20.2 per cent of world production), tea (9.4 per cent), cocoa (56.3 per cent), palm oil groundnuts (16 per cent), rubber, tobacco, sisal, timber and sugar (3.28 per cent) are the main crops.[27]

The problem is that too many African countries depend on the export of one or two crops for 50 per cent or more of their foreign exchange[28] as is indicated in Table 11.19:

Table 11.19: Major Resources of the Arab World, 1970 and 1978

Countries	Main Resources	% Total Exports	
		1970	1978
Algeria	oil	67.5	91.7
Iraq	"	92.2	98.7
Kuwait	"	94.2	90.8
Saudi Arabia	"	99.6	99.7
UAE	"	96.3	94.9
Libya	"	99.7	99.9
Bahrain	"	75.0	78.2
Oman	"	99.6	99.4
Qatar	"	96.4	98.9
Other countries			
Egypt	Cotton/rice	54.7	22.2
Jordan	Phosphate	18.4	21.4
Morocco	Phosphate/citrus fruit	37.7	45.4
Syria	Cotton/oil	56.6	78.3
Tunisia	Oil/phosphate/olive oil	53.6	53.4
Somalia	Bananas/meat	84.1	95.1

Sudan	Cotton/beans	75.2	75.8
Mauritania	Iron/fish	79.0	97.8
North Yemen	Cotton/coffee	87.2	68.4
South Yemen	Oil products	75.0	83.2

Source: Arab Development Fund, 'Arab Development Growth in the 70s', *Chou'un Arabiyyah*, 21 (November 1982), p. 60

Many giant agricultural schemes are being carried out in Africa by the major agri-business concerns: Kenana, Bura, Savannah and almost always the same half-dozen company names recur: Brookers, Tate and Lyle, Lonrho, Mitchell Cotts, Nestlé, Del Monte, the Commonwealth Development Corporation (CDC). They are operators, financiers (CDC) or full partners.

Apart from cash crops, African agriculture does not feed its population. Imports of wheat, rice and coarse grains were, according to the FAO estimates, likely to rise from 15 million tons in 1981 to 17 million in 1983. A 1977 IFPRI study estimates that the calorie gap would be equivalent to approximately 13 million tons of cereals by 1990.[24]

Meat might well be lacking if serious emphasis is not put on the development of cattle rearing. African beef cattle production represents 11.23 per cent of the world's; and sheep production, 9.8 per cent. But pork production does not exceed 0.75 per cent of world production.

If the current trends persist, the situation would become intolerable. This is why both the Economic Commission for Africa and the Organisation of African Unity have been vocal in drawing attention to the continent's vulnerability to hunger and uncontrolled famine. It is understandable that Africa's food problems are accorded a central place in the Lagos Plan of Action, adopted by the OAU extraordinary Economic Summit in April 1980.

Scope for Increasing Afro-Arab Co-operation

Arab-African co-operation has been confined to financial flows from the Arab oil exporting countries to the African states. At any rate, Arab oil exporting countries '*seem to resent* their confinement to the role of mere lenders'.[31]

To maintain and increase the real value of their assets 'they are aware that they must get involved in the capital formation process, especially through the creation of new productive capabilities'.[32]

Table 11.20: Major Exports of Selected African states (% total exports, 1965, 1975)

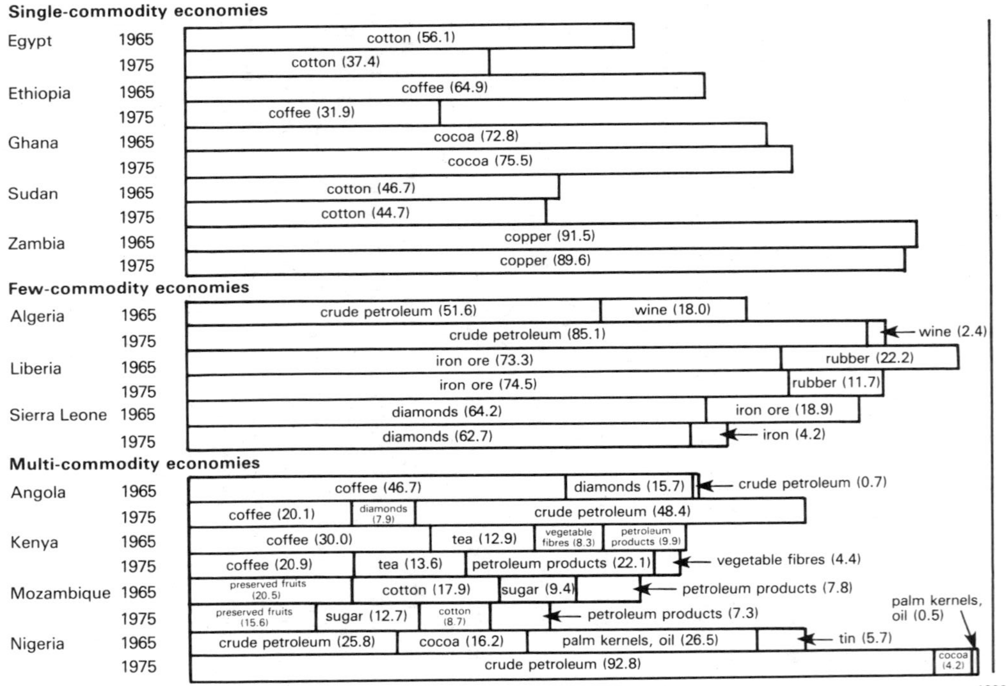

Source: *UN Statistical Yearbook*, 1977

Until now, Arab money has been attracted by Western industries, and Arab trade has been increasingly directed towards Western countries.

I would like to suggest that Arab money, which is a transient feature, should find its way into African economies.

Many reasons suggest the wisdom of such an approach:

a. Arab aid derives from a *temporary situation* and not true wealth resulting from a great and renewable productive capacity. For that reason, Arab aid to Africa represents a greater sacrifice than the aid given by the industrial countries. Dr Shihata elaborates this point in a very lucid way:[33] On the one hand, aid is deducted from *income which is in reality a cash exchange for a depletable natural resource*. On the other hand, Arab aid is not given, except rarely, *to encourage the donor's exports*, but is used chiefly to finance purchases from third countries, which are usually the developed countries, i.e. this aid represents a transfer of wealth to the industrial countries in exchange for goods and services exported to the recipient developing countries.

   Such a situation cannot last. Africans might come to believe that Arab aid is a mere compensation for higher oil prices, which is an unacceptable argument; while the Arabs might be tempted to reduce the volume of their aid because their financial assets are drying up.[34]

b. If Arab aid should be expected to have a lasting impact, on Arab and African economies alike, it should be based on solid, long-range economic foundations and not only on temporary and transient political considerations.

c. Arab aid to Africa *has to be repaid*. Then it is in the interest of the Arabs to help creating sound and productive economies in Africa, capable of coping with the growing problems of this continent and its international obligations.

d. From the African point of view, aid is only one possible method of acquiring the resources and the foreign exchange which they need to finance their economic development. Generally speaking, African countries are more interested in the expansion of trade than of aid. The opening up of Arab markets to African raw materials, semi-manufactured products, and agricultural crops would have a more lasting effect on Afro-Arab co-operation.

e. Aid can, therefore be used to *stimulate trade.* Among aided projects, projects with an export potential toward the Arab world could be specially emphasised. Also, aid could be given more on a *regional basis* and for multinational projects or groups of projects, thus encouraging the trade of developing countries with each other. The techniques of regional aid are still practically unexplored by Arab Funds, but they may be suggested for study now.

f. Tying up Arab aid to trade expansion is not hypocritical, since it is suggested that a policy by aid donors of using aid to help trade would be accompanied by a trade policy giving easier access to their markets.

New Avenues for Afro-Arab Co-operation

There appear some areas where Arab aid can play a role to ensure 'the maximum economic return for the donor countries' while at the same time allowing the recipient countries to benefit:

Arab Aid Should Promote the Import of Raw Materials

It is hard to see why African countries should have any difficulties in interesting Arab investors in Africa's plentiful raw materials. The present low level of industrialisation in most Arab countries sets limits to the demand for raw materials from Africa. However, the Arab countries have ambitious plans to build up a metallurgical industry and to exploit cheap energy costs in the construction of energy-intensive industries. Arab countries will need to import raw materials such as copper for the smelter at Bahrain and for projects underway or planned in the steel and aluminium sectors.

A good existing example is that of Saudi Arabia. The country's Third Year Plan places particular emphasis on developing the productive sectors of the economy to reduce the kingdom's heavy reliance on oil exports. The country's industrial planning is focused on two huge new towns, Jubail and Yanbu, where massive petrochemical plants are being planned or built, and on the industrial sites located at Jeddah, Riyadh and Damman.

Among the many industrial projects the most advanced is the reduction steel complex being built with Korf Stahl of West Germany. Another major project under way is the 600,000 tons a year methanol plant being built by a Japanese consortium led by Mitsubishi Heavy Industries. Another methanol plant is to begin operating in 1984 under an agreement signed in 1981 with the American company Celanese-Texas Eastern. A fertiliser plant is being built under the guidance of a partnership between SABIC (Saudi Iron and Steel Company) and the Taiwan Fertiliser Company. Cement plants are under construction at Abqaiq and Jizan. The National Pipe Company, a joint venture between Sumitomo Metal Industries and the Sumitomo Corporation, in partnership with the Ali Reza Group, has started production at a new mill in Dhahran.

Since Africa's reserves of iron ore are said by the US Treasury to total twice their own and two-thirds of those of the USSR it would seem natural for a country like Saudi Arabia to look across the Red Sea to Africa for a permanent source of supply of that essential raw material.[35]

The Saudis may well set up a vast programme of co-operation with African countries by investing in resource development programmes in the supplying countries, for instance in the Kudremukh project (1974) between Iran and India.[36] This was designed to develop and extract iron-ore deposits from the Kudremukh mines in Karnataka, which were to be processed and exported from the port of Managalore to Iran for use by the Iranian steel industry. The Iranians provided a US$300 million loan to cover the entire capital cost of the project, with a provision to double the investment. The market was to be secured through long-term purchase contracts between the Steel Authority of India and the National Iranian Steel Company for sale of iron-ore at a price slightly higher than the world price. Thus the project involved Iranian commercial investment, marketing guarantees and the opening up of new resources within the framework of South-South solidarity.[37]

The present policy of developing energy-intensive industry within the oil exporting Arab countries holds promise for African bauxite, copper or iron-ore exporters. It would be feasible to tie in a long-term procurement contract and project development loan for each Arab project likely to use imported raw materials from Africa. A joint Afro-Arab company could be floated to develop a particular deposit, process the raw material, transport it, and then convert it into a finished product. The exporting African countries and importing Arab countries could be partners in this project.

Not only could Arab money help buying African raw materials for industries located in the Arab world, but it could help setting up new industries in Africa itself. Africa has an important labour force in every part of the continent that desperately needs to solve its growing unemployment problem. Moreover, Africa is blessed with limitless cheap hydro-electric power potential. Finally, Africa, as any other continent, does not want to confine itself to the role of raw materials exporter. It has the will to process its own raw materials, selling aluminium instead of bauxite, steel instead of iron ore, electric wires instead of copper, precision tools instead of diamonds, etc. Some of these processed and transformed raw materials could then be exported to the Arab countries provided that they did not compete with local Arab industries.

Arab countries, in general, are not sufficiently aware of the economic potential of the African continent. And if they are aware, they do not show the required political will to embark on a vast programme of co-development. This is indeed the key concept on which should be founded long-term Afro-Arab solidarity. Two adjacent continents, with so many comparative advantages cannot afford the luxury of ignoring one another. Contingent aid policies are no longer sufficient. One has to think in terms of decades, not in terms of years.

One must, of course, acknowledge that some Arab efforts have already been made in this direction. Suffice to note the co-operative ventures between Libya and Guinea; the participation of Saudi Arabia in building a joint Guinea-Algeria oil refinery project; the participation of Egypt in forestry development; the establishment of a paper mill in Guinea; and the proposed Arab project of floating a Guinea-Arab aluminium company. Other examples could also be cited. It should be the task of the Arab League to prepare a detailed list of Arab-African joint ventures in order to assess their efficiency and future viability, and to identify the problems of an economic, political and social character facing them, exploring ways of solving them.

Compared with Asia, whose growth in the relative share of the South in terms of manufacturing exports has been the most impressive during the last decade, Africa has rather a weak industrial base. Given financial and technical assistance from the Arab world, however, Africa should be in a position to alleviate the misery of its population. But we should always keep in mind that the Arab countries as a whole, are also inadequately or insufficiently industrialised, and that charity begins at home.

Arab Aid Should Stimulate Arab Trade

Expanding Afro-Arab trade, in raw materials, in processed goods, through joint ventures, stems from the necessity of diversifying Arab and African import and export markets, creating a supply capacity to cater specifically to Arab demands for African minerals, and solving the capacity constraints in the African exporting countries, integrating investment decisions with a long-term marketing arrangement, thus providing the necessary element of security for these investments.

But the Arab oil exporting countries' own development plans are likely to create serious problems for at least some among them. Countries like Saudi Arabia, Libya, Bahrain, the Emirates and Kuwait are so small, as is their population, that the big investments in downstream ventures designed to add value to their oil and gas products, could run into serious external marketing problems. These investments are specifically designed for export, particularly for the 'low absorbers'.

I have analysed elsewhere the difficulties of selling Arab refined oil and other by-products in the traditional markets of Western Europe.[38] Western European countries are going through serious problems due to the under-utilisation of their refineries and the devastating crisis in their petro-chemical industries. One could not reasonably expect them to aggravate their own unemployment problem by widely opening up their markets to Arab-transformed products. Their protectionist policy, un-economic in its nature, and unfriendly in its shaping, is the stumbling block of Euro-Arab dialogue.

But diversifying Arab potential markets becomes an obligation. For example, Saudi Arabia's programme of investments in petrochemicals can only remain viable if it can export its output of ethylene-based products.

High construction costs, high operating costs (due to heavy expenditure on expatriate personnel tied to industrial projects) and high transport costs are not likely to make Arab industrial projects competitive. If all these negative constraints can be combined with a global underutilisation of capacity, then Arab industrialisation would remain wishful thinking, or a plan doomed to failure.[39]

African markets offer a golden opportunity to the Arab oil exporting countries. But as Mohammed Omer Beschir points out: 'as long as the present structures whereby exports and imports and trade routes are geared to the industrialised countries exist, very little improvement in the trade can be expected'.[40]

Arab Aid Should Stimulate Commercial Investments by Arab Aid Donors

It has been argued that for their own self-interest and for the benefit of the African peoples, Arab aid donors should give priority in their investment policies to productive projects in African states. The argument has been reinforced by the recent confrontation between the US and Iran, following the freezing of the latter's assets in US banks. As Beschir comments: 'the action underlined the fact that investments by OPEC countries are not necessarily secure. Domestic and foreign policy considerations in the industrialised countries could lead to similar and perhaps more extreme actions. Hence the need for the oil exporting countries to rethink their prevailing investment strategies and give serious thought to the political and economic gains from rediversifying their resources towards Third World countries and institutions.'[41]

It is usually believed that Arab investments do not run the danger of encroaching upon African sovereignty, particularly because the oil rich countries are militarily weak and usually poor in other resources, indeed poorer in some instances than the countries which seek their assistance. Consequently 'the investing of resources of the oil countries in other developing countries for profit provides the obvious form of co-operation which can further the interests of both sides, as opposed to the giving of grants or concessional loans, which represent a financial loss to the aid-giving countries, and a net gain to the recipients.'[42]

In spite of arguments which work towards the promotion of Arab investments in Africa, it has been proved that only a small proportion of Arab surpluses has been invested in Africa. Thus African expectations that Arab investments will be more forthcoming and less demanding in terms and conditions than other investments have not been realised. Nor were the expectations of Arab countries that they would be given better treatment and better guarantees for equitable distribution of profits; state guarantees for investments; compensation in the case of nationalisation; legal and judicial guarantees for investors; exemption from customs duties on production machinery; and exemption from income tax for a definite period.

The problem of guarantees can easily be tackled through the establishment of an Investment Guarantee Fund for Africa, similar to the Arab Authority Investment Guarantees. More embarassing and thorny are the discouraging factors attributable to political instability and lack of infrastructure, whether of material facilities or appropriate institutions and legislation.

It is, then, 'one of the basic tasks of the Arab national aid institutions to assist the recipient countries which are likely to host investment of the Arab donor countries, to carry out [such] infrastructure projects as ports, roads, electrical transmission and communication systems, and to develop their institutions.'[43] 'This approach will have obvious effects on the choice of beneficiary countries and sectors which would receive finance, according to Shihata. It will also require continuous co-ordination between the aid agencies and the investment institutions in the donor countries, since the latter will acquire a direct interest in the continuation of aid and will become a source of support for the former.'

It is true that a good percentage of Arab aid has been concentrated on financing infrastructure projects. However, 'this was not based on a policy of linking aid with future investments, and is not the result of co-ordination with local investment institutions, but is rather a direct result of the soft terms of the financing provided, which by its very nature is appropriate to infrastructure projects which are difficult to finance through commercial banks.'[44]

As could be expected, bi-lateral channels of Arab aid should bear the brunt of such a dynamic approach, by directing their aid towards serving Arab investments in the African countries.

Thus Arab aid should serve as:

a tool to promote Arab imports of raw materials;
a stimulus to Arab exports; and
a stimulus to Arab investments.

Unless Arab aid is set within such a comprehensive strategy, its perpetuation in the 1980s becomes problematic, even impossible. The Arab oil countries would prefer to be stockholders rather than bondholders. They do not want to be passive donors, mere 'money-lenders'. They are interested not only in income but also in the implementation of the projects they finance. They would like to have a say in the policy-making and management of the projects and programmes which are financed by them. They think that any participation by a non-Arab country in contracts financed by them should have their concurrence.

These requirements should constitute the prerequisite in choosing the projects to finance or the countries to assist. As Beshir has put it:

'This is a world of give and take and therefore it is just and natural that the Arab countries should also expect the recipient country to reciprocate in one form or another.'

In view of this, African countries will succeed in attracting Arab foreign capital only if they offer sufficient incentives which will guarantee good return on capital invested.

The point has been made that the African countries have commanded only a small share of trading opportunities opened up within the Arab countries, and that Arab investments in Africa are still very limited.

Such a situation is justified by the attraction of Arab surpluses by the developed countries and the domination of the latter on Arab trade patterns, on outdated assumptions of the superior competitive worth of the developed countries' products and services. But it is also justified by the general ignorance of the Arabs of African mineral and agricultural potential,[45] and by the inability of the African countries better to inform the Arab ones of the sectors which are in need of capital injection.

In conclusion, it must be kept in mind that Arab aid to Africa has reached a volume which requires a comprehensive outlook[46] so that it may be perpetuated into the eighties to the benefit of both the donors and recipients.

Perhaps the worst way of setting the problem is to consider aid as a charity, or as compensation. Conceived as a charity gesture, aid will create an increasing feeling of frustration in the Arab countries which might rightly come to believe that they are the milch cows of the world, since after all they are not responsible for the devastating problems of African economies. No-one can reasonably argue that it is the responsibility of the Arab world to cater for the needs of the entire Third World.

If conceived as compensation, Arab aid might be looked at as a right, and African countries might feel entitled to it. Such an assumption would create a strained relationship.

Arab aid can really be regarded as an instrument for the promotion of South-South relations only if it helps create a more balanced, mutually beneficial pattern of co-operation between the Arab countries and the African ones. Only then can Arab aid be regarded as a means for the distribution of income on a world-wide scale for the benefit of the poorer countries.

Naturally, the Arab donors do expect a return from their aid policies, but this does not contradict the principles of South-South solidarity. If conditions of reciprocity are respected, mutual understanding prevails.

Until now, Arab aid has been generously provided without a clear vision of how it should be utilised. I would suggest that multi-lateral aid should be developed through a limited number of organisations to avoid duplication, and that it should pave the way for Arab investments. It would be advisable, on the other hand, that bi-lateral aid should be directed toward the financing of infrastructure projects in those countries which are particularly suitable for investment by Arab states.

Direct investments by the capital-surplus Arab states in Africa must be encouraged because of sound economic considerations, not only as a matter of concern for the plight of African countries. A strategy of investment diversification is in the interest of all countries, because of their interdependent economic relations.

Notes

1. See the address of Chedli Ayari to the 13th African-American Conference, Harare, Zimbabwe, 10–14 January 1983.
2. Ibrahim Shihata, *The Other Face of OPEC; Financial Assistance to the Third World* (Longman, London, 1982) p. 14.
3. Victor T. Le Vine and Timothy W. Luke, *The Arab-African Connection: Political and Economic Realities* (Westview Press, Boulder, Colorado, 1979) p. 92.
4. Shihata, p. 3
5. Ibid.
6. Ibid.
7. Bichara Khader: 'Energie et dialogue euro-arabe', *Cahiers du Monde Arabe Contemporain* (CERMAC, Louvain-la-Neuve, 1982) p. 1.
8. See *Amex Bank Review*, 29 March 1982.
9. See Dr Zalzala, 'Prospect of Afro-Arab Co-operation' (in Arabic), in *Chou'un Arabiyyah*, no. 6, 1980.
10. See Rehman Sobhan, 'Enhancing Trade between OPEC and the Developing Countries of Asia', *Third World Quarterly*, October 1982, pp. 719–35.
11. There is an abundant literature on this subject. For example: Giuseppe Pennisi, *Development, Manpower and Migration in the Red Sea Region: the Case for Co-operation* (Deutsches Orient Inst., Hamburg, 1981) p. 264; CETRI, *Les migrations de travailleurs dans les pays producteurs de pétrole du Golfe Persique* (Louvain-la-Neuve, 1982) p. 42; S. Al Din, R. Tabbarah, A. Labib and N. Farjani, 'The Transfer of Arab Human Resources' (in Arabic), in *Al Mustaqbal Al-Arabi*, no. 1, 1983, pp. 66–148; J.B. Birks and C.A. Sinclair, *International Migration and Development in the Arab Region* (ILO, Geneva, 1980) p. 175; Saad Eddin Ibrahim, *The New Arab Social Order* (Croom Helm, London, 1982) p. 208; ILO/ECWA Seminar: *Manpower and Employment in Arab Countries, Some Critical Issues* (Beirut, 1975) p. 229; Anne Findlay and Allan Findlay, *The Geographical Interpretation of International Migration: a Case Study of the Maghreb* (Centre for Middle Eastern and Islamic Studies, University of Durham, 1982), p. 131.

12. Nigeria literally drove out of the country 2 million Africans in January and February 1983.

13. Le Vine and Duke, p. 115.

14. See J. Bhagwat (ed.): *The New International Economic Order: the North-South debate* (MIT Press, Cambridge, Mass., 1977).

15. Jeffrey B. Nugent: 'A Programme of Arab-African-Asian Co-operation in Industrial Development and Trade', Paper presented to the International Conference on Afro-Arab Co-operation at the Jordan Center for Studies and Information, Amman, 11–14 September 1982, p. 1.

16. I. Shihata, p. 24.

17. The indebtedness problem is the subject of an ever-widening literature. See, for example: Jonathan David Aronson (ed), *Debt and the Less Developed Countries*, (Westview Press, Boulder, Colorado, 1979); Laurence Franco and Marilyn Seiber (ed.): *Developing Countries' Debt* (Pergamon Press, New York, 1979); Miguel Wionczec (ed.), *LDC External Debt and World Economy* (Colegio de Mexico, Mexico City, 1978); *World Development* has published a special issue on *International Indebtedness and World Economic Stagnation*, (February 1979) pp. 91–224; International Monetary Fund, *External Indebtedness of Developing Countries*, Occasional paper no. 3, (May 1981).

18. The Brandt Commission, *North-South: a Programme for Survival*, p. 117.

19. The Middle East countries spend much more than the average on arms. According to the Stockholm International Peace Research Institute (SIPRI) figures, Saudi Arabia spends annually about $2,700 per capita, the UAE about $1,700, Oman about $1,200, Kuwait about $950; cf. *Middle East Review* (London, 1982) p. 33.

20. Marvin G. Weinbaum, *Food, Development and Politics in the Middle East* (Croom Helm, London, 1982) p. 3; Dr Ziyad Al Hafez, *The Food Crisis in the Arab World* (in Arabic) (Institute of Arab Development, Beirut, 1981); Dr Mohamed Mahmoud Al Sayyad, 'Toward an Arab strategy for food security', in *Al Mustaqbal Al-Arabi* no. 6 (Beirut, March 1979) pp. 76–85.

21. John Parker, 'North Africa-Mideast Fastest Market for Agricultural Imports', in *Foreign Agriculture* (US Department of Agriculture, 1 January 1979) p. 2, quoted by Weinbaum, pp. 3–4.

22. 'Saudi Farm Imports Head Toward $4.5 billion', in *Foreign Agriculture* (September 1980) p. 14, quoted by Weinbaum, p. 4.

23. For the year 2000 predictions indicate that the Third World countries will consume 2.5 billion tons of oil. According to a recent study, total consumption of oil in Third World countries in the year 2010 will be equivalent to the current world oil consumption. See Jean Romain Frisch, *Third World Energy Horizons 2000/2020*, Report to the Conservation Commission of the World Energy Conference, München, 1980, p. 39.

24. Fehmy Saddy 'OPEC Capital Surplus Funds and Third World Indebtedness: the Recycling Strategy Reconsidered', *Third World Quarterly* vol. 4, no. 4, (October 1982) p. 749.

25. Nugent; pp. 3–4.

26. Guy Arnold, 'The Grip of Transnational Agri-business', *Africa Guide* (1982) p. 33.

27. Percentages of output are provided by Beaujeu-Garnier.

28. The Arab world suffers from the same distortion, as is shown in Table 11.19.

29. See Beaujeu-Garnier.

30. Quoted by Dr Jenny Dey, 'Is Food Security in Africa No More Than a Dream?', in *Africa Guide* (1982) p. 37.

31. I. Shihata, p. 133.

32. See Shihata and also several lectures delivered by Al-Hamad, Director-

General of the Kuwait Fund for Arab Economic Development, reproduced by Kuwait Fund Publications.

33. See Shihata, pp. 18 and 39.

34. In an interview given by Mr Mohammed Aba Al-Khail, Minister of Finance and National Economy, to a group of foreign journalists, Mr Al-Khail highlights this point: 'The costs of development are very high. Oil production is increasing but we believe the absorptive capacity is going up even faster. We can see the point where we will have to dip into the surplus.' *International Herald Tribune* (30 May 1977).

35. E.C. Chibwe, *Arab Dollars for Africa* (Croom Helm, London, 1976) pp. 65–6.

36. See Subhan: p. 729.

37. Unfortunately this project became a casualty of the Iranian revolution. One of the key policies of the new regime was the scaling down of the ambitious development projects initiated by the Shah. This has left India with considerable surpluses of processed iron-ore, which have to find alternative export markets or be absorbed within the domestic steel industry in India.

38. Bichara Khader, 'Energie et dialogue euro-arabe', *Cashier du Monde Arabe Contemporain* no. 2 (CERMAC, Louvain-la-Neuve, 1982) p. 48.

39. This problem is discussed more fully by Louis Turner and James Bedore, in 'The Trade Politics of Middle Eastern Industrialisation', *Foreign Affairs* (Winter, 1978–9).

40. Mohamed Omer Beschir, *Terremedia: Themes in Afro-Arab Relations*, (Ithaca Press, London, 1982) p. 155.

41. Ibid., p. 152

42. Reham Sobhan, 'Institutional Mechanisms for Channelling OPEC Surpluses within the Third World', *Third World Quarterly* vol. II, no. 4, (October 1980) p. 245, quoted by Beshir, p. 152.

43. Shihata, p. 212.

44. Ibid.

45. Zalzala, p. 65.

46. See the excellent article by Dr Abdel Ghaffar Rachad Mohamed 'The Arab League and the future of Afro-Arab Co-operation', (in Arabic), *Chou'un Arabiyyah*, no. 18, (August 1982) pp. 151–74. Badea has also prepared a remarkable report on '*Prospects of Development in the Sahel Countries and the Role of Arab Aid*,' and a summary of this has been published by the Arab journal *Al-Dirasāt Al-I'lāmiyah*, (March 1982) pp. 112–58.

12 LAFICO AND THE LIBYAN CONTRIBUTION TO DEVELOPMENT ASSISTANCE

Yousef Abdelmula

This chapter deals primarily with the Libyan Arab Foreign Investment Company's efforts and accomplishments in the field of economic development in the Third World, with emphasis on Arab countries, endeavouring to describe the company's policies, functions, limitations, and performance, and with a brief look into its background and objectives. It is worth noting, however, that LAFICO is only two years old.

The Libyan Arab Foreign Investment Company was established by an Act of the General People's Congress on 4 December 1981. Its purpose, as stated in the Act, is 'the investment of Libyan Arab Funds abroad in agriculture, industry, tourism, transport, marine fisheries, mining, communication, and other various sectors'. Moreover, it is 'to carry out any other activities which ensure the fulfilment of its aims or activities delegated . . . within the framework of co-operation between the Socialist People's Libyan Arab Jamahiriya and others'.

LAFICO is, therefore, geared mainly towards investment in profit-oriented ventures; hence, sound business practice has become its reigning principle. Its capital is 500 million Dinars divided into 5 million shares owned by the state.

Upon its creation, LAFICO came into possession of a large number of joint companies operating in several countries; in addition, it created a host of new companies. The function of these is to carry out economic development projects in various sectors, in harmony with the overall development programme.

Economic Partnership

LAFICO adheres to the principle adopted by the Jamahiriya in the area of economic co-operation with Third World countries, namely partnership between two or more of them to ensure effective commitment. Economic partnership, a new concept in economic co-operation, designed specifically for Third World countries, had its genesis in the universal doctrine of the Great Fateh Revolution, complementing the Green Book dictum 'Partners and not wage workers'. It is straightforward, practical and mutualistic. As such it adds a long absent, but necessary dimension to economic development—sound business practice, objective assessment and mutual responsibility. For performance results of each company, published annual reports should be consulted. Projects under consideration are privileged information.

The company's financial participation worldwide amounts to 240 million Dinars, its *holding companies* being worth 110 million Dinars. These include Arab Libyo-Burundias Holding Co. Ltd, Libyan Arab Uganda Holding Co. Ltd, Libyan Arab Maltese Holding Co. Ltd, Pak-Libyan Holding Co. Ltd, Fiat, Libyan Ghanaian Holding Co. Ltd, International Holding Co. Ltd, and Libyan Malagasian Holding Co. Ltd.

Investment companies, worth 41 million Dinars, include Libyan Maltese Investment Co. Ltd, the Libyan-Greek Investment Co. Ltd, Arab Petroleum Investment Corporation, Banque Arabe et Internationale d'Investissement, the Arab Investment Company SAA, and Compagnie Arabe et Internationale d'Investissement.

Maritime transport companies (34 million Dinars) include Turkish-Libyan Joint Maritime Transport Stock Co., Compagnie Algero-Libyenne de Transport Maritime, Société Arabe Libyo-Tunisienne de Transport Maritime, Romanian-Libyan Joint Stock Company for Maritime Transport, Sea Malta Co. Ltd, Pan Arab Shipping Co., and Arab Maritime Petroleum Transport Co.

Fishing companies (4 million Dinars) include Société Togolaise Arabe Libyenne de Pêche, Maltese Libyan Arab Fishing Co. Ltd, Société Arabe Libyenne Mauritanienne des Ressources Maritimes, Guyana-Libyan Fishing Co., Société Benino-Arabe Libyenne de Pêche Maritime, Seychelles Libyan Arab Fishing Co. Ltd, the Yemen Libyan Arab Fishing Co., Société Tchado Arabe Libyenne de Pêche, and the Arab Fishing Co.

Industrial companies (10 million Dinars) include Libyan Maltese Insecticide Co., Medisan Ltd, Ethio-Libyan Joint Sugar Co., Rotos Zirayia Pumps Co. Ltd, Mediterranean Power Electric Co., Medelec Switch Gear Co. Ltd, Arab Company for Drug-Industries and Medical Appliances, Arab Industrial Investment Co., Arab Ship Building and Repair Yard Co., and Asteris SA Industrial and Commercial Corporation.

Mining companies (11 million Dinars) include Société Libyenne

Centra Africana des Mines, Ethio-Libyan Joint Mining Co., Société Benino-Arabe Libyenne des Mines, Arab Petroleum Services Co., Société Arabe des Mines de l'Inchiri (Samin), Arab Mining Co., Société des Mines de Fer de Guinée pour l'Exploitation des Monts Nimba, Arab Potash Co. Ltd, Libyan Ghanaian Mining Co.

Agricultural companies (11 million Dinars) include Société Mixte Rwando Arabe Libyenne pour le Développement et la Commercialisation des Produits Agricoles et d'Elevage, Société Tchado Arabe Libyenne pour la Production et Commercialisation d'Elevage, Société Agricole Tchado Libyenne, Société Agricole Togolaise Arabe Libyenne, Cameroon Libyan Arab Agriculture Company, Société Arabe Libyo Guinéenne pour le Developpement Agricole et Agroindustriel, Société Arabe Libyo-Nigerienne pour le Développement et la Commercialisation des Produits Agricoles, the Joint Turkish Libyan Agricultural and Livestock Co., Société d'Economie Mixte Centre Africaine Libyenne des Produits Agricoles, Libyan Sierra-Leonean Agricultural and Livestock Production Co., Syrian Libyan Industrial and Agricultural Investment Co., Sri Lanka Libya Agricultural and Livestock Development Co., Guyana-Libyan Agricultural Development Co., Ethio-Libya Joint Agricultural Co., Société Agro-Animale Benino Arabe Libyenne, Somal-Libyan Agricultural Development Co., Sudanese Libyan Arab Agricultural Co., Société Mauritanienne Arabe Libyenne de Développement Agricole, Libyan Ghanaian Agricultural Co., Libyan Malagasian Agricultural Co., Acropeçuaria-Nicaragua Arabe-Libya para el Desarrollo.

Hotels and tourism companies (17 million Dinars) include Svipa-Pantelleria SpA, Jerma Palace Hotel, Société Mixte Rwando-Arabe Libyenne de Promotion, Hôtelière et Touristique du Rwanda, Corinthia Group of Companies, General Touristic and Building Construction, Société Tourgueness, Farah El Maghreb Société de Promotion Touristique, Libyan Syrian Arab Company for Hotels and Tourism, Arab International Company for Hotels and Tourism.

Real estate companies (0.2 million Dinars) include the Arab Real Estate Co. (ARESCO) and the Pan-African Real Estate Co.

Other companies (2 million Dinars) include Mediterranean Aviation Co. Ltd, Société Arabe Libyenne-Centrafricaine d'Import-Export, Bahar-U-Sewwi Ltd, Swan Laundry And Dry-cleaning Co. Ltd, Gambian-Libyan Arab General Transportation Co., Mediterranean Publishing Co.

These companies serve more than forty countries in three-continents, the arithmetic mean of LAFICO participation being about 42.9 per cent of their capital. LAFICO shares range from 1.1 to 100 per cent, with its share in about half of the companies being 50 per cent of the capital or over.

LAFICO Activities in the Arab World

The Arab world is paramount to the company's activities, and it therefore comes as no surprise that out of $1,317 million invested worldwide by LAFICO, $400 million are invested in Arab countries in the form of participation in joint Arab companies. These are mainly involved in development programmes, in various sectors.

Emphasis on economic co-operation and co-ordination in the Arab sphere stems from an utter commitment to Pan-Arab aspirations in the areas of food, industry and technology. Such aspirations are consistent with LAFICO's major position in the field of Pan-Arab economic sufficiency. LAFICO's investment in the Arab world is covered by the joint companies listed below:

Holding and Investment Companies

The Syrian Libyan Industrial and Agricultural Investment Company was established in February 1978, with a capital of $200 million, fully paid. Its headquarters are in Damascus. LAFICO's participation is 50 per cent, and the company works in the fields of agriculture and industry.

The Arab Petroleum Investment Corporation was established in September 1974, with a capital of 1200 million Saudi Riyals, fully paid. Its headquarters are in Dhahran. LAFICO's participation is 15 per cent, and the field of activity is petroleum industrial projects.

The Arab Industrial Investment Company was established in July 1978, with a capital of 150 Million Iraqi Dinars. It headquarters are in Baghdad. LAFICO's participation is 8 per cent, and the company works in industrial projects, such as the manufacture of railway coaches, air conditioning, generators and iron pipes.

The Arab Investment Company SAA was established in July 1974, with a capital of $300 million. The headquarters are in Riyadh. LAFICO's participation is 6.66 per cent, and the company is interested in the investment of Arab money to develop Arab resources.

Compagnie Arabe et Internationale d'Investissement was established in 1973, with capital of $70 million. Its headquarters are in Luxembourg. LAFICO's participation is 2.86 per cent, and the field of activity financial co-operation between Europe and the Arab countries.

Industrial and Mining Companies

The Arab Mining Company was established in June 1974, with capital of 100 Million Jordanian Dinars. Its headquarters are in Amman. LAFICO's participation is 10 per cent. The company funds industrial and chemical projects.

The Arab Potash Company Ltd was established in July 1956, with a capital of 63 million Jordanian Dinars. Its headquarters are in Amman. LAFICO's participation is 5 per cent. It is engaged in the development of Dead Sea minerals and chemical resources.

Société Arabe des mines de l'Inchiri (SAMIN) was established in December 1980, with a capital of $72 million. Its headquarters are in Nouadhibou. LAFICO's participation is 10 per cent. The company works in copper mining and treatment.

The Arab Company for Drug-Industries and Medical Appliances was established in March 1976, with a capital of 60 million Jordanian Dinars. Its headquarters are in Amman. LAFICO's participation is 8.3 per cent. It works in the manufacture of drugs, etc.

Agricultural Companies

Société Mauritanienne Arabe Libyenne de Développement Agricole was established in January 1977, with a capital of $8.5 million. Its headquarters are in Nouakchott. LAFICO's participation is 49 per cent. It works in the cultivation and marketing of cotton and sugar cane.

The Somal-Libyan Agricultural Development Company was established in January 1972 with a capital of $8 million. Its headquarters are in Mogadishu. It is concerned with land reclamation and livestock development.

The Sudanese Libyan Arab Agricultural Company was established in April 1976, with a capital of $14 million. Its headquarters are in Khartoum. LAFICO's participation is 49 per cent. The company works in cultivation of coffee, tea, rice, etc.

Real Estate and Tourism Companies

Farah El Maghreb Société de Promotion Touristique was established in October 1973, with a capital of $45 million. Its headquarters are in Casablanca. LAFICO's participation is 27.77 per cent. It works in the development of the tourist industry.

Société Tourgueness was established in January 1970 with capital of 3 Million Tunisian Dinars. Its headquarters are in Tunis. LAFICO's participation is 46.67 per cent. It is involved with all business and industrial activities related to tourism.

Arab International Company for Hotels and Tourism was established in January 1975, with a capital of $51 million. Its headquarters are in Cairo. LAFICO's participation is 7.88 per cent. It is concerned with all activities related to hotels and real estate in tourism and housing.

The Arab Real Estate Company (ARESCO) was established in 1974, with a capital of 6 million Lebanese Pounds. Its headquarters are in Beirut. LAFICO's participation is 66.67 per cent. It is involved in real estate.

The Libyan Syrian Arab Company for Hotels and Tourism was established in April 1976, with a capital of 40 million Syrian Pounds. Its headquarters are in Damascus. LAFICO's participation is 15 per cent, and it is concerned with all tourism activities.

Fishing Companies

Société Arabe Libyenne Mauritanienne des Ressources Maritimes was established in August, 1978, with a capital of $50 million. Its headquarters are in Nouadhibou. LAFICO's participation is 50 per cent. It is involved with all fishing-related activities.

The Arab Fishing Company was established in October 1979, with a capital of 70 million Saudi Riyals. Its headquarters are in Jeddah. LAFICO's participation is 15 per cent. It is concerned with all fishing-related activities.

The Yemen Libyan Arab Fishing Company was established in February 1981, with a capital of $10 million. Its headquarters are in Aden. LAFICO's participation is 40 per cent. It is concerned with all fishing-related activities.

Maritime Transport Companies

The Arab Maritime Petroleum Transport Company was established in January 1973, with a capital of $500 million. Its headquarters are in Kuwait. LAFICO's participation is 13.56 per cent. It is involved with the transport of oil and oil products.

Compagnie Algero-Libyenne de Transport Maritime was

established in March 1972, with a capital of $50 million. Its headquarters are in Algiers. LAFICO's participation is 50 per cent. The company works in maritime transport and related activities.

The Pan Arab Shipping Company was established in December, 1967, with a capital of $18 million. Its headquarters are in Baghdad. LAFICO's participation is 14.7 per cent. It is concerned with shipping between Arab countries.

Société Arabe Libyo-Tunisienne de Transport Maritime was established in October 1973, with a capital of 1.5 million Tunisian Dinars. Its headquarters are in Tunis. LAFICO's participation is 50 per cent. It is concerned with passenger conveyance.

The Arab Ship Building and Repair Yard Company was established in December 1979, with a capital of $340 million. Its headquarters are in Manama. LAFICO's participation is 1.25 per cent. It is involved in ship building, and training.

Companies

The General Assembly of LAFICO consists of:
Secretary, General People's Committee for Treasury — Chairman
Secretary, General People's Committee for Planning — Member
Secretary, General People's Committee for The People's Bureau for Foreign Liaison — 2 Members
Governor, Central Bank of Libya
Three experts in financial, economic and legal matters, appointed by the General People's Committee

The Board of Directors consists of:

Mohamed Taher Hammuda Siala	Chairman and General Manager
Smeida El-Hosh El-Naili	Participation Manager
Yousef A. Abdelmula	Planning Manager
Mohamed Bubaker Al Dahmani	
Mohamed Hussein Layas	

Executives:

Abuzeid Ramadan Omrani	Administrative Manager
Taher Mohamed El-Ghorbi	Financial Manager

LAFICO's Branch Offices are in Sliema, Malta; Rome, Italy and Athens, Greece.

13 THE ARAB ASSISTANCE ORGANS AND THEIR ROLE IN ECONOMIC DEVELOPMENT

Abdul Razek Hassan

The constitution and the development of the Arab development organs (both banks and Funds), national and regional, are closely related to the economic conditions which saw their birth, and to the intricate relationships of capital in the Arab and international markets.

Bank financing in the Arab countries before independence was essentially due to affiliates of various foreign banks: English, French, Belgian, Italian, Greek etc. These were primarily interested in operations involving foreign trading and anything connected with this. Besides these affiliates there were some mortgage banks which granted credit on guarantees binding agricultural land or real estate. These banks, because of their very nature, were not interested in the economic development of the countries in which they operated. Because of this their activities were limited and inspired by the policies decided by the relative central head offices, which were of course situated abroad.

Banknotes themselves were issued by some of these banks or else by using organs or commissions whose activity was organised and supervised by foreigners. Moreover, the original banknotes were all in local currencies which could only circulate in the country of origin, even if they were all tied to one of the foreign currencies, and monetary reserves were mainly made up by deposits in the currency of the dominant state or else by vouchers from its treasury. Monetary exchange abroad was carried out across the zones of the currency tied to it: sterling, French francs, Italian lire.

The institution of the Bank of Egypt, the first national Arab bank, in 1920, represented a type of revolution with respect to the then existing banking situation, not only in Egypt, but for the whole Arab world. This bank began by being run totally by Arabs, both in management and operations. The bank based itself on the German banking system, that is, entering into various fields of activity, and not limiting itself only to the commercial environment. Since its setting up the bank has not limited itself merely to the granting of credit, but has also contributed to and participated in the constitution and financing of various industrial, commercial and service companies operating in fields concerned with metal extraction, the textile industry and connected businesses, air and sea transportation, insurance, printing, theatre, cinema, etc.

It also seems that the setting up of this bank was a stimulus for the constitution of other similar banks in other Arab countries. This has happened in stages, under difficult conditions and against strong resistance on the part of foreign banking organs and from conservative religious groups. We do not now remember that two banks were set up in the Arab world in the 1930s and another group in the 1940s and 50s, involving Iraq, Egypt, Kuwait, Saudi Arabia, Syria, Lebanon and Morocco. By the 1960s national commercial banks were spread over most Arab countries. Besides these, some national development banks were established, whose first step was towards the elimination of foreign economic hegemony. They wanted to guarantee the mobilisation and direction of national savings, and to guarantee its flow in the various production sectors in a balanced manner, especially at a time when the banking system was becoming one of the principal components of any modern economic system based on the monetary element, and considered the life-blood of a complex economic social organ.

Tendencies for Arab Integration

The approval of the Common Defence and Economic Co-operation Pact between the countries of the League of Arab States, in April 1950 and what was said there about the diffusion of peace and tranquility and the insurance of the well-being of Arab states and the improvement of the standard of living, implies these states' co-operation. To confirm this the Economic Council, afterwards called the Economic and Social Council, was formed. One of its most important initiatives was the constitution of the Council of Arab Economic Unity in 1957, followed by the unification of Egypt and Syria in 1958. This prepared the atmosphere for broader initiatives.

With the completion of the main structures of the banking system for every Arab state and with the widening of the Arab financial market, action was directed towards the constitution of organisations which operate in wider environments, for ingrated Arab development and for co-operation abroad.

One of the first initiatives, in this environment is represented by the deliberation of the Arab Economic Council in the middle of May 1968 regarding the constitution of an Arab regional financial body, the Arab Fund for Economic and Social Development.

The agreement on it, which has gathered the support of all countries which are members of the League of Arab States, expresses their commitment and determination to construct an Arab economy on a solid basis, and make it able to face the needs of economic and social development in the respective countries, applying the Charter of the League of Arab States.

To complete this co-operation in the fields of finance and Arab development, the Arab ministers of finance and of the economy approved, in April 1976, the constitution of the Arab Monetary Fund, which largely follows the model of the International Monetary Fund. It has the responsibility of straightening out the balance of payments of the Arab countries; reinforcing the policies and forms of monetary co-operation; providing advice regarding how far they should relate to the policies of foreign investments; developing Arab financial markets and co-ordinating the policies of Arab countries regarding monetary and international economic problems; and regulating the payments being made between these countries.

With the aim of reinforcing relations with the group of African states which are tied to the Arab countries by economic, social and civil bonds, the Summit of November 1973 approved the constitution of the Arab Bank for Economic Development in Africa with the duty of financing economic development projects in Africa and supplying the technical assistance necessary for this.

The Credit Fund of African Countries was then added, assigned by the Arab states to cover the increase in the price of oil imported from African countries; it had a capital of $350 million. It is intended to help the non-Arab African states of the Organisation for African Unity. In order to do this, the Arab summit of October 1974 approved the institution of the Arab Fund for Technical Assistance for African and Arab countries in the field of practical economic development.

Monetary Surplus and the Widening of the Institution of Banks and Funds

The rapid growth of a monetary surplus in the oil producing

countries and these countries' inability to absorb this, have forced them towards the constitution of a group of banks and Funds operating in the Arab world and the Third World, as well as in the international financial market. Actually, while the surplus of six Arab countries (Saudi Arabia, Kuwait, the United Arab Emirates, Qatar, Iraq and Libya) was $8.8 billion in 1972, this figure reached roughly $270 billion in 1981.

The distribution of the monetary investments in various directions, both those carried out using monetary institutions and those through direct intervention, was normal practice. It mitigated the effects of economic dangers on the one hand, and pleased the various sectors stimulated by the increase in the price of oil on the other.

It must be noted that the banks and the Funds have taken different forms. There are those which are constituted only in the Arab environment or in the joint Arab-foreign environment (even if the Arab quota is dominant), or else they are bi-lateral or at the national level.

I will not attempt here to list these financial institutions, but will question only the most important.

In the Multi-lateral Environment

Arab/Arab. There are nine financial institutions, instituted between 1964 and 1981. Participation in them varies from three Arab states (as with the International Arab Bank and The Arab Bank for Investment and Foreign Commerce) to all the states (as is the case for the Arab Fund for Economic and Social Development). All these institutions operate in the environment of the Arab countries, with the exception of the Arab Bank for Development in Africa which operates in the environment of the African countries, and the Gulf Fund for the United Nations which supplies assistance internationally to some organisations of the United Nations, in the fields of food, education, culture and the environment (Table 13.1).

Arab/foreign. The two most important funds in this field are those of the Organisation of Petroleum Exporting Countries (OPEC) and the Islamic Development Bank. The first was founded in 1974 and brings together the OPEC countries (13, of which 7 are Arab), with registered, stock of $4,000 million. It supplies credit to non-oil producing countries, especially to those who have been hit by the increase in the price of oil.

The second was founded in 1975 by all the Islamic countries (22 Arab and 19 Afro-Asian), with registered stock of 2,000 million Islamic Dinars. (The Islamic Dinar is one of the special withdrawal right units, equivalent to $1,080). The idea of the Islamic Bank has been met and taken up in many Arab countries and has already led to the constitution of similar banks with their own mode of thinking on investments, safeguarding religious principles which forbid money-lending and interest (Table 13.2).

Besides the OPEC Fund and the Islamic Bank, many banks and joint Arab/foreign investment organisations have been formed. They have begun to function fully, beginning with the constitution of the Union of Arab-French Banks (UBAF) in Paris. This has played an important part in the institution of a network of banks in London, Luxembourg, Italy, Hong Kong and the US, and its capital exceeds $7 billion. Besides the UBAF group there is a group of Arab-European Banks, Arab-Asian Banks, Arab-Spanish, Arab-Greek, Arab-Turkish, Arab-Latin American etc. In addition, almost every year sees the birth of an Arab-foreign bank or the purchase of shares in foreign banks by Arab capital, or else the constitution of a financial organisation in one of the centres or most important financial markets in the world.

In the Bi-lateral Environment

The increase of the economic and social links between the various Arab countries has led to an increase also in the constitution of banks and associated financial organisations. We find, for example, banks common to Bahrain and Kuwait, to Bahrain and Oman, to Egypt and Kuwait, to Egypt and the United Arab Emirates, to Libya and Tunisia, to Morocco and Tunisia, and to Saudi Arabia and Yemen. Obviously the activities of these are tied to the development of financial relationships between the countries which have established them to serve their own needs.

In the National Environment

It is probable that the most important group of financial institutions constituted in order to facilitate Arab development and that of developing countries, is the national funds of the principle oil producing countries, Kuwait, Libya, Saudi Arabia, the United Arab Emirates and Iraq. All these, with the exception of Kuwait, were constituted in a two-year period 1973–4, during which the price of oil was doubled (Table 13.3).

National and Regional Funds and Relative Financial Activity

There are various forms of national and regional funds. There are those which concentrate in granting short-term credit for well-specified activities regarding balance deficits, as, for example, the Arab Monetary Fund. And there are those which grant credit with various terms and for many development objectives, as does the Arab Fund for Economic and Social Development. And there are also those which operate only within the framework of Arab countries, such as the Arab Monetary Fund and the Arab Fund for Economic and Social Development. Then again there are those which operate in Africa like the Arab Fund for Development in Africa. Finally there are those whose operation is apparent in various continents.

In general, the states which use the services supplied by these funds are the 98 developing countries spread over the various continents (Table 13.4).

In the case of the Arab Monetary Fund its duty is limited, as we have seen, to the granting of short-term credit to Arab countries which have a deficit in their balance of payments. Besides this, the fund works for the stabilisation of the exchange rate between the various Arab currencies, and for the strengthening of the policies and the forms of Arab monetary co-operation; for the supplying of advice regarding foreign investment policies, and for the development of Arab financial markets; for the co-ordination of policies in the face of international economic and monetary problems; to regulate the current payments of member countries; to study means which allow the widening of the use of the Arab Dinar (representing three units of special withdrawal rights); and to regulate Arab interventions and in this way to prepare the way for the institution of a unified Arab currency.

The credits allowed by the fund vary from spontaneous ones in the measure of 75 per cent of the quota of participation of each state to the capital of the Fund, to normal credits to the limit of 225 per cent; to lengthened credits, which can reach 325 per cent; to indemnity credits to the measure of 100 per cent of the quota paid to the capital of the fund. In May 1982 the Fund instituted a new way of facilitating the development of trade between Arab countries, conforming to the treaty for the development and facilitation of commercial exchanges. The Fund foresees an interest rate which varies from $3\frac{3}{4}$ per cent to 7 per cent, according to credit conditions. Besides this, the payment terms vary and can be as much as seven years.

The increase in credits granted by the Fund from its constitution up until June 1982, has reached about $448 million divided between seven Arab states (Morocco, the Sudan, Somalia, Democratic Yemen, Mauritania, Egypt and North Yemen).

The main aim of the Fund, however, has not yet been reached, because of the economic and political conditions which obstruct the Arab world, and because of the brevity of the period in which it has operated. The other regional institution which carries out an important role in supplying credit and assistance to Arab states is the Arab Fund for Economic and Social Development. This finances Arab economic projects, usually specific projects, facilitating credits, and encouraging the development of Arab capital investments in such a way as to encourage economic development, and supply experience and technical assistance. Their credits are long-term, varying from $12\frac{1}{2}$ to 20 years, while the interest fluctuates between 4 and 6 per cent. Besides this, the Fund allows a delay in payment which varies from $2\frac{1}{2}$ to 5 years.

At the end of September 1982, the value of operations carried out by the Fund reached $1,525 million. The greater part of this investment is in the transport, communications and warehousing sector, with 35 per cent, followed by the energy sector with 22 per cent, and water with 15 per cent. To the agricultural, industrial and metallurgical sectors, 26 per cent has been given. As can be seen, the aim has been to concentrate on structural projects which are at the base of projects whose actualisation is not the responsibility of the Fund, and which therefore may be neglected by the individual states in their public and private sectors.

Finally, the Fund has been charged with the responsibility of controlling the treaty of development for which the Amman Summit of November 1980 appropriated $5 billion destined for the less-developed Arab countries.

The Islamic Development Bank, supplies its own facilities to the group of 41 Islamic countries. It has its head office in Saudi Arabia, and does not provide financial services. In its operations the Bank trades and speculates. It does not ask for interest on its operations, only for expenses due for the services supplied; these consist of bureaucratic-administrative ones.

At the end of September 1982, the value of operations carried out by the Bank reached had $2,350 million, divided between the Arab, Asian and African countries, in the measure of 45 per cent, 38 per cent and 17 per cent.

Its operations principally involved energy projects (44 per cent), followed by industry and metallurgy (33 per cent). Transport, communications and warehousing spent almost as much as agriculture — 7 per cent.

Despite the fact that the non-Arab states of OPEC participate in the OPEC Fund, the greater contribution to it is made by the Arab oil producing countries, since this fund was constituted in order to supply facilities and grant guarantees to developing countries which have been particularly hit by the increase in the price of oil.

The credits for the projects are granted with an interest rate of $\frac{3}{4}$ per cent, while for those which are granted for deficits in the balance of payments, the interest rate is $\frac{1}{2}$ per cent.

At the end of September 1982, the credits granted by the Fund had reached $1,659 million, to which must be added about $450 million destined for the international Fund for Agricultural Development in Rome. Of the first figure 43 per cent went to aid the balance of payments of some affected countries, and to facilitate the importation of necessary goods; 27 per cent was destined to be spent on energy and 10 per cent on industry and metallurgy.

In January 1981, the Fund proposed the opening of an investment agency in the service of the Sahara states which face vast economic and financial problems.

The credits granted, on the other hand, by the national Funds (except for the Libyan Fund about which I do not have adequate or sufficient documentation) are all long-term, and are characteristically low-interest.

The Kuwait Fund grants credits with an interest rate which varies from $\frac{1}{2}$ to 4 per cent for periods as long as 40 years, with payments deferred for up to 6 years. The Saudi Fund fixes the level of assistance in such a way as not to exceed half the cost of the projects which need financing; the interest rate asked fluctuates between 2 per cent and 3 per cent for periods of 20 to 30 years, with payments deferred for 5 to 10 years. Credits granted by the Abu Dhabi Fund are characterised by the fact that about 30 per cent of them are gifts, while the credit granted does not exceed half the cost of the project. The interest rate foreseen varies from 3 per cent to 5 per cent for a period which lasts from 15 to 20 years, with 5 years of deferred payments. In addition, it is the only Fund whose statute demands participation in the projects.

The credits from the Iraqi Fund are charged at an interest of $2\frac{1}{2}$ per cent. Their duration is about 15 years, with payments deferred for 3 years. In addition, the Fund allows credits without interest to developing countries for the purchase of Iraqi oil.

The total amount of credits allowed by these national funds is equivalent to $985 million, of which 39 per cent comes from the Kuwait Fund, followed by the Saudi Fund, with 36 per cent, and then those of Iraq and Abu Dhabi. The credit quota conceded by these funds to Arab countries is equivalent to 53 per cent, while 27 per cent went to Asiatic countries and 17 per cent to African ones. The remainder was almost all paid to Latin American countries.

From the indications obtained from the financing, it is seen that about 30 per cent went to transportation, communication and warehousing operations, followed by energy, which received 23 per cent, with the productive, agricultural, industrial and extraction sectors receiving not more than a third.

The Assistance of Oil Producing Countries and of Funds

There is much discussion concerning the assistance supplied by the oil producing countries to the developing ones which are going through a difficult period because of recession and inflation.

There has been an attempt by advanced industrial countries to make the oil producing countries bear the burden of the world's economic problems; more precisely, blame has been attached to the surplus-holding Arab countries. This matter must be viewed within the framework of the present economic and political situation. The advanced industrial countries do not want to recognise that the problem of recession and the consequent increase in unemployment levels is due mainly to the structural dysfunctioning of the international economic system, the result of the Industrial Revolution of the beginning of last century. This imposed an unfair distribution of wealth and of earnings, and the imposition of a certain type of production involving a certain type of work, both between industrial and raw material producing countries. It also produced internal changes in industrialised countries, and those without industry. The injustice of the resulting distribution has provoked imbalance in modes of production and consumption. In the absence of a planned economy the result can only be a cyclical economic and social crisis.

Many theories have analysed the effects of such economic cycles, and their causes. Without going into the merits of competing theories, it can be said that they all enter into one of the two opposing currents of economic thought: socialism or capitalism.

Developing countries have borne the weight of Western colonialism for a long time, knowing, without the support of scientific and philosophical analysis, that they are the losers in their relations with the industrialised countries. The latter receive raw materials at low prices from them, without the developing countries having the chance to block their extraction or impose conditions to their advantage for their exploitation. Meanwhile, the industrialised countries sell the developing ones finished products at a price which does not correspond with that of the materials, even less with the cost of production. At the same time the developing countries are not able to do without these products, for they are beginning to play an important role in the production process. They also require civil trade and consumption relations with the outside world.

The present recession and the economic crisis which follows from it is a link in the long chain of development of the capitalist economy. This situation will remain also after the disappearance of oil from the mode of production and consumption, unless the world decides to face the problem more seriously by reviewing the present world economic system.

In any case the operations of the Arab financial institutions to which we have made reference do not include how much is offered and given by the Arab countries to international organisations such as the World Bank, bodies set up for international assistance, the International Monetary Fund and the Agricultural Assistance Fund. They do not include amounts given through bi-lateral accords with some states, and those deposited in the banks of some countries in order to help them overcome their own monetary difficulties (for instance, the deposits of Saudi Arabia and Kuwait in the Central Egyptian Bank and Saudi deposits in one of the French banks).

We have seen that the amount of aid from the Arab oil producing countries through their national and regional funds, is equivalent to about \$16 billion divided between a number of developing countries spread over three continents. The aid given by Arab countries for the year 1981 is valued at about \$7,770 million, a figure which, even if \$146 million less than what was given in 1980, represents 2.81 per cent of the Gross National Product (Table 13.7) of the countries supplying aid, varying from 0.16 per cent to 4.77 per cent (Table

13.6). American aid, meanwhile, does not exceed 0.2 per cent and is less than the 0.35 per cent of the OECD countries. This last figure represents half the percentage established by the United Nations as a target for the 1970s. And yet if we return to these surpluses we find that they are due to oil wealth — that can be exhausted, and is not replaceable unlike that of the industrialised countries. Their aid comes from renewable earnings. There are observations to be made regarding the use of oil surpluses, and it must be said that these are invested in the construction of a solid and integrated economy which allows the oil producing countries to go ahead with their own development in a period which will see the exhaustion of oil, predicted to be within 56 years. We also know that the greater part of the oil producing countries is made up of desert, without any productive sources apart from oil.

I will not enumerate the problems and risks which weigh on surpluses deposited or invested abroad, and are a consequence of the political relations which exist between Arab countries and those in which capital is deposited or invested; or the risks due to fluctuations in the exchange rates of those countries where this capital is deposited which the financial organisations could fix as a result of unplanned-for increase in the concessession of guarantees.

Up to this point I have outlined the role of the Arab national and regional development Funds. Obviously, the tendency is to give greater importance to national Funds and those operating in the Arab world in particular. In fact, while the regional funds have supplied $5,965 million, of which $2,851 million went to Arab countries, national Funds have supplied $9,985 million of which $5,358 million went to Arab countries. However, greater attention has been paid to the granting of credit and to the supplying of facilities and guarantees. And it has only been occasionally that the Funds have invested directly in development projects.

It seems that they are continuing to follow the Anglo-Saxon system of advising financial institutions against direct participation in development projects, the opposite of the German and Japanese systems. The former is valid when there is a wide financial market and when it is possible for projects to find finance without any difficulty. This is not the case for Arab countries and for developing countries in general. There are additional economic difficulties facing these latter in as much as they must face large multinational companies as well as protectionist legislation which all industrialised countries have in various forms. There are no guarantees for projects, or even possibility of their success, if there are no adequate conditions, and if they do not manage to impose their own development and their own action. So the laws of the state are not sufficient to supply facilities for capital, exemption from payment, of taxes for example. They prefer to purchase their own products for their own consumption even if at higher cost, within certain limits, instead of imported products. It may be that to obtain facilitated credits with low interest rates, and facilitation of transportation, or assistance in the formation of industrial and technical groups against foreign competition, is much more important than fiscal exemptions. Because taxes are usually paid on a surplus; and if because of an increase in the cost of production, for monetary or technical reasons there is no longer a surplus, fiscal exemption will not have any meaning.

In any case, the granting of credits and of aid will have little effect if it does not take place within the framework of a general development plan where the productive and service sectors are balanced. In some cases, at a certain level, this must happen within a group of regional states, and not at the level of individual ones.

In addition, that which is granted by the national and regional funds must be in agreement with that granted by international organisations, since each unbalanced development brings with it problems and social burdens.

There is also the question of the increase in the price of oil, which has serious consequences for developing countries without their own energy supplies. There were those who supported the application of two prices, one low for such countries, the other declared as the market price. However, most of those with oil interests were opposed to the idea, declaring that it was not in agreement with freedom to contract. In addition, they added, there is the risk that price differentiation might bring with it cheap oil for others, influencing prices in general; on the other hand, they continued, this differentiation does not go hand in hand with the law of supply and demand.

The truth is that it would have been possible to fix a quota for the countries which enjoy price facilitation, one equivalent to their needs and increasing each year in proportion to the increase in their needs. It is unthinkable that a state should sell oil at a low price in exchange for other products and in the face of other obligations, because this would bring the economy of the seller to eventual crisis. The question is different. The law of supply and demand is not applicable to the present economic situation subject to limited supply and demand in the absence of sufficient alternatives, information or adequate time permitting the consumer or the producer to move from one position to another in order to guarantee the required balance.

Despite this, and due to pressure from some of the developing countries, the International Monetary Fund has formed a special account so as to allow the countries hardest hit by the increase in the price of oil to obtain credit at facilitated prices. The OPEC Fund was set up with the same aim in mind. It has ample possibilities for conceding guarantees to developing countries. In the same way, the Iraqi Fund has directed itself towards facilitating interest-free guarantees to non-oil producing countries hit by the increase in the price of oil.

But these international, regional and national provisions have not provided a solution to the problems of these developing countries, and they have been forced to close their debts in currency with an elevated exchange rate, from the moment at which the prices of their products plunged. This has led to a situation in which a great number of these countries are not able to close their own debts, forcing them drastically to reduce their consumption, and to face a rapid fall of the quotations of their own currency. This has forced the banks and the crediting countries to postpone credit in order to avoid the collapse of the world economy, meaning that the institutions proposed for development, in this environment, were not equal to the situation.

In any case, it cannot be denied that the Arab development organs, both national and regional, have played an important part in finance and assistance given to developing countries, with better conditions with respect to international institutions, and to the advanced industrial countries, especially in the light of the fact that all aid granted by Arab institutions is free of conditions, meaning that the benificiary is totally free to use what is granted to him, from whatever state, without limit.

References

General Secretariat of the Arab League, *The Unified Arab Economic Report* (1982) (Arab Monetary Fund, Arab Fund for

Economic and Social Development, Organisation of Arab Oil Exporting States).
Arab Fund for Economic and Social Development, *Ten Years at the Service of Arab Development and Integration* 1972–81.
General Secretariat, League of Arab States, *Guide to the Specialised Arab Organisations.*
General Secretariat, League of Arab States, *Guide to Common Arab Programmes and to the Qualitative Arab Unions; Guide to the Common Arab-Foreign Programmes* (1979).
Secretariat for the Co-ordination between Arab Development Organs, *Financing Operations of the Arab Development Organs up to 31 December* 1981.
Arab Economic Development Bank in Africa, *Annual Report* (1981).
Chase World Information Corporation, *Arab Investor*, vol. 1.
Arab-British Chamber of Commerce, *Journal* (January 1983); *The Economist* (21 November 1981).
'Financial co-operation among Islamic Countries', *Journal of Economic Co-operation*, January 1982.

Table 13.1: Collective Arab Banks and Funds

Name	No. of countries	Year of foundation	Nominal cap. in local currency (millions)	in millions of dollars
1. Arab-African International Bank	5	1964	500 D	500
2. Arab Fund for Economic and Social Development	22	1968	800 DK	2,749
3. Arab International Bank	3	1973	100 D	100
4. Arab Investment Company	15	1974	300 D	300
5. Arab Bank for Investment and for Foreign Trading	3	1974	60 DM	16.3
6. International Gulf Bank	7	1975	40 DB	106.1
7. Arab Bank for Economic Development in Africa	17	1973	738 D	738
8. Arab Monetary Fund	22	1976	230 DA	745.2
9. Gulf Fund for the United Nations	7	1981	91 D	91

D = US Dollars
DK = Kuwait Dinar
DM = United Arab Emirates Dirham
DB = Bahrain Dinar
DA = Arab Dinar, which is the special withdrawal rights unit
The dollar exchange rate is that of 3 February 1983.

Table 13.2: Institutions which Finance Arab Development and the Countries which Participate in Them

	1	2	3	4	5	6	7	8	9	10	11
Jordan	x	x	–	–	–	x	x	x	x	–	–
United Arab Emirates	x	–	x	x	x	x	x	x	x	–	x
Bahrain	x	–	x	–	x	x	x	x	x	–	–
Tunisia	x	–	–	–	–	x	x	x	x	–	x
Djibouti	x	–	–	–	–	–	x	x	–	–	–
Saudi Arabia	x	–	x	x	x	x	x	x	x	–	–
Sudan	x	–	–	–	x	x	x	x	x	–	
Syria	x	–	–	–	–	x	x	x	x	–	–
Somalia	x	–	–	–	–	–	x	x	–	–	–
Iraq	x	x	–	x	x	x	x	x	x	–	–
Oman	x	–	x	–	x	x	x	x	x	–	–
Palestine	x	–	–	–	–	–	x	x	x	–	–
Qatar	x	x	x	x	x	x	x	x	x	x	–
Kuwait	x	x	x	x	x	x	x	x	x	–	–
Lebanon	x	–	–	–	–	–	x	x	–	–	–

Table 13.2 — *Continued*

	1	2	3	4	5	6	7	8	9	10	11
Libya	x	–	–	x	–	x	x	x	x	x	x
Morocco	x	–	–	–	–	x	x	x	x	–	–
Egypt	x	x	–	–	–	x	x	x	x	x	–
Mauritania	x	–	–	–	–	–	x	x	x	–	–
Yemen Arab Republic	x	–	–	–	–	–	x	x	–	–	–
Democratic Yemen	x	–	–	–	–	–	x	x	–	–	–

1 = Islamic Bank. 2 = Arab-African Bank. 3 = Gulf Bank. 4 = OPEC Fund. 5 = Gulf Fund for the United Nations. 6 = Arab Investment Company. 7 = Arab Monetary Fund. 8 = Arab Development Fund. 9 = Arab Bank for Africa. 10 = Arab International Bank. 11 = Arab Investment Bank.

Table 13.3: Arab National Funds

Fund	Year of Constitution	Capital in local currency (millions)	in millions of dollars
Kuwait	1962	2,000 DK	6,872.9
Libya	1973	43 D	43
Abu Dhabi	1974	2,000 DM	544.5
Saudi Arabia	1974	25,000 RS	7,256.9
Iraq	1974	677 D	677

Table 13.4: Countries Benefiting from Aid Granted by Arab Development Institutions

Institutions	Arab	African	Asian	Latin-American	Others	%
Regional and international						
Arab Fund for Development	15	–	–	–	–	15
Arab Bank for Africa	–	35	–	–	–	35
Islamic Bank for Development	17	11	6	–	–	34
OAPEC Fund	11	37*	16	15	**	79
National Funds						
Abu Dhabi	12	17	9	–	1	39
Saudi Fund	12	24	11	1	1	49
Iraqi Fund	8	12	10	–	1	31
Kuwait Fund	16	22	13	–	3	54
Total of countries	18	41	20	16	3	98

Sources: Financing operations of the Arab national and regional development institutions and the Economic Society for West Africa

* The Fund has agreed aid with the Brandt Commission, with the Oceanographic Institute at the Oxford Conference for Energy at the Oxford Centre for the study of the new economic system and with the International Fund for agricultural development.

Table 13.5: Countries Benefitting from Aid Granted by the Arab Institute for Development (to 30 September 82)

Aggregate of Countries / Institutions	Arab	African	Asian	Other	Total	%
Arab Development Fund	1,525	–	–	–	1,525	9.6
Arab Bank for Development in Africa	–	430	–	–	430	2.7
Islamic Development Bank	1,067	397	886	–	2,350	14.7
OAPEC Fund	259	591	614	194	1,659	10.4
Total, International and Regional Funds	2,851	1,418	1,500	195	5,964	37.4
Abu Dhabi	758	83	156	7	1,004	6.3
Saudi Arabia	1,563	631	1,278	88	3,560	22.3
Iraq	1,099	314	230	90	1,733	10.9
Kuwait	1,938	675	1,054	21	3,688	23.1
Total, National Funds	5,358	1,703	2,718	206	9,985	62.6
General Total	8,209	3,121	4,218	401	15,949	100
%	51.5	19.6	26.4	2.5	100	

Sources: Secretariat for Co-ordination between National and Regional Development Institutions; Financing operations of the Arab National and Regional Development Institutes. Data relative to January — September 1982.

Table 13.6: Financing Operations Granted by Arab National, Regional and International Development Institutions to 30/9/82, According to Sectors of Action (US$M)

Aggregate of Countries / Institutions	Transport, Communication, Warehousing	Energy	Water and channels	Agriculture	Industry and Nutrition	Other	Total	%
Arab Development Fund	538	334	236	214	182	22	1,525	9.6
Arab Bank for Development in Africa	162	55	16	108	84	5	430	2.7
Islamic Development Bank	169	1,037	38	170	784	152	2,350	14.7
OAPEC Fund	152	460	28	131	170	719	1,659	10.4
Total, International and Regional Funds	1,021	1,886	318	623	1,220	898	5,964	37.4
Abu Dhabi	131	395	16	109	528	25	1,004	6.3
Saudi Arabia	1,441	825	322	500	320	151	3,560	22.3
Iraq	221	124	5	321	186	876	1,733	10.9
Kuwait	1,094	976	174	749	656	40	3,688	23.1
Total, National Funds	2,887	2,320	517	1,679	1,490	1,092	9,985	62.6
General Total	3,908	4,206	835	2,301	2,710	1,991	15,950	100
%	24.5	26.4	5.2	14.4	17.0	12.5	100	

Table 13.7: Aid Supplied by Arab Oil-producing Countries (1981)

Country	Value	$M % of the product
Saudi Arabia	5,798	4.77
United Arab Emirates	799	2.88
Kuwait	685	1.98
Qatar	175	2.64
Iraq	143	0.37
Libya	105	0.37
Algeria	65	0.16
Total	7,770	2.81

14 THE ARAB FUND FOR TECHNICAL ASSISTANCE TO AFRICAN AND ARAB COUNTRIES

Abdallah Adam

I will be discussing the role of the Fund and its activity in the Third World. I would first like, however, to thank those who follow up the work of the Funds for the sensitivity shown towards the theme of world development, which has as one of its major aims the training of men in the economically weaker countries. In fact, giving priority and precedence to training (human development) is the first step in every kind of development, implying the creation of a technically advanced framework.

Over the past two decades, the group of developing countries has confronted various attempts on the part of the larger industrialised ones for leadership, control and exploitation. It has now become evident that behind this pressure on developing countries is the industrialised countries' desire to escape from the economic crisis they are living through, a crisis represented by monetary inflation, falls in production, fierce competition among Western industries and increases in the price of raw materials produced in developing countries.

In their attempts the major industrialised countries have resorted to a mixture of threats and flattery and to using their own international influence and their old colonial connections and relationships in order to bend the small countries to their will, to plunder their wealth and to humiliate them. This was done at a time of growing national feeling in the Third World and an increasing need for political and economic independence and autonomy of choice, in accordance with the interests of these countries and their respective development plans.

During this same stage, and in an attempt to break out of the encirclement of the major industrialised countries, some ideas have emerged upon which are based the hopes and aspirations of the developing countries. They have set up an institutionalised organisation which was represented by the establishment of the 77 Group and by international and regional conferences, during which development possibilities were discussed in the light of the present international economic system. This system is characterised by injustice, inequity and exploitation, and hits the small countries hardest, thwarting their potential and making them, at the end of the day, docile tools to be bent to the will and interests of the major industrialised countries.

At a time when there is a growing demand for a change in the present international economic order in political, economic and intellectual centres, the developing countries, as a group, have started up a dialogue amongst themselves in order to face the challenge made to them, organising their own scientific conquests and producing a series of methods which have been carried out around the following key ideas: In order to free themselves from the rapaciousness of the major industrialised countries, there is no other way out but to establish a relationship of collaboration between the developing countries themselves, with the intention of relying collectively and firmly on one another, and on the confirmation of the principle which declares that the right to benefit from possessions and wealth goes, as priority, to the nearest. In confirming this principle, the developing countries will find themselves in a position of dignity equal to that of other states, and they will be able to impose their conditions as holders, referring to the Western industrial machine, of both the most important levers: that is, raw materials and markets. Furthermore, they represent three-quarters of the total number of states in the world, with all that involves in terms of weight and influence in the sphere of international needs and the formation of international public opinion.

Knowing that they are responsible for the development of their own economy, and on the basis of the realities of the unjust international economic system, the developing countries were pushed to take their own initiative, and in March 1977 the wishes of the two groups, Arab and African, representing two-thirds of the Third World, took a concrete form. They called the first Arab-African Summit; this made a series of decisions and adopted orientations which reconfirm the meaning of collaboration and solidarity in the interests of their peoples, for combined utilisation of their wealth and collective enjoyment of relative resources.

And with the same spirit of responsibility, enthusiasm and equity, the Arab countries managed successfully to crown this attempt by forming institutions and organisations appointed to supply aid to African countries, based on the same principles and orientations which are common to both groups. As the Arab countries are an integral part of this same group of developing countries, they are struggling in the same way as other members in order to expand and confirm their sovereignty and independence.

Arab assistance reaches the various countries of the Third World through numerous national, regional and international organisations. These include the Arab National Funds, the Arab Bank for Economic Development in Africa, the Arab Fund for Economic and Social Development, OAPEC, and the Islamic Bank with its related funds.

The overall Arab commitment to aid to the individual African countries reached approximately $7,000 million at the end of 1981, in the form of credit facilities, contributions and concessions.

Assistance and aid supplied by the Arab states to the countries of the Third World, and especially to African countries, is greater than that granted by Western industrialised countries. Furthermore, the ratio between the amount the Arab states spend on foreign aid each year and their national income is greater than the maximum contribution established by the international organisations concerned. Nor are there unjust conditions and pressures, however camouflaged, in the supply of Arab aid, for it is not conditioned by political aims, whims or pretensions of any kind.

Suitable methods and instruments for guaranteeing the success of technical assistance projects have not been neglected, either. In effect, the Arab Fund for Technical Assistance to African and Arab Countries was set up on the deliberation of the Arab Summit in Rabat in 1974. Its aim is to link Arab assistance projects to the needs and exigencies of the development plans of Third World countries. This Fund is thought of as one of the instruments of the Arab-African Collaboration Programme and the Arab Technical Collaboration Programme, under the aegis of the Arab League.

The importance of the human component, when assured of necessary movement opportunities, potential training and experience, is obvious. The Fund has given priority to those less developed countries which have particularly bad economic conditions. It also takes an interest in the concrete and material opportunities aimed at refining and forming frameworks capable of handling the responsibilities of management in the respective countries of origin. The general orientation which directs the Fund's activities and its responsibilities is based on the principles of the Arab-African Summit Manifesto of 1977. The recommendations of the General Secretariat of the League of Arab States concerned the preparation and carrying out of Arab technical collaboration projects and the League

Council's and Economic Council's relevant deliberations.

Constitution of the Fund, Objectives and Suitable Means of Achieving Them

The Arab Fund for Technical Assistance to Arab and African Countries is one of the organisations of the League of Arab States' General Secretariat. It is the responsibility of the Arab League's Council to follow its administration and fix the general policies and principles which govern it.

The seventh Arab Summit in Rabat (29 October-November 1974), approved the Fund's statutes. In April 1975 the Arab League's Council nominated the First Fund Administration Council. In 1976 the Fund began to supply technical assistance.

Objectives and means

The Fund's objective is to supply technical assistance within the framework of the economic and scientific development of African and Arab countries. The intention of the Arab kings and presidents in setting up this Fund was to strengthen human relationships and bonds with African countries, and to re-establish the value of Arab-African co-operation.

The Fund works towards its objectives using means which it judges appropriate, in particular:

1. Co-ordinating and financing technical assistance programmes presented by the General Secretariat and by the organisations concerned.
2. Preparing general studies on development plans in African and Arab countries and making it possible for them to be carried out.
3. Supplying consultancy services, and putting experts at countries' disposal while organising the exchange of experts between African and Arab countries.
4. Co-ordinating African countries' efforts towards scientific and technological development and the development of production methods and means.
5. Creating new fields of co-operation for development between African and Arab countries.
6. Raising the level of technical and administrative training and

preparation, offering study and training scholarships to African and Arab citizens.

7. Co-operation and co-ordination with African, Arab and international corporations and organisations working within the framework of development and technical assistance.
8. Directing Arab capital into African and Arab project investments.

Fund Resources

The Fund's resources consist of:

1. Allocations to the Fund from the Arab League.
2. Voluntary contributions from Arab states.
3. Contributions from states which make use of the Fund.
4. Offerings and contributions from international organisations, Arab institutions and corporations which the League decides to accept.

Fund Strategy and Work Plan

In order to strengthen Arab-African cooperation with its relative present and future requirements, and with the aim of increasing the Fund's efficiency as the main, important instrument of the Arab League in the field of Arab-African cooperation itself, the following arrangements and orientations were deliberated and accepted.

1. Strategy objectives shall be continued according to a series of plans, the first of which covers the three-year period 1981–83.
2. For the time being and for the period established, selection shall be made of the Fund's policies and work programmes.
3. In carrying out its duties, the Fund shall give priority to the development of human resources which can urge on development of African and Arab countries, for example, supplying experts and study and training scholarships, respecting the following priorities:
   a. *Education*: to concentrate on general, professional and technical teaching.
   b. *Public Health*: to undertake the fight against epidemics and widespread disease in general hospitals.
   c. *Development of Agriculture*, irrigation, rural co-operatives, cattle breeding and veterinary medicine.
   d. *Consultancy services*, research and censuses for general economic and social development.

e. *Training Programmes*: priority in this sector to be given to the training of a national nucleus to undertake the restructuring and organisation of state administration and the public sector, and to create administrative structures for rural development, for workers' unions and for means of information.
f. *Scholarships*: to establish these in the field of secondary and university teaching, with the aim of giving opportunities to Arab and African citizens to train people and develop experience in those sectors of their countries in which it is lacking.

In order to achieve this strategy and reach its objectives in the best possible way, the Fund keeps to the following principles and criteria:

1. Acting as a centralising organ for available Arab experience, the Fund will prepare a programme for supplying Arab technical assistance and the necessary resources for carrying this out. It will follow its various stages, making the relevant Arab organisations and local agencies responsible for doing so in conformity with instructions from their own managing body.
2. It will ensure a renewable influx of finances to the Fund.
3. It will multiply efforts towards co-ordinating the Fund's activities at all levels concerned with Arab-African co-operation, such as governments and financial and executive organisations.
4. It will concentrate on the less developed African and Arab countries in conformity with standards set by the United Nations.
5. It will give priority to newly-independent states and those in greatest need of technical assistance.
6. It will co-ordinate total technical assistance received from the countries concerned from various sources, Arab or other.
7. It will aim for a degree of correspondence of technical assistance granted, with priority established for Fund programmes and the countries' own national plans.

The Fund gives a certain flexibility to its strategy's general guiding principles and to the resulting work plans, in order to be able to absorb possible innovations which may occur in the field of Arab-African collaboration. This strategy is defined with the collaboration of all relevant Arab League organisations which the Fund considers as a source of experience in assistance and the instrument for carrying out its programmes. Moreover, the Fund pursues and developes co-ordination with all bodies interested in Arab-African co-operation at national, regional and international level.

Fund Work Method

1. The Fund makes use of information and reports prepared and put together by Arab and African experts for Arab and international organisations. These concern the situation of the states concerned and enable them to evaluate priorities in granting assistance.
2. The Fund organises, at various levels and in various ways, a network of collaboration and co-ordination relationships with relevant Arab organisations, and with the financial and technical bodies, funds and organisations working in the sphere of Arab-African technical co-operation and Arab co-operation.

   This leads to the Fund regularly convening an annual conference to which representatives from all sides are invited in order to compare and exchange information and to regulate levels and methods of collaboration and co-ordination.
3. The Fund believes in collaboration with regional and international organisations working in the Arab world and on the African continent, with the aim of exchanging experience and information.
4. Each year, the Fund convenes an advisory meeting which involves a number (no greater than twenty-three) of experts in the field of technical assistance and Arab-African co-operation, in such a way that these experts are equally divided between the two sides, Arab and African. The people attending the meeting express their opinions and their evaluations of experience and suggest new means of strengthening relationships and bonds between Arabs and Africans.

Fund Activity

The Arab Fund for Technical Assistance to African and Arab Countries represents the main Arab organisation working within the sphere of the Arab League. It finances technical assistance programmes for economic, social and scientific development and supervises and co-ordinates these programmes, especially within the framework of Arab-African co-operation, but also including, as its own activity, various Arab countries.

The Fund started its activities in 1976, supplying technical assistance to Arab and African countries and then following up the work and the bi-lateral and multi-lateral assistance granted by Arab states through their own institutions. Given that its financial resources are limited, it was necessary to place a priority on some specific activities. Therefore, the Fund Administrative Council decided to grant technical assistance in the field of the development of human resources. This consists of:

1. Making available Arab experts, doctors, teachers, engineers, technicians;
2. Offering of scholarships;
3. Preparing training programmes, set up and carried out by the Arab organisations concerned, in collaboration with the Fund.

The following tables shows assistance granted by the Fund to African and Arab countries, from its foundation to the present day.

Table 14.1: Assistance Granted to African and Arab Countries by the Fund

Supplier States	Type of Assistance	Observations
Djibouti	86 teachers 5 Maritime Inspectors 5 Doctors 2 Radio-TV Technicians	from 1977 to now
Somalia	61 Teachers 14 Doctors 5 Scholarships for 3 years	from 1976 to now
Sudan	10 Professors	
Jordan	2 Experts in Social Development	during 1978
North Yemen	4 University Professors 1 Statistics expert	from 1981 and for 2 years
Palestine	93 Experts 55 Experts 4 Scholarships	working in Uganda, Equatorial Guinea, Guinea-Bissau, Ghana. With costs for 1 year of teaching staff at Nablus University

Table 14.1 — *Continued*

Supplier States	Type of Assistance	Observations
Mauritania	100 Teachers 9 Professors 9 Doctors 4 Scholarships	from 1978 to now from 1977 to now from 1977 to now
Comores	32 Teachers + an Arab Press Centre	from 1977 to now with Scholastic books
Uganda	66 Experts in various disciplines 6 Scholarships	in 1977 in 1978 Engineers, Doctors, Teachers
Burundi	48 Teachers 5 Scholarships	in 1977–8
Zambia	45 Experts in various disciplines 5 Scholarships	in 1977–9 Engineers, Doctors
Kenya	2 University Professors 1 Surgeon 1 Scholarship	from 1977 to now with Scholastic books and a Typewriter
Ghana	2 Scholarships	in 1977
Guinea-Bissau	2 Teachers 20 Scholarships	in 1977
Niger	31 Experts in various disciplines	in 1978–9 (Doctors, Engineers, Teachers)
Lesotho	1 Postal Expert 2 Scholarships	in 1977
Sierra Leone	34 Training Scholarships	in 1977
Liberia	2 Postal Experts 2 Scholarships	in 1977 in 1978
Mauritius	4 Professors	in 1978–80
São Tomé and Principe	1 Postal Expert	in 1977
Mali	1 Expert in Mechanical Calculations	in 1978
Equatorial Guinea	16 Teachers 36 Scholarships	in 1978–9
Cape Verde	15 Training Scholarships	in 1978–80

Tanzania	11 Scholarships	in 1978
Nigeria	1 Scholarship	in 1978
Cameroon	2 Scholarships	in 1978–9
Senegal	6 Teachers	in 1979

Table 14.2: Assistance being Carried out, Having already been Deliberated by the Administrative Council in Previous Sessions (overall cost $20 million approx.)

Supplier States	Type of Assistance
North Yemen	2 Experts
Jordan	6 Scholarships
	2 Experts
Sudan	5 University Professors at Juba University
	10 Teachers
	1 Professor of Communications and Journalism
	5 Scholarships
	1 Expert
	an Optical Instruments and Audio company
Oman	9 Experts
Morocco	2 University Professors
	1 Expert in Arabising Statistics Centre
Burundi	12 Teachers
	6 Engineers
Senegal	8 Scholarships
	6 Engineers
Mauritania	100 Teachers for the 1981–3 Scholastic year
	15 Doctors for one year and until 1 November 1983
	9 Professors for the 1982–3 Scholastic year
	5 Experts
	2 Scholarships
Comores	32 Teachers for the 1982–3 Scholastic year
	1 Press Expert
	1 Translation Expert
	1 Expert in the Introduction of the Arab Language
	1 Preacher
Rwanda	15 Scholarships
	14 University Professors
Zambia	45 Experts in various disciplines (Engineers, Doctors)
	21 Scholarships
Somalia	20 Scholarships
	15 Doctors
	27 Teachers
	61 Teachers (renewal for the 1982–3 Scholastic year)
Djibouti	1 Arab Press Centre
	4 Judges
	86 Teachers for the 1982–3 Scholastic year
	3 Experts

Table 14.2 — *Continued*

Supplier States	Type of Assistance
Niger	7 Teachers
Kenya	4 University Professors
	9 Scholarships
Mauritius	4 Professors
	1 Expert
Ghana	1 Professor in Arabic
Guinea-Bissau	2 Professors
	1 Preacher
São Tomé and Principe	1 Expert
Chad	5 University Professors
Liberia	34 Scholarships
	4 Doctors
Central African Republic	1 Expert
Cape Verde	5 Engineers
Ivory Coast	1 Expert
People's Congo	21 Scholarships
African University Union	25 Scholarships

15 THE ROLE OF THE ARAB BANK FOR ECONOMIC DEVELOPMENT IN AFRICA IN ARAB-AFRICAN CO-OPERATION

Hussein Elsayed Osman

At the outset let me state a number of rather obvious concepts regarding Afro-Arab co-operation: The first is that such cooperation is as old as the peoples of Africa and those of the Arab nation. Since the dawn of Islam to the present day, Arabs and Africans have been in constant contact, with varying degrees of intensity. Cultural ties based on Islam apart, it is perhaps significant to note that at present Arabs constitute 29 per cent of the population of Africa excluding South Africa (27 per cent if South Africa is included); while, with respect to the population of the Arab world, Arabs in Africa constitute 69 per cent of the total population.

The second concept is that Afro-Arab relations have continually been subjected to systematic and calculated misrepresentation by world imperialist and racist forces, starting with distortion of the historic cultural ties between the Arab and African nations, and depicting them as contradictory. These forces have even invented the idea of Negritude in order to cloak the African entity in a folkloric framework, reducing it to tourist artefacts. The European finds a museum of equatorial curiosities: wooden masks, animal skins, birds' feathers and totems, with the sound of drums and flutes providing the background. This is supplemented with misleading historic lies about the slave trade, branding Arabs as slave-traders whose relations with Africa were based on exploitation, the Africans being bought and sold. Furthermore a thick, dark curtain is drawn over the intellectual activities of Africans, and their contribution to an international cultural movement. A deliberate attempt is also made to ignore Africa's great cultural heritage, illustrated by manuscripts which are to be found in international libraries, particularly European ones. So Africans themselves are being persuaded that their cultural life actually started with the introduction of an alien culture. The purpose of all this is an abominable distortion of facts and a premeditated misrepresentation of history in a naïve attempt aimed at dismembering the nations of Africa, destroying their national pride and weakening them, with a view to subjugating and permanently controlling them. But Afro-Arab relations continue to defy all distortion, for one simple reason: they represent a historic fact between these nations, a fact which cannot be obliterated by disregard, changed by explanation or altered by interpretation.

The third concept is that the case for Afro-Arab co-operation does not rest merely on historical considerations, but is also a present-day requirement. The sixth decade of the present century witnessed the emergence of African independence. African countries have together thrown off the colonial yoke and a new dawn has been ushered in. The Arab countries were justly proud of the achievement of their sister countries, in which they played a significant role. The common struggle waged against the twin enemies of imperialism and racism has riveted the links of eternal solidarity between Arabs and Africans and opened new grounds for more positive and fruitful interaction and mutual support. The advent of oil and the boom it achieved in the early 1970s has enhanced the Arab capacity for rendering help and assistance to their African brothers. At the beginning, Arab aid to Africa was sporadic and arbitrary, but it was gradually rationalised and institutionalised, as it gathered momentum. Methods were evolved, criteria established and institutions set up with a view to making aid a genuinely effective agent in the overall development of African recipient countries. There are at the moment nine institutions for development co-operation in the Arab world, some national and some regional.

The co-operation they institutionalise is a present-day requirement simply because it concerns countries which were once colonised, a large number of which have barely emerged from a state of domination, and whose people have been subject to exploitation for too long. They are now living through the frustration of being under-equipped, and wish for a better economic and social future. The present-day requirement is part of the overall effort which is being made by Third World countries to establish a New International Economic Order which is equitable and just.

The fourth concept, which is a corollary of the third, is that Afro-Arab co-operation is, to all intents and purposes, a unique fact in that it is a partnership in development in which resources are transferred from one group of developing countries to another. Evidence of this unique partnership is the observation that the wealth of the Arab aid donors is derived from a depletable resource, oil, unlike that of other aid-givers, which is based on industrial power, rooted in colonial history, and more or less motivated by commercial interests. In effect, therefore, Arab aid could be taken as synonymous with the act of the USA donating the proceeds from selling the Statue of Liberty, France giving away the Eiffel Tower and Italy offering as a gift of the Leaning Tower of Pizza. All of them, once lost, can never be recovered.

The fifth concept, which in turn is a corollary of the fourth, is that Afro-Arab co-operation, being unique in its own right, has laid the exemplary foundation for a viable institutional framework for South-South co-operation by creating a novel multi-lateral agency for the chanelling of aid to Africa in the form of the Arab Bank for Economic Development in Africa (BADEA). This stands as a unique example of multi-lateral co-operation, not only between Afro-Arab countries, but between all Third World countries. Its example is unique in that it was established by eighteen Arab countries which are themselves developing. None of these, or for that matter, any Arab country, no matter where it may be geographically located, can benefit from BADEA's operations. And yet, it is not a commercial enterprise; nor is it a profit-seeking organisation. It is merely a development institution whose sole purpose is to assist in the speedy development of non-Arab African countries, thereby strengthening the bonds of friendship and solidarity between the Arab nation and the African peoples. The unique example of BADEA becomes very striking when we realise that some of the Arab countries which contributed to its share capital are among the least developed countries of the world. Furthermore, its example assumes a much greater significance, and takes on a much wider dimension, when you realise that the valiant people of Palestine, who are still engaged in a bitter struggle to regain their fatherland and establish their own state, have subscribed to its capital and have paid their share in full.

The sixth concept, is that Arabs and Africans, apart from sharing, as previously highlighted, the great cultural heritage of a glorious past and a common experience of a bitter struggle against the evil forces of colonialism, racism and foreign domination, are both engaged in a ceaseless fight to consolidate their political and economic independence, to master their own destiny and to realise their great hopes and aspirations. It is these common bonds of past and present history that unite Arabs and the Africans. It is this community of ideals, hopes and aspirations which provides the solid foundation for Afro-Arab co-operation and solidarity.

The above concepts, self-evident as they are, should serve as an argument to dispel any lingering suspicions regarding the spuriousness of the frequently-cited accusation that Afro-Arab co-operation is promoted by base motives: profiteering and shameful bargaining. To quote H.E. Douda Diallo of Niger, 'There is hardly any need for me to stress here that the African states have not been waiting for financial aid from the Arab peoples in order to manifest their support for the just cause of the Arab peoples in the Middle East crisis. . . Afro-Arab co-operation is a natural objective alliance which transcends the minor designs and calculations and the minor contingencies of the moment.'

Understood as a natural objective alliance Afro-Arab co-operation is not meant as a substitute for other forms of co-operation between Africa and the rest of the world, developed or developing, and it is most certainly not an attempt at the creation of a 'splendidly isolated block'. Rather, it is a form of co-operation with distinctive features which we believe cannot fail to enrich international relations and contribute to the rationalisation of the on-going North-South dialogue.

Let me hasten to add that the objective of this modest endeavour is neither to establish in a definitive way the record of Arab aid to Africa, important though this is in its own right, nor to evaluate it. Rather, this endeavour has the limited aim of highlighting some of the salient features of the role of BADEA in this unique relationship, with a view to clearing the path for future efforts.

BADEA's Role

The decision to create a specialised Arab agency entrusted with the task of providing aid to the non-Arab African countries was taken at the Sixth Summit Conference of the League of Arab States, meeting in Algiers in November 1973. The Board of Governors of the nascent Arab Bank for Economic Development in Africa held its first meeting in Cairo in January 1975.

The General Agreement establishing BADEA spells out in a lucid way the motivation for its creation. Thus 'The Governments of the League of Arab States on whose behalf this Agreement is signed:

—Believing in the need to strengthen the ties between African States and the Arab Nation;
—Seeking to further the economic development of African

countries within a framework of solidarity and mutual interest;

—Recognising that co-ordinated efforts aimed at bringing about the economic independence of African countries are a crucial factor in achieving our national goals;

—Seeking to give African-Arab solidarity a concrete and efficient shape, based on equality and friendship;

—Being convinced that the establishment of a financial institution to support the economic development requirements of African countries constitutes a major step towards stimulating Arab-African co-operation',

[agree to its establishment]

In short the motivation for its establishment is a special case of the effort to establish a New International Economic Order.

The role assigned to BADEA, according to Article 4 of the General Agreement, is 'to foster economic, financial, and technical co-operation between African countries and the countries of the Arab World'. In carrying out this purpose, BADEA shall:

I. Assist in financing economic development in African countries,

II. Stimulate the contribution of Arab capital to African development,

III. Help provide the technical assistance required for African development.

The rest of this brief survey seeks to elucidate the salient features of this role. Before proceeding, however, it may be useful to note a few points which form the set of parameters in the context of which BADEA's role should be understood and perhaps evaluated:

a. On 31 December 1982, BADEA's subscribed capital amounted to US$738.25 million, while its paid-up capital amounted to approximately US$735.5 million.

b. A total of forty-one countries are eligible for BADEA aid. These are member states of the Organisation of African Unity which are not at the same time members of the League of Arab States.

c. BADEA's share of financing cannot exceed 40 per cent of the total cost of any project nor go beyond a ceiling of US$10 million for any given intervention.

d. The Bank's terms of lending vary according to the nature of the project and the economic situation of the recipient country. It is however important to note that the interest rate has so far varied from 1 to 8 per cent.

The Assistance Role

By the end of December 1982, the cumulative net commitments of BADEA amounted to US$728.2 million, of which US$514 million constituted project loans, while US$214.2 million was in the form of balance of payments-SAAFA loans. (SAAFA was established by the Arab petroleum producing countries to aid African countries with balance of payments difficulties. Its total resources amounted to US$350 million, of which US$214 million had been disbursed by 1977 in the form of emergency aid.)

Table 15.1: BADEA's Commitments And Disbursements, (1975–82) (US$ M)

Year	Gross Commit-ments	Net Commit-ments	SAAFA Loans	Cumulative Total Net Commitments	Cumulative Disbursements
1974	–	–	79.8	79.8	79.8
1975	84.1	71.6	64.65	216.1	144.5
1976	61.9	61.9	56.5	334.4	203.1
1977	66.29	66.24	13.244	413.884	223.962
1978	72.87	55.27	–	469.154	279.643
1979	49.07	44.07	–	513.224	331.593
1980	71.95	63.95	–	577.144	379.447
1981	71.026	61.026	–	638.2	412.429
1982	90.00	90.00	–	728.2	449.24
Total	567.206	513.956	214.244	–	–

Excluding 1974, where 100 per cent disbursement was achieved, the average ratio of disbursement to net commitment over the period 1975–82 was 62 per cent. We have no doubt that this ratio could be improved.

In terms of geographical coverage, out of 41 eligible countries, BADEA's operations reached 34, with a total of 68 projects. If we take the coverage of SAAFA loans into account then only two countries, Nigeria and Malawi, have not benefited from the specialised Arab aid agencies for Africa. It seems fair to argue, then, that over the period 1975–82 BADEA, broadly defined, succeeded in achieving one of its objectives in a relatively short period of time.

Using the information already referred to together with BADEA's records on repayment, we have a net transfer of resources, defined as disbursements minus repayments, in favour of Africa by the end of 1982, amounting to US$443 million.

Needless to say, we are aware of the rather limited size of our operations, given the estimated aid requirements of African development. However, we are also aware that we are but one, and the smallest, of nine Arab financing institutions active in this field. Data available on total Arab aid commitments to Africa over the period 1973–81 indicate a cumulative total commitment of approximately US$7 billion. Thus, for the relevant period of comparison, and excluding SAAFA commitments, the BADEA share in total Arab aid to Africa equals 8 per cent. If, however, SAAFA operations are included, our share in total Arab aid to Africa increases to 14 per cent, which by any standard is not a paltry contribution.

As far as the sectoral reach of our finances is concerned, and without getting involved in the semantics of what a given sector is, we note that over the period 1974–82, BADEA contributed to the funding of seven economic and financial sectors. The percentage distribution of commitments over them, including SAAFA loans, is such that 29.4 per cent went for balance of payments support and 31.8 per cent for infrastructural projects. Energy, industry and agriculture received respectively 13.1 per cent and 10 per cent, while lines of credit and technical assistance accounted for 2.8 per cent and 0.2 per cent respectively. The pronounced emphasis of our lending programme on infrastructure is, we believe, appropriate, given the realities of the present stage of development of the African continent.

In considering the concessional nature of BADEA's aid we note, to begin with, that SAAFA loans had a grant element of 71.3 per cent. The weighted average grant element for BADEA's project loans over the period 1975–82 is 31.2 per cent. This gives a weighted average of 43 per cent as a grant element for the combined operations of project financing and SAAFA. In assessing the concessionality of BADEA's aid we should not forget that this aid is completely non-tied aid. As is probably well known, the additional cost of tied aid has very serious implications on the net benefit embodied in it.

To place BADEA's role in a proper perspective it is perhaps important to look at the trend of Arab aid commitments to Africa. Over the period 1973–81 Arab aid commitments recorded a substantial increase, from approximately US$150 million in 1973 to US$1.26 billion in 1981. The trend, however, was not uniform: an increasing one over the period 1973–5 was followed by a decline over the period 1975–9. In 1979 aid commitments registered a trough of US$529.1 million, climbing, however, in 1980 to a peak of approximately US$1.3 billion.

Despite these fluctuations, and according to our calculations, the general trend for Arab aid commitments to Africa was one of growth, where for the whole period an annual rate of increase of 16 per cent was achieved. This, we suggest, is an important result in view of the recommendation of the World Bank's Study *Accelerated Development in Sub-Saharan Africa* that 'aid to Africa must be augmented in the 1980s.'

Using the World Bank's global model to project development trends in oil-importing Africa, and assuming extensive policy reform, the report concludes that in order to achieve annual rates of growth of 5 per cent, 2.1 per cent, 3.8 per cent, 5.2 per cent and 3.9 per cent for GDP per capita, agriculture, exports and imports respectively 'the required ODA disbursements would have to increase from US$4.9 billion in 1980 to US$17.8 billion in 1990'. This implies an annual rate of increase of 13.8 per cent in current prices or 6.4 per cent annual rate of increase on 1980 prices. The report concludes that 'while these aid flows will require a major effort by all donors, the rate of growth is less than was achieved in the previous decade. It should be feasible to achieve these increases, but they will require early action to increase commitments.'

Thus, using these projections as rough indicators for the job that awaits donors, it seems fair to conclude that given their record the Arabs have already far exceeded the rates of increase projected. It thus remains for the other sources of aid to rise to the challenge.

The 'Stimulation' Role

Let us recall that Article 4 of BADEA's General Agreement specifies its second role as being to 'stimulate the contribution of Arab capital to African development'. One way of interpreting this could be to look at the co-ordination between BADEA and the Arab Funds in providing aid of Africa. Obviously a much more elastic interpretation could be offered; however, for our purposes we shall stick to this narrow version.

This being understood, it is perhaps worth quoting at length Dr

Ayari, The President and Director-General of BADEA, on BADEA's understanding of this particular role:

> If BADEA has a special role to play as far as Arab aid to non-Arab Africa is concerned this does not mean that Arab Funds will not use their initiative. . . Arab Funds are absolutely free and in no way restricted by any special role entrusted to BADEA as a co-ordinator of aid. There have been many cases when an African project was brought to the attention of the group by an Arab Fund other than BADEA. An example of this was the Maseru airport project in Lesotho which the Abu Dhabi Fund first initiated and sponsored.
>
> We are not the only source of information about Africa for the Arabs. We cannot be that. Arab countries have bi-lateral relations with African states which may lead to Arab interest being aroused in respect of a project.
>
> There have been cases where BADEA took second place to some other funds because at the time we lacked expertise. For instance, in the case of the Selingue Dam in Mali, to which we had commited an exceptionally large loan of US$15 million in 1976, BADEA did not have any experts on dams. We then agreed that KFAED (Kuwait Fund), which had such experts, should take the lead among the Arab funds co-financing the project and act as a leader in the course of implementation.
>
> But we had been promoting the Selingue Dam. We had been talking about it at our meetings with other Arab Funds, we were able to raise money for it — and that is the most important part of co-ordination. When we play the role of co-ordinator this above all means organising finance so that the project can get off the ground.
>
> In other cases we had not only introduced the project to Arab Funds and sponsored it, but also administered the entire Arab contribution, as with the cement project in Guinea which we are co-financing with the Abu Dhabi Fund and the IDB.
>
> Our role has been particularly important in respect of African countries which were not very well known in the Arab World, such as Mauritius and Seychelles, or even might have been under some suspicion for their policies, such as Angola and Mozambique. We first brought these countries to the attention of the other Arab Funds.

See A. Sylvester, *Arabs and Africans* (The Bodley Head, London, 1981, pp. 68–9)

The above, we suggest, is an almost comprehensive view of BADEA's 'stimulation' role as originally designed in the Articles of Agreement. Institutionalised co-ordination among the Arab Funds started in earnest in April 1977, when the first co-ordination meeting was held in Kuwait. During the period April 1977-December 1982, four meetings at the level of Presidents-Directors-General, were held in addition to fifteen meetings at the level of Directors of Operations. Such meetings served the objective of allowing the exchange of information among Arab Funds, orchestrating action and streamlining policies and practices. As the learning-by-doing process embodied in these meetings matures it is expected that well-defined roles for individual institutions *vis-a-vis* co-operation will emerge.

This co-ordination among Arab Funds has already drawn attention and gained respect. The OPEC *Development Co-operation Review* (1981) had this to say:

> Meanwhile our colleagues in the Arab development funds, with whom the members of DAC have been meeting annually for the past four years, have set us a daunting example. The ten institutions involved meet regularly at both policy and technical levels; they have adopted standardised documentation and procedures for project appraisal, loan agreement, procurement and disbursement; they commonly undertake joint operational missions and routinely interchange appraisal and supervision reports and other relevant information. Moreover, in jointly financed ventures, the Arab Funds are now starting to concentrate the bulk of the loan administration responsibility on a single co-operating institution. This arrangement, which borrowers, contractors, consultants and banking community all are said to welcome, is formalised by a standard loan administration letter exchanged among the co-operating financiers.

The results of this concerted effort at co-ordination in terms of commitments has recently been investigated by BADEA (1982) in a study entitled *BADEA's Co-Financing During the Period 1975–81*. The study notes that:

> Since the inception of its operations BADEA has striven to co-

> ordinate its development efforts with those of Arab financing institutions operative in Africa with a view to promoting African development and consolidating Afro-Arab co-operation. . . (Thus) 29 out of a total of 72 BADEA commitments during the period (1975–81), were co-financed with the participation of one or more Arab financing institutions. Whilst BADEA financed these 29 projects to the tune of US$202.68 million, Arab financing to the same projects reached US$554.8 million.

BADEA's co-financing with Arab institutions covered large, medium and small-sized projects. Large projects include Sonichar Energy Project in Niger, Kpong Dam in Ghana, Selingue Dam and Savari-Gao Highway in Mali, paper pulp (Cellucam) in Cameroon and chemical industries in Senegal. The total cost of each ranges between US$116 million and US$260 million. However, on average it is calculated that the total cost of a project co-financed with Arab institutions is US$77 million.

The Technical Assistance Role

Using any definition of 'technical assistance' BADEA has yet to start addressing itself to the ways and means by which it can fulfil this role. Its 1981 Annual Report had to keep virtually silent about this, noting, as if apologetically, that 'Technical assistance operations remained at a low level during 1981. Even though the planned allocation for technical assistance was not attained, the project aid programme was over-fulfilled.'

Without in any way trying to be evasive or apologetic, we may be able to explain this short-coming in terms of the so-called Development Aid Community. It seems fair to argue that the decade of the 1970s was a period during which the international community was persuaded that somehow investment in human capital is a futile endeavour, and the building of training institutions is synonymous with wasting scarce foreign resources. Physical capital accumulation was emphasised as the ruling development paradigm.

This, however, is now changing. Regarding the likely place of technical assistance in development aid, it has recently been argued rather forcefully by the ADSSA Report that

> *accelerated Growth in Africa depends more than anything else on training people and building institutions. Although technical assistance can help overcome particular scarcities in the*

> *short-run, its major purpose is, and should be, training and building up of institutions*. . . A production oriented strategy will require greater reliance on technical assistance in the decade ahead. Substantial increases in project lending will require increases in technical assistance in most of Africa, as will the formulation of sectoral investment programmes and the evaluation of the policy framework. . . Some modifications in the general approach do seem appropriate e.g. *strengthening project related training; and shifting technical assistance more decisively in the direction of training*.

Taking the cue from the World Bank, the OECD *Development Co-operation Review* (1982) echoes the same sentiment:

> Skilled manpower at all levels is a critical factor in development and in many cases more critical than availability of capital or natural resources. Hence training assistance will continue to be central to economic and technical programmes and must be a key factor in technical and capital assistance. The challenge is to ensure quality and relevance in the training that is provided.

The extent of our success or failure, in achieving the above roles is perhaps best judged by others. Needless to say that we, like any other organisation, have had our share of frustrations, disappointments, mistakes and mishaps; some of these are purely internal matters while others pertain to the African domain in the context of which we operate.

As far as the internal difficulties are concerned, let me say that our learning-by-doing curve is asymptotically approaching the optimum. Despite this we are indeed proud that we were able to establish ourselves as a development institution which enjoys a fair amount of respect on the African continent, in the Arab world and indeed throughout the international financial community as a whole.

Difficulties pertaining to the African domain have largely to do with the time-lags involved in the chain of approval-signature-effectiveness of fundable projects, the availability of fundable projects and the slowness of disbursements. With regard to the time-lag between approval and signature, we are happy to report that over the years we have been able to reduce this from an average of one-and-a-half years to an average of three months. This improvement, however, does not apply to the time-lag between signature and effectiveness. The reason for the length of this lag is, we believe, the lack of prompt action on the part of recipients, which in turn may be due to the deficiency of their project-implementation capabilities. There are obvious implications for the place of 'technical assistance' in aid-giving. This reason also applies, *mutatis mutandis*, to the difficulties related to the availability of fundable projects, as well as the slowness of disbursements.

Be that as it may, and without pre-empting opinions to the contrary, let me once more quote at length the views of Dr Ayari on what we were able to fulfil of our role in Afro-Arab cooperation:

> We have been able to enhance the interests of the Arab countries in Africa. This I believe is very important. More than once we have been instrumental in throwing yet another bridge between non-Arab Africa and Arabs. We have been active as spokesmen of the Arab states in Africa and of Africa in the Arab region. We have been able to spread the message of Afro-Arab co-operation so that this is now better understood by public opinion in Africa and in Arab countries than it had been a few years ago. . . Thanks to our contacts and our relations with the public and with the media, we have also no doubt contributed to better co-operation between the Arabs and Africans in regard to OAU and the Arab League (see Sylvester).

The intensive developmental efforts of the two sister organisations, the OAU and the League of Arab States have materialised in the Lagos Plan of Action for the Economic Development of Africa 1980–2000, and the Amman Strategy, respectively. These two documents are the embodiment of the hopes and aspirations of these peoples for shedding the fetters of backwardness and attaining the commanding heights of development and advancement. The fact that BADEA is entrusted with reconciling these two plans, with officiating, as it were, in their marriage, is further evidence of the goodwill it enjoys in both camps.

Given the size of our institution we entertain no illusions about the single-handed impact we may have, and given the state of African development we have no cause for complacency regarding what has been achieved.

16 EURO-ARAB CO-FINANCING

Bernard Petit

The European Community, which is particularly attached to the efficacy of its co-operation with developing countries has participated actively in co-financing from the start, but especially so since 1975 which saw the multiplication of co-financing projects with institutions in oil producing countries, particularily Arab countries. It is worth examining the experience of this collaboration between the EEC and the Arab Development Funds over the years.

My purpose will be three-fold: Having first outlined the EEC's Development Policy and the extent and nature of the means involved, I will highlight the conditions that have pertained to and governed Euro-Arab co-financing projects to date. Finally, I will outline the overall considerations governing the new approach which the EEC intends to adopt in its Development Policy.

The EEC Development Policy, Characteristics and Means

The Development Policy constitues one of the most significant and satisfying elements of Common Market reality. Having originally come into being almost by accident, it has matured through the experience of conventions which developed from unilateral, and thus precarious, preference and aid agreements, to a contractual programme, and, finally to the breadth of a global co-operation policy. This last hinges on two pivots:

World-level actions, which include:

a. a generalised preferential tariff system with the EEC;
b. financial and technical assistance to 'non-associated' countries in Asia and Latin America;
c. food aid;
d. certain specific actions, such as co-operation with non-governmental organisations and emergency assistance in the event of natural disasters or similar circumstances.

Regional and contractual agreements that are periodically

reviewed and concern the different aspects of co-operation, whether commercial, financial, industrial or agricultural.

I refer first of all to the agreements signed with the Southern Mediterranean countries concerning which new financial drafts have been negotiated which total some 1 billion ECU for the 1983–4 period (Commission Budget and European Investment Bank Funds combined).

They also cover the successive conventions signed with the African, Carribean and Pacific countries (ACP), the second of which, the second Lomé Convention, is without doubt the most elaborate example of the EEC's Development Policy. Resulting from negotiations between two equal partners and with inbuilt institutional structures to ensure ongoing dialogue between the two groups at both government and parliamentary level, the Lomé Convention's Policy can be summed up as:

a. respecting each partner's sovereignty in the conduct of its external relations and economic and social policies;
b. binding the partners on a long-term basis and thus guaranteeing a stability in the relationship;
c. encompassing all forms of co-operation (aid, trade relations, stabilising export earnings, energy and mining co-operation, capital transfer, institutions, etc.).

With a 1980–5 allocation of 5.6 billion ECU of which 4.7 billion were from the European Development Fund and 0.9 billion from the Bank's resources, the Lomé Convention has at its disposal such a choice of financial techniques that it can answer the needs of any situation with the required flexibility. It can deal with grant aid, normal loans at going market conditions, Stabex transfers, special loans, special loan facilities, equity stakes, semi-capital grants or subsidised loans.

EEC co-operation and Development Policy is considerable in terms of the means, institutional, financial, technical, commercial, that it controls and in terms of the number of partners it addresses and the new and original forms of co-operation that it has conceived and put into operation. As the *Commission Memorandum on Community Development Policy* (Brussels, September 1982) says:

Today it is a manifestation of Europe's identity in the world at large and a major plank in the Community's external policies generally; it is an earnest of solidarity with poorer countries, of awareness that international interdependence has a political and humanitarian dimension as well as an economic one, and that industrialised and developing nations have mutual interests.

I would now like to turn to the question of the role that this policy has played in co-financing operations, particularily with Arab Development Funds.

How Euro-Arab Co-financing is Organised

Naturally, the different financial means at the Community's disposal can be used jointly. But they can also be used in the context of co-financing operations that are conceived and executed with third party sponsors. In this area, the Commission has been particularily active in developing the use of such co-financing, in particular with Arab countries. Unlike the situation in certain other financial institutions, co-financing is not an obligation for the Community. Indeed, the general rule is that it assumes total financial responsibility for a given project, even including the local, in the field, costs, which a great number of donors are not in a position to do.

This co-financing policy has been developed voluntarily over the past few years, and its main features and results are:

The foundations of Co-financing Policy

There are three fundamental elements:

a. Firstly, in the face of the high level of investment required, co-financing is the only means of realising large projects, and it is thus an efficient way of contributing to nations' development. When properly conceived and economically justified, these large projects can be of great interest to the developing country through the unit cost reduction achievable in execution, management and production.

   This concept has resulted in some very large projects, some of which have been realised by Italian firms. In particular, I can refer to the trans-Cameroon railway, the Upper Tana reservoir in Kenya and the Goluen-Gelib road in Somalia.

b. Secondly, co-financing encourages international co-operation and thereby brings together various organisations specialised in development aid. It thus contributes to a harmonious co-ordination of such aid.
c. Lastly, through co-financing agreements the different financial agencies can extend their activities to a particular country and thereby contribute to a maximum deployment of available Development Funds.

Means Available from the Community for Co-financing

There are four major areas:

a. The Community's capacity to give financial assistance for a given project under very favourable terms can enable the conclusion of economically interesting operations even when profitability is low (in the EDF, the ratio of grant aid over special loans and risk capital is 80/20);
b. The Community's procedures are well tested, particularly in the area of specifications which result from the harmonisation of the principal European regulations and their adaptation to the individual conditions of developing countries and to the constraints peculiar to internationally financed projects.
c. The Commission can give important administrative and technical assistance to the co-sponsors for projects that are undertaken in countries where it has representation in the form of a 'delegate', i.e., ACP and Southern Mediterranean countries.
d. The Commission can be very flexible with regard to its normal terms and is willing to adapt them to the constraints of the co-lending organisations. In this manner, it will accept bids for tender that are open to outside countries (that is, outside the ACP-EEC area for example), on condition that is, that the co-financiers should make the same concessions and therefore admit European companies.

   In the same way, the Commission is open with regard to the form of co-financing if it considers that the joint financing, where all partners participate in the same conditions, is more advantageous than parallel financing, in which each participation is related to a distinct part of the project, treated in isolation.

Naturally, the considerable development of co-financing,

especially with Arab Funds, springs from these characteristics of the Community Assistance Programme.

The Results

While not pretending to be an exhaustive list of past actions, a few noteworthy figures will illustrate the importance of co-financing, and with Arab Development Funds in particular.

In the framework of the first Lomé Convention, some fifty projects were co-financed, of which more than half were with Arab Funds. Overall, Euro-Arab co-finance was used in some thirty projects, totalling close on 4.5 billion ECU and in which Arab participation is much the same as the Community's (*c.* 20 per cent).

It is a sure sign that systematic co-operation with the Arab Funds is beginning to bear fruit from the increasing Arab participation in co-financing projects with the Community over the past few years. Looking more closely at this evolution one sees that Arab participation in this type of co-operation was strong from the outset. This can be explained by the possibilities offered to the Arab Funds to participate in projects that had been drawn up under the Yaoundé Convention, which preceded the First Lomé Convention. The Congo-Ocean railway, Douala Port, the Goluen-Gelib road, and the Selenge barrage are examples. Over time a certain consolidation can be observed, but with lower rates of participation. It is only from 1978 onwards that the combined European and Arab efforts developed co-operation between the two groups, with the result that in the co-financed projects where they were involved, the Arab participation grew to be identical to the Community's.

It is since that time that both on a technical and political front, the number of meetings between the Commission and different Arab Funds has increased considerably. At a technical level, co-ordination meetings (in principal, annual ones) are organised between the Arab Funds and the Community to examine questions of specific projects together with certain other problems of a more general nature, such as sectoral policy. The last of these meetings was held in Brussels in June 1982 with participants from the Commission and the European Bank on the one hand, the Saudi-Arabian, Kuwait, Abu-Dhabi, OPEC, BADEA and AFESD Funds on the other.

Other, more specific meetings are also held to examine particular problems such as procedures. For in co-financed projects, each financing partner has a tendency to impose his own complex procedural grid on the recipient country. This can work to the detriment of correct execution of a project and constitutes a heavy burden on the recipient country's administration.

The need for harmonisation of procedures is quite obvious, whether it is for parallel financing or for co-financing, where procedural homogeneity is particularily important. Two meetings have already been held in Kuwait during which the Commission and most of the Arab Funds examined questions as precise but also as general as rules of elegibility, comparison of offers, arbitration, contract terms, terms of payment, terms of quantity, modifications in mid-project or terms of temporary caution money payments. This Euro-Arab co-ordination also takes place on the ground, that is, at meetings between all Funds participating in a given project, whether these take place in the recipient country, in Brussels, Vienna, Khartoum or Washington.

One begins to see the distance covered and all the important efforts conceded by both sides to ensure that this co-operation between the European Community and the Arab Funds became a reality. No doubt further efforts must be made: greater degrees of integration are needed, more frequent meetings, etc., and for its part, the Commission will do all it can. This will be done within the framework of the new approach to its Development Policy which it intends to pursue and which is aimed at intensifying the collaboration between the Community and Arab Funds in a manner that goes beyond the mere financing of a specific project. With this in mind, a top-level meeting is scheduled for next spring between the Commission and the representatives of the BADEA, in order to sound the latter out on their views on this new approach. I therefore feel that it is the right moment to give you an outline of the main features of this approach.

The Commission's Recommended New Approach to Development Policy

Presented in September 1982 in the *Commission Memorandum on Community Development Policy* already mentioned, this new approach springs from a stark fact: whatever progress may have been achieved in developing countries over the last twenty years (average income per capita, life expectancy, degree of literacy, etc.), there has been a dramatic increase in the gap separating middle-income countries from the poorest nations, which have suffered, to a greater degree than others, the effects of global international deterioration. These countries have dangerously increased their food dependence while their natural heritage has continued to deteriorate. In parallel with this, the number of starving people has continued to increase. In effect, the efforts that have been made have not yielded the substantial results hoped for. While no doubt needing to be encouraged and developed, the Community's Development Policy also needed to be readjusted in terms of its objectives and practical applications. For this reason the Commission proposed to reinforce co-operation, and to undertake more efficient development actions.

On the first issue, the Commission considers that the Community should reinforce and standardise the network of contractual links already established with developing countries while continuing to give a privileged position to the co-operation agreements with ACP countries and Southern Mediterranean ones. As to the second issue, with regard to the Development Programme, the Community should re-examine its priorities, means and methods in order to contribute more significantly to the autonomous and long-term development of the recipients, particularly the poorest countries. It is on this last point, i.e., the concrete realities of development, that the most fundamental renewal is called for.

This concern with autonomous development means that the first priority must be the effective application of a rural Development Policy. This in turn conditions both the regression of hunger and poverty and the creation of an economic matrix without which no real take-off will ever occur, however much external aid is injected. Other fundamental priorities will include actions designed to develop human resources, to exploit natural resources, and restore ecological balances, as well as to develop autonomous scientific research.

To be efficient, this greater concentration on the basic actions that condition development must start from a change in methodology. To quote the *Commission Memorandum*: 'To step up development action requires more than a mere increase in aid resources . . . nonetheless very necessary.' In substance, what the Commission is proposing is to go beyond the present situation in which the two parties are only concerned with the definition and financing of a project, and to arrive at a mutually approved policy, to be defined by the recipient country, to which a real commitment is made by the nation concerned to the same degree as the Community. One could thus arrive at a more coherent mix between external aids and internal policies, and a better chance of establishing a structural rather than a cyclical Policy. As a result, donors would necessarily achieve better co-ordination of their actions and the different forms of aid that they control. This approach, as recommended by the Commission, has been put into practice by the Community in several African states on an experimental basis in the context of food aid strategies designed to take into account interdependence and complementarity. In the Commission's view, this new effort at defining and implementing food aid assistance programmes can be extended to other areas, such as mining, energy, and industrial development programmes.

These are the outlines of this new approach, which is designed to arrive at a better deployment and more efficient use of available resources. It will have a chance of success if it involves other donor organisations from outside the Community.

My hope is that as a result of our respective thoughts on the subject, whether we are Arabs or Europeans, the objective remains one and the same: millions of people are struggling for survival and will continue to need external aid for a long time to come. We can give them that aid. When speaking of efficiency and collaboration, those are the people we must think of first.

17 UNICEF AND THE ARAB FUNDS: PERSPECTIVES FOR THE FUTURE

S. Tayyarah

The Arab Funds (both the national Funds such as the Kuwait Fund and the multi-lateral funds such as the Arab Fund) have become some of the largest donors in the world to developing countries. According to HE Mr Al-Nowais, Director-General of the Abu Dhabi Fund, the Arab oil countries gave 4 per cent of their GNP as ODA during the period 1975–80 against 0.35 per cent for the industrialised countries. Most of these funds were channelled through the Arab Funds.

UNICEF started as an emergency fund for children in war-torn Europe and China, and has evolved into a development organisation for the Third World. UNICEF's assistance is humble in financial terms (expenditures totalling approximately $322 million in 1982), but it reaches 112 countries. Through concentrating on advocacy, low-cost programmes and pilot activities that can be extended countrywide, UNICEF tries to optimise its impact.

In view of the increasing importance of Arab aid both in terms of sectoral and geographical coverage it was natural that discussions be started between UNICEF and several of the Funds, concerning how to initiate joint efforts. These discussions have so far resulted in concrete project co-operation with the OPEC Fund in Vienna and the Arab Fund for Economic and Social Development in Kuwait.

AGFUND

In 1980 another important development occurred in the relations between UNICEF and the Arab countries when HRH Prince Talal bin Abdul Aziz, the brother of HM King Fahd of Saudi Arabia, accepted the assignment as Special Envoy for UNICEF. Since then HRH Prince Talal has become a spokesman at the highest level for the interests of children, in addition to raising large amounts of money for UNICEF. The Prince in 1981 announced the establishment of the Arab Gulf Programme for the UN Development Organisations (AGFUND); this comprises the seven Arab Gulf

States. AGFUND has so far allocated $36.25 million from its governmental resources to UNICEF and pledged to collect $15 million from private and other donors. The government of Italy in 1982 made a first allocation of 1 billion lire to UNICEF through AGFUND. In accordance with its Charter, AGFUND gives assistance only to UN development organisations in the humanitarian and social field.

UNICEF's Methods of Co-operation

Country Programming

There are no UNICEF projects, only government projects with UNICEF co-operation. This is a long-standing UNICEF policy which ensures that the projects will strenghten the capacity of the recipient country and continue after the termination of the assistance. This also ensures that the project fits into the priorities of the recipient country. All UNICEF projects are prepared by field offices, reviewed at headquarters and approved by UNICEF's Executive Board, with members both from donor and recipient countries.

General Resources/Noted Projects

UNICEF can receive funds either as general resources (its regular budget) or for noted projects. A noted project means that the UNICEF Executive Board has noted the project as worthy of funding and authorises the Executive Director to seek financing from other donors.

Opportunities

The Arab Funds' assistance is almost entirely directed towards projects in the field of economic development. Some, such as the Arab Fund for Economic and Social Development, have indicated an interest to do more in the area of social development. In this area, UNICEF, through its more than 100 field offices, an efficient supply system, and long experience in social development, represents an efficient partner.

Potential Obstacles

Some of the Arab funds, because of their mandate, may have difficulties in financing activities in the social sector. Secondly, projects involving social and human resource development are much more difficult to assess and quantify than investments in infrastructure. Thirdly, most of the Arab Fund financing is on a concessionary loan basis, whereas UNICEF extends only grants. In view of the difficulties in financing many social development projects with loans this may pose an obstacle to increased engagement of the Funds in the social sector. In cases, however, where the recipient government would request loan financing for a specific project, a mechanism has been found for channelling such funds through a UNICEF project. (See below).

Future Co-operation

There should be good possibilities for strengthened co-operation between UNICEF and the Arab Funds in the future. This co-operation could take many different forms such as (in ascending order):

a. A Fund finances a large-scale project, based on the extension of a UNICEF-funded pilot project. The World Bank has done this in India.
b. A Fund finances certain components of a project which is partly financed by UNICEF (parallel financing). An example is Wad Al Magboul Water Institute in Khartoum (AFESD).
c. A Fund finances a project by extending a loan to the recipient government, which in its turn allocates the proceeds of the funds to a UNICEF noted project (AFESD).
d. A Fund extends a grant directly to UNICEF to finance a noted project (the OPEC Fund).
e. A Fund extends grants to sectoral programmes of UNICEF such as the programme for women's development (AGFUND).

Since the Arab Funds, the recipient governments and UNICEF have a joint interest of learning from each other's experience and pooling their resources, UNICEF regards its co-operation with the

Arab Funds as an area of the highest priority which will be of great benefit to the children of the world. Since the organisations concerned have different mandates, an imaginative approach is necessary in order to achieve the desired results.

Thanks to the efforts of the Arab Fund, the OPEC Fund and AGFUND, however, we have already begun well. UNICEF regards this as a significant development since it has been shown, for example, by the World Bank (*World Development Report*, 1980) that investment in human resources is not only called for on humanitarian grounds, but may have higher economic returns than investments in infrastructure. Because of the squeeze in the social budgets of the recipient countries, however, innovative methods in programming and implementation may be required. UNICEF feels that it has come a long way towards meeting this challenge, as witnessed by the recent emphasis in its report on the situation of the children of the world.

18 CO-OPERATION BETWEEN THE OECD, DAC MEMBER COUNTRIES AND THE ARAB DEVELOPMENT FUNDS *

J.M. Bartsch and R. Stock

The OECD Secretariat has been co-operating with the Arab Development Funds for many years, and this co-operation between the OECD, its member countries and the Arab Development Funds will be the subject of this chapter.

I would like to mention briefly the origin and functions of the OECD's Development Assistance Committee (DAC). In 1960, ten governments, seven from Europe, including Italy, together with those of the USA, Canada and Japan, and the Commission of the European Communities, formed the Development Assistance Group. The aim was to provide a meeting place where suppliers of bi-lateral aid to less developed countries could consult together and exchange experience on common problems. When the Organisation for European Economic Co-operation was re-organised as the OECD in 1961, the Development Assistance Group became incorporated as the Development Assistance Committee. The DAC now has eighteen members. The World Bank and the International Monetary Fund attend DAC meetings as regular observers.

The DAC itself is not an aid-giving agency, and has no development fund of its own. Its main purpose is to stimulate a common effort in development assistance and to assess member governments' policies, with particular respect to the volume, terms, conditions, geographical and sectoral distribution of the aid. It regularly reviews each member's aid policies, and seeks to set quantitative and qualitative standards for aid, to encourage better co-ordination among aid donors, and to find ways of improving the effectiveness of development assistance. The statistical system built up by the DAC has become the primary source of information on financial flows to developing countries.

Every year, the Chairman of the DAC publishes a report on the development co-operation efforts and policies of DAC members,

*The views expressed in this chapter are those of its authors and do not represent the official view of the OECD or its member countries.

who until 1973 provided over four-fifths of total aid to developing countries. When in 1973–4 Arab OPEC countries became an important source of aid, with a share of 16 per cent of world ODA, the OECD Secretariat began to monitor systematically the aid efforts of Arab countries and Development Funds. From 1974 onwards the annual reports by the DAC Chairman have contained a chapter on non-member countries, largely devoted to a description of the aid provided by the national and regional Arab Development Funds and by Arab governments. In compiling this information the OECD has benefited from the co-operation of the Funds.

The first direct contact with an Arab Development Fund dates back to 1974 when an official of the Arab Fund for Economic and Social Development visited the OECD. It was followed by visits from other Arab institutions, and since 1976 the OECD Secretariat has frequently visited the national and regional Arab Development Funds.

In 1978 the Chairman of the OECD's Development Assistance Committee invited the Director-General of the Kuwait Fund and the Managing Director of the Saudi Fund for Development to address the Committee. This invitation led to the first meeting of the DAC with the heads of Arab/OPEC aid agencies in June 1978.

Since that date a joint meeting has been held every year (the last one in June 1982) with a view to offering Arab/OPEC DAC and multi-lateral aid agencies the opportunity of discussing (a) broad aid policy issues; (b) policies pursued by the different aid agencies; (c) technical problems encountered in day-to-day aid implementation and (d) specific problems related to a particular geographic area (for example, sub-Saharan Africa), or a sector (such as aid to energy development, re-afforestation or transport development). Moreover, these meetings have offered the opportunity of getting better acquainted with one another and enhancing mutual understanding and confidence.

One of the main topics discussed during these meetings has been the co-financing of development projects between Arab/OPEC, DAC and multi-lateral aid agencies, the problems involved and possible ways and means to alleviate the administrative burden which they impose on both recipient and donor countries.

Since the emergence of Arab/OPEC countries as a major source of aid in 1973–4, co-financing of development projects by DAC and Arab/OPEC aid agencies and international financial institutions has become an important technique for increasing the flow of resources to developing countries. By the end of 1981, over 350 co-financed projects involving external finance of almost $23 billion had been agreed upon or were in an advanced stage of negotiation. Co-financing arrangements have fluctuated considerably from year to year in terms of both the funds involved and the number of new projects undertaken, reaching a peak in 1979 when $4.4 billion was committed to 67 projects. Excluding 1979, co-financing arrangements averaged annually some $2.6 billion spread over 40 projects. It should also be noted that the number of co-financed projects has decreased in recent years from 67 in 1979 to 33 in 1981, but that the amounts committed, which had declined sharply in 1980, were again on the increase in 1981, reaching their second highest level, mainly because of large additional commitments to the Senegal River Development Project.

The amounts contributed by individual donors have been extremely unequal, as have the financial conditions. The number of participants has also varied from project to project, ranging from two to sixteen. Usually the number of co-financiers has been greater for infrastructure projects. International financial institutions, usually the lead agencies in co-financing arrangements, accounted for over two-fifths of the funds involved, followed by Arab/OPEC countries and institutions with about one-third, and DAC member countries with nearly one-fifth. International financial institutions continued to play a major role in organising co-financing arrangements, participating in some 90 per cent of all such projects. The bulk of funds for co-financing was provided by half a dozen international financial institutions and donor countries: the World Bank, Saudi Arabia, Kuwait, Germany, the Asian Development Bank and the EEC. Together, these agencies provided about 60 per cent (or $13.5 billion) of total co-financing flows.

Arab/OPEC aid agencies continue to place heavy emphasis on co-financing with international financial institutions and/or DAC aid agencies, in particular with regard to large-scale projects situated in countries where they have little experience. On average, about two-thirds of their development finance goes into projects co-financed with a multi-lateral and/or DAC aid agency. Saudi Arabia and Kuwait have been the leading contributors, accounting together for over two-fifths of Arab/OPEC funds committed to such projects (i.e., cumulative totals of $2 billion and $1.6 billion respectively). They are followed by the OPEC Fund, the commitments of which have come close to $900 million spread over 169 projects. BADEA, the Islamic Development Bank, AFESD and the Abu Dhabi Fund have also participated actively in co-financed projects in recent years, contributing to 51, 40, 39 and 39 projects respectively. Except for AFESD, however, the amounts involved have remained relatively small.

Although 14 DAC Members had participated in at least one project with an Arab/OPEC financial institution by the end of 1981, three countries, Germany, France and Japan together accounted for over two-thirds of DAC members' overall total contributed to co-financed projects (i.e., $1.4 billion, $866 million and $782 million respectively), while participating in 50, 40 and 16 projects. Other DAC members who have participated in a relatively important number of projects are Canada, the USA and the UK.

In contrast with Arab/OPEC donors, multi-participant projects represent less than 4 per cent in DAC members' total project assistance. However, for Germany's and France's main executing agencies, the Kreditanstalt für Wiederaufbau and the Caisse Centrale de Co-opération Economique, the percentage is much higher (i.e., 10 and 16 per cent respectively).

The geographic distribution has remained stable in recent years. About one-half of each of the projects undertaken and the funds committed were devoted to Africa, about one-third to Asia, about one-eighth to Latin America, while the rest was spread over Europe and Oceania. Although Arab countries remained major recipients of co-financed projects, it should be noted that there was a movement of funds away from them to non-Arab countries in both Africa and Asia. This movement was particularly noticeable for Arab aid agencies: through 1979 over 93 per cent of their co-financing monies had gone to Arab states while in 1980 and 1981 only 28 per cent did.

The sectoral distribution of co-financed projects has remained stable in recent years: infrastructure projects have continued to engage 60 per cent of total committed funds, industry and mining about one-quarter and agriculture about 7 per cent. Although the promotion of alternative sources of energy has been designated as a desirable sector for increased co-operation among donor groups only one such project had been negotiated by the end of 1981.

The co-financing with non-concessional sources of finance and in particular commercial banks, was felt to be another area which needed further exploration and co-operation among donor groups.

It will be the main topic to be discussed during the next joint DAC/OPEC meeting to be held for the first time at the OPEC Fund's headquarters in Vienna.

Another subject to which a great deal of discussion has been devoted concerns the harmonisation of aid procedures. While the Arab/OPEC aid agencies have achieved a large degree of harmonisation, a similar standardisation of aid procedures is difficult to achieve for DAC members since their historical background and the budgetary and administrative circumstances under which their aid agencies work are different. Under these circumstances it was felt preferable on the DAC side to try and overcome these obstacles in a pragmatic way, although there is still some scope for harmonisation, in particular with regard to project identification and appraisal, the sending of joint appraisal missions and the drawing up of joint project reports.

Maintenance and recurrent cost financing has become a crucial problem for most of the poorer developing countries and was felt to be particularly well suited for effective co-operation between DAC and Arab/OPEC donors. It implies little in terms of exports from the industrialised countries and has as a prime objective the interest of the developing countries, which the Arab/OPEC donors, being developing countries themselves, claim to defend in a more genuine way.

In addition to the joint annual meetings at the OECD, many DAC member countries have established and maintained contacts with the Arab Development Funds on a bi-lateral basis. The French Caisse Centrale de Co-opération Economique and the German Kreditanstalt für Wiederaufbau have developed particularly close relations, but there are also contacts with several other DAC aid agencies, notably the United States Agency for International Development, the Canadian International Development Agency and the Scandanavian aid agencies. The seminar on 'Financing New and Renewable Sources of Energy' in October 1981 jointly sponsored by the Nordic aid agencies and the OPEC Fund is one concrete example of this co-operation. It was during this seminar that Dr Shihata made his proposal to establish an international non-governmental fuelwood research centre to conduct research on the afforestation of sub-Saharan Africa; this was welcomed by participants from both the DAC and Arab donors. The Nordic countries are currently investigating the practical arrangements for collaboration in the fuelwood sector.

Other subjects of common interest are being discussed among donor groups, including the difficult question of procurement restrictions, felt to be one of the major obstacles to effective co-financing arrangements by Arab/OPEC donors. Their enumeration would however go beyond the scope of this chapter.

19 INTERNATIONAL CO-FINANCING AND INTERNATIONAL CO-OPERATION

Rainer B. Steckhan

In the 1980s developing countries confront unprecedented financial requirements. These countries have to adjust to a markedly deteriorated world economic climate and to maintain a minimum of long-term growth. This requires both economic policies conducive to facilitating the required structural adjustment and additional external finance.

The World Bank as an Instrument of International Co-operation[1]

The World Bank can assist in this process but its possibilities are necessarily limited. By its nature, the World Bank is a co-operative institution owned by 147 sovereign states: developing and industrialised countries, OPEC and OECD countries, market-oriented and socialist countries. In one of its main decision-making bodies where 21 Executive Directors represent its member countries there is a clear desire to avoid confrontation and to reach a consensus on the issues before them. The co-operative nature of the World Bank is also reflected in its dealings with borrowing member countries where dialogue and mutual learning predominate.

In the field of economic policies, the World Bank has always maintained with its client countries a policy dialogue designed to help formulate appropriate policy measures. About three years ago, the World Bank began to support programmes of financial and structural adjustment measures through so-called structural adjustment loans. As of the end of the fiscal year 1982 (i.e. 30 June 1982) the World Bank had lent over $2 billion for this purpose in 13 countries. However, the bulk of World Bank financing has been and will be for well-designed, carefully prepared, thoroughly appraised and closely supervised development projects.

Since the spring of 1947 when it approved its first lending operation, the World Bank has approved loan commitments in an aggregate principal amount totalling the equivalent of about $110 billion. It has suffered no losses on its loans, and delays in the payment of loan charges have been insignificant. The World Bank has a firm policy against debt rescheduling and does not participate in such exercises.

Impact of World Bank Activities

In its technical and financial assistance the World Bank has exercised great care in helping to identify, prepare, appraise and supervise World Bank financed projects. Ex-post audits of these projects show that they have been largely worthwhile. For the last ten years the World Bank has operated an independent Operations Evaluation Department (OED), to check ex-post on the success and failures of these projects. OED is headed by a Director-General who reports directly to the Executive Directors as representatives of the (nation) owners of the World Bank. For a number of years OED has published and distributed to the public its Annual Reviews. OED's *Sixth Annual Review of Project Performance Audit Results*, the fourth to be distributed to the public, was published in November 1980.

OED's *Seventh Annual Review of Project Performance Audit Results* was published in December 1981. The sixth and seventh Reviews covered 217 projects with a total cost exceeding $15 billion to which the World Bank had contributed $4.2 billion. As in earlier reviews, OED concluded that these projects were, with few exceptions, either successful in achieving their principal objectives or well on the way to doing so, and that they had contributed substantially to the development of both material and human resources in the countries concerned. In addition, 109 agricultural projects reviewed by OED in the last three years benefited approximately 18 million people. Projects more specially designed than others to reach small farmers offered average economic rates of return of about 26 per cent, and carried smaller dollar costs per farmer benefited.

Last last year a report *IDA in Retrospect*[2] was published covering 20 years of IDA activities in the poorest countries and showing 'its record of solid achievement and its ability to learn from past mistakes'.

Co-financing with the World Bank[3]

Despite the World Bank's capacity for policy dialogue and for successfully financing high-return priority projects it can meet only a small proportion of the costs of the required investments from its own resources.

In recent years, the World Bank has helped to meet the growing needs of its borrowing member countries by becoming increasingly active in stimulating the flow of external capital to them. Co-financing, one of the most important ways by which these flows can be tapped, directly associates Bank funds with those provided by other sources in financing specific projects or programmes in developing countries. Co-financing has become a regular feature of the World Bank's work. It is another aspect of the co-operative nature of the Bank.

The three main categories of co-financing partners with the World Bank are: (a) official sources, which include governments, their agencies, and other multi-lateral financial institutions; (b) export credit institutions, which are directly associated with financing the procurement of certain goods and services from a particular country; and (c) private financial institutions, primarily commercial banks.

World Bank co-financing operations have expanded steadily during the past decade with the number of operations increasing from 37 in fiscal year 1973 to 99 in fiscal year 1982. During the same period, the total volume of co-financing rose from about $\$\frac{1}{2}$ billion in fiscal year 1973 to a record \$7.4 billion in fiscal year 1982. Of this \$7.4 billion, co-financing with private financial institutions comprises \$3.3 billion, export credit agencies account for about \$2.1 billion and another \$2.1 billion will come from official sources. Forty per cent (99 of 247) of the projects approved by the World Bank in the fiscal year 1982 involved some co-financing.

Co-financing with Official Sources

Historically, bi-lateral and multi-lateral official aid agencies have been the major contributors to World Bank co-financing. Co-financing with OPEC institutions has been concentrated on Africa. In fiscal year 1982, the agencies from industrialised and OPEC nations provided about \$2.1 billion for 76 World Bank projects.

The World Bank also engages in aid co-ordination activities. While these are not immediately related to promoting the co-financing of particular projects, they can facilitate co-financing. Activities include participation in the meetings of aid co-ordinating groups for a particular country as well as consultative meetings on co-financing co-operation which the World Bank holds regularly with various donor governments and their aid agencies and with other multi-lateral institutions. In addition, the World Bank has entered into several formal co-financing arrangements with official aid bodies. Of particular interest is the fact that Italy and the World Bank last year signed an agreement under which Italy will make available 450 billion lire (about $321 million) for co-financing World Bank projects through June 1985. This type of support is, obviously, greatly appreciated.

Co-financing with Export Credit Institutions

Export credits have been an important source of co-financing, particularly for capital-intensive projects in the energy, industrial, public utilities, and transportation sectors. In fiscal year 1982 nearly $2.1 billion in export credits was distributed among 26 World Bank operations.

In order to increase the awareness of export credit opportunities information is now being sent regularly by the World Bank to export-finance institutions on projects suitable for export credits. Furthermore, discussions were held in Washington in mid-December 1982 to explore whether the procedures and objectives of bilateral export-finance agencies can be better matched with World Bank procedures and those of international competitive bidding, and whether measures can be taken to increase co-financing with these agencies.

Co-financing with Commercial Banks

World Bank co-financing with private sources has increased substantially in recent years. The volume has grown from $84.7 million in fiscal year 1974 to $3.3 billion in fiscal year 1982, and the number of operations with potential for co-financing from private sources has grown from two in 1974 to 16 in 1982.

Past Co-Financing Programme

For the past several years, the World Bank has pursued a co-financing programme aimed at encouraging participation of the private sector in IBRD lending operations. In typical co-financing operations, the IBRD and the commercial banks have entered into separate loan agreements with the borrower. The commercial loans are on market terms and are negotiated *directly* by the co-financier with the borrower. In most of the cases, but not in all, they are linked to the IBRD loan through an optional cross-default clause and a memorandum of agreement signed by the IBRD and the agent for the commercial banks. The memorandum of agreement provides for the exchange of information on the projects, and serves to keep the World Bank and the co-lender in contact during the inplementation of the project.

More than 200 commercial banks participated in co-financing operations involving formal arrangements during the fiscal years 1974–82. These banks provided about $2 billion worth of funds. Of this total, private banks with headquarters in Japan provided the largest share (30 per cent) of funds. United States banks provided 23 per cent, United Kingdom banks 8 per cent, and Canadian banks 7 per cent. Italian banks have so far participated only in a very modest fashion in co-financing operations (Italian banks have contributed only $20 million over the last 10 years). An additional $1.7 billion has been arranged in conjunction with World Bank projects, but without formal links to the World Bank loan. Another $4.8 billion in private co-financing is envisaged, but yet to be arranged, for World Bank projects that have already been approved. Projects in the power sector have historically attracted the largest amount of private co-financing. Recently, however, more private co-financing loans have been directed to projects in other sectors: agriculture and rural development, industry, transportation and energy development.

New Co-financing Instruments

The World Bank has announced the introduction of a set of new instruments designed to increase the participation of commercial banks in World Bank project loans to developing countries. These new instruments are intended to help increase the flow of private capital to developing nations; they will supplement the World

Bank's present methods of co-financing with the private sector. Under the existing system, if co-financing for a World Bank-financed project is needed and desired by the borrower, the Bank will assist in arranging for such financing. However, the World Bank and the commercial banks enter into separate loan agreements with the borrowing country. The commercial bank loans have been on market terms.

The new instruments, approved by the World Bank's Board of Executive Directors, will mean that in selected cases the World Bank, in addition to making a direct loan for a project, will also participate in the financing from commercial sources. This programme will be tested for the next 12–24 months. During this time, the World Bank is authorised to provide up to a total of $500 million for participation in commercial co-financing loans.

Three New Approaches for Co-financing

These have been approved and are all intended to provide better maturities to developing country borrowers than are available from a direct market operation:

Direct Financial Participation by the World Bank in the Later Maturities of a Commercial Loan

To supplement the direct World Bank loan, the World Bank would participate in a commercial bank loan, in the range of 15–20 per cent. The resulting maturities would be significantly longer than available in the market. Annual repayments of principal would be made by the borrower first to commercial lenders until their share of the loan is fully repaid; then, in later years, principal payments would be applied to the World Bank's share. As the loan is amortised, the World Bank's share would be available for sale to the commercial lenders.

Contingent Participation by the Bank in the Later Maturities of a Commercial Loan which would be Initially Financed Entirely by Commercial Lenders

Annual debt service of the commercial bank loan to the borrower would be fixed even though the interest rate would be variable. If the interest rate rises above the initial rate, the amortisation will not be completed on the original schedule. The World Bank's contingent commitment would be to finance the balance of principal, if any, at the end of the term of the initial loan if rates turn out to be higher than anticipated. The benefit of this approach, in addition to extended maturities, is that it provides borrowers with a fixed payment schedule for their debt service, enabling better planning. The commercial lenders would have the opportunity to purchase the outstanding balance for their own account.

Guarantees of the Later Maturities of a Private Loan by the World Bank instead of Direct Funding

Under this option, the World Bank, to supplement its direct loan, would not participate in the commercial bank loan directly but would guarantee repayment of the later part of the loan. This approach, too, is designed to extend maturities. As the loan is amortised, and the guaranteed portion comes within the normal range of market maturities, the guaranteed share can be reduced.

It is expected that the pilot phase of the programme will include 15 to 20 lending operations, and will be completed within a two-year period. Estimating that the World Bank's share of each commercial transaction would be approximately 20 per cent, the pilot programme could result in total co-financing of about $2.5 billion. These finds will be used to finance high-quality investment projects already deemed suitable for World Bank lending in those countries which the Bank judges to be credit-worthy.

Notes

1. Unless otherwise indicated references to the World Bank include both the International Bank for Reconstruction and Development (IBRD) and the International Development Association (IDA).
2. Libreria Ledi, Piazzale Dateo 6, 20129 Milan; Libreria Scientifica, via Meravigli 16, 20123 Milan.
3. For details see the World Bank's Annual Reports and other publications, excerpts of which are contained in the following.
4. See *World Bank News*, vol. II, no. 2.

20 EUROPEAN COMMUNITY FINANCIAL CO-OPERATION IN THE ARAB COUNTRIES: THE ROLE OF THE EUROPEAN INVESTMENT BANK

Christopher Lethbridge

For those unfamiliar with our Bank it may be useful briefly to explain what the European Investment Bank is, before describing something of its particular activities in Arab countries.

The European Investment Bank was created by the Treaty of Rome in 1958 and its members are the ten member states of the Community. These members have also subscribed to its capital which today stands at 14.4 million ECU. (The ECU, European Currency Unit, is made up of the sum of a number of EEC national currencies and was equivalent in value at the end of December 1982 to US$0.97.) The EIB raises the bulk of the funds required for its lending operations on the capital markets of the Community and on international ones. The main objective of the Bank is to contribute to financing projects for the balanced development of the EEC and for this purpose the Bank grants long-term loans to enterprises, public authorities and financial institutions to finance projects for regional development, for converting existing undertakings, or for creating fresh activities by means of projects of interest to one or more member states of the Community.

By special authorisation from the EIB Board of Governors, who comprise the Ministers of Finance of the member states, operations *outside* the Community may be financed by the Bank. These non-Community operations may be for single projects of special importance to the EEC, as, for example, the provision of energy supplies from outside the Community. They may also be authorisations for loans to individual countries or groups of countries granted under the terms of specific EEC agreements or conventions. These conventions or financial protocols have, over the years, extended the Bank's theatre of operations to such countries as Turkey, Portugal, Spain and Yugoslavia as well as to the countries of Africa, the Caribbean and Pacific who are members of the ACP group, and who are the EEC's partners in the Lomé Convention. Since 1978 the Bank has additionally been authorised to make loans to the Maghreb countries (Algeria, Morocco and Tunisia) and to the Mashrak group

(Egypt, Jordan, Lebanon and Syria).

At the present time the EIB activities in the Arab countries are concentrated in the Maghreb/Mashrak countries and in certain countries of the Lomé group. This chapter will be concerned primarily with the Maghreb/Mashrak operations of the Bank.

As mentioned earlier, the Bank operates in the Maghreb and Mashrak under the terms of co-operation agreements signed between the individual countries concerned and the European Economic Community. These agreements contain, in addition to trade and other arrangements, a financial element in the form of a protocol. The first financial protocol with the Maghreb/Mashrak countries came into force in 1978 and comprised a package of financial aid extended from the Community to the countries concerned within the framework of an overall EEC/Mediterranean co-operation policy.

The objective of these financial protocols is to provide a form of financial assistance enabling a wide range of different projects to be suitably supported by the European Community. Each protocol contains provision for loans from the EIB at its normal lending terms, as well as grants from the European Commission and loans on concessionary terms. Grants and special loans are provided from the budget of the European Community and in the case of grants, managed by the European Commission. The Commission is concerned primarily with projects requiring a very soft or grant-oriented approach, e.g. social infrastructure, basic rural development and funds for studies and technical assistance of various kinds. The EIB's loans, on the other hand, are concentrated on finance for the development of economic infrastructure, the expansion of the production sector, development of energy resources and other similar initiatives for which financing by loans is normally appropriate. Some projects are of the type which call for a blend of different types of finance; in these cases money from the Commission and the Bank can be utilised jointly to provide an appropriate blend for the project concerned.

The first financial protocol with the Maghreb/Mashrak countries covered the period 1978–81. A second protocol which has very recently come into force continues the previous co-operation until 1986. Taken together, these two protocols provide for a total amount of Community financial assistance of 1.68 billion ECU of which nearly 1 billion has been or will be provided by the European Investment Bank from its own resources. The remaining 720 million (or 42 per cent) is made up of very soft loans (1 per cent interest rate, 40 year repayment period, ten year grace period) or grants. As mentioned earlier, these grants are used either for direct project investment in special sectors or for technical assistance, but a substantial proportion is available for subsidising the interest rate of the EIB loans. These subsidies have the effect of reducing the Bank's normal interest rate by a maximum of 3 per cent so that the borrowers receive loans on more favourable conditions than the Bank itself could afford to give, bearing in mind that it must raise its funds on the financial market and to do so must offer a competitive interest rate to its own lenders. Within the Community, the Bank's loans closely follow, as far as interest is concerned, the movement of the market. From its own borrowings, the Bank applies a very small margin to enable it to cover its own operating costs and to contribute to reserves. It thus sets its own lending rate to member countries on a basis enabling it to fulfil this requirement but, in the case of the Maghreb/Mashrek countries, thanks to the Community grants, it can afford to reduce its interest rate by up to three percentage points.

The mix of financing referred to earlier includes not only subsidised loans from the EIB, but the very soft-term loans from the Community budget. These loans are in many cases managed, on behalf of the Community, by the EIB (except where they are applied to social and basic rural development). Special loans can be made available for a project alongside an EIB loan from its own resources so that the overall financial burden on the project is greatly reduced.

A special arrangement in the financial protocol allows also for the use of special loans to finance 'risk capital' operations. Essentially this is a technique which enables the Bank, using Community budget funds, to finance a shareholding or to lend to a government or national development agency so that it, in turn, may increase the equity base of suitable projects, thus enabling the project to provide a more balanced borrowing foundation for its activity.

The experience of the Bank in project financing in the Maghreb/Mashrak countries has now extended over the past four years. It has resulted in a pattern of project financing which is likely to be repeated during the coming second financial protocol period, to 1986. Broadly, the Bank's financing has been concentrated in the four sectors of transport, energy, industry and agriculture. This wide range of economic activity has been chosen to try to give maximum impact to the relatively modest sums of money available.

Transport projects have so far been financed in all the

Maghreb/Mashrak countries, except Jordan and Lebanon, where the governments concerned preferred to concentrate Bank lending in industry (Jordan) and energy (Lebanon). Briefly, in Morocco the transport sector benefited from two major loans to help the construction of port facilities at Jorf Lasfar and the expansion of the existing ports at Agadir and Safi. These projects have been aimed at aiding Morocco's phosphate exports, as well as developing general purpose port facilities for the agricultural and general import/export trades.

Two railway projects in Tunisia have benefited from EIB loans. A new railway between Gafsa and Gabes has been built for transporting phosphate rock to the port of Gabes. On the Tunis-Algiers main railway line the EIB has financed the re-location of a section of the track which had to be moved to allow the filling of a major irrigation reservoir.

The EIB made a contribution in Egypt, to the deepening and widening of the Suez Canal, a project in which a number of major international institutions provided co-financing. The EIB loan was particularly aimed at the provision of ship repair and maintenance facilities at Port Tewfik and the removal of obstructions and wrecks from the Canal.

Road projects in Syria and Algeria have both been financed by the Bank. In Syria the new alignment of the Aleppo Tall-Kojak Highway is now in its final stages, providing an important link and reducing the transport cost between the farming areas in Eastern Syria and the main population centres in the western part of the country. In Algeria the Bank loan involved highway improvements between the major centres of Constantine and Jijel.

The financing of *energy supplies and energy development* in general has been given high priority by the Maghreb/Mashrak countries and it is appropriate therefore that EIB financing has already been applied to energy projects of various kinds and is likely to be equally concentrated in this sector in the future.

In Egypt the Bank contributed to the financing of the power station development at Shoubra-el-Kheima near Cairo, a 600 megawatt generating plant, and to the development of Egyptian natural resources in the form of off-shore gas at Abu-Qir near Alexandria. In Algeria five Saharan oasis towns are increasing their electricity generating capacity by the provision of mobile diesel units financed by the Bank. In Jordan, electricity transmission and distribution facilities to assist the development of small-scale industry north of

Amman provided an opportunity for the Bank to participate in the financing of this priority objective.

The Bank has been able to respond to the desires of the Maghreb/Mashrak countries in the *industry* sector by developing the financing of small and medium-scale industry through lines of credit (global loans) to development banks.

In Morocco, Egypt, Tunisia, and Jordan loan facilities have been extended to local development investment institutions for on-lending to small industries operating in a wide variety of sectors, including food, metal-working, mechanical engineering, transportation, leather, etc. These small ventures have helped to create a large number of local job opportunities and have enabled the EIB to participate in the financing of very small-scale industries which would not normally warrant direct financing by the Bank. In Morocco and Jordan a number of small handicraft businesses have benefited from the flexibility of the EIB's global loan technique and in Morocco part of the funds were made available as a risk capital contribution so that the government-owned corporation responsible for share participation could finance equity holdings with local entrepreneurs. In another type of lending, of indirect benefit to industry, the Bank provided a loan for the construction of an industrial zone near Amman so that modern and tailor-built factory space could be made available to replace the inefficient and crowded manufacturing conditions in the city.

Finally although the *agriculture* sector is mainly supported by means of grant funds from the European Commission, the Bank has committed some financing to it. The Syrian road project and the Tunis/Algiers railway project mentioned previously both have indirect agricultural development as their motivation but, in addition, in Tunisia, a loan has been extended (through the Banque Nationale de Tunisie) for on-lending to various agricultural activities aimed at increasing food supplies to the domestic market.

The above brief review of some of the Bank's activities to date should be seen in the context of the relatively short period within which it has been financing in the Maghreb/Mashrak Arab countries. In contrast with the agreements signed between the individual Maghreb/Mashrak countries and the EEC, co-operation between some 60 countries in tropical Africa, the Caribbean and the Pacific is governed by a single treaty, the so-called Lomé Convention, which was first signed in 1975, then renewed in 1979.

Only four members of the League of Arab States are signatories to the Lomé Convention — Djibouti, Mauritania, Somalia and the Sudan and I will, therefore, only make a few remarks about the lending activities of the EIB in these countries.

In Mauritania the Bank has provided finance for the development of a large iron-ore mine. The project is of great importance for the country's development, and the financial agreements, exemplary from the point of view of international co-operation, have entailed the support of a large number of lenders, including the Islamic Development Bank, the governments of Iraq and Morocco, the Arab Mining Company, the Kuwait Foreign Trading and Contracting Investments Corporation, the OPEC Special Fund, the Saudi Fund for Economic Development, the Kuwait Fund for Economic Development, the Arab Fund for Economic and Social Development, and the Abu Dhabi Fund, as well as the World Bank, the African Development Bank and others.

In close co-operation with the Sudan Development Corporation and the International Finance Corporation, the EIB has participated in the financing of a new textile mill in the Sudan. In Somalia the Bank has provided long-term funds for the rehabilitation of the dairy industry and in Djibouti we have helped finance power generating facilities to provide energy for further industrial development.

In many ACP countries, the Bank provides lines of credit to national development banks for on-lending to small and medium-scale projects in the fields of manufacturing and agro-processing. Examples of this policy are a project preparation facility made available to the Somali Development Bank and the provision of loan and equity funds for the establishment of a new development bank in Djibouti.

Altogether these operations in the Mediterranean and ACP Arab countries have represented a total commitment of some 390 million ECU from the EIB's loan resources in the past few years. As mentioned earlier, a second generation of financial protocols between the Community and the Mediterranean Arab countries is now coming into force. The second phase of financing provides for an increase of approximately 50 per cent in the amount of aid available from the European Community. Discussions with the governments concerned to identify priority projects for this new money are now under way and the EIB is already actively appraising and presenting to its Board projects for financing under the new protocols.

It cannot be too strongly emphasised that while the amounts

authorised by the Bank's governors for lending to the Maghreb/Mashrak and other Arab countries seem modest in comparison with the undeniable development needs of these countries, the Bank itself tries to maximise the impact of these funds by the flexibility of its approach to sectoral project financing over a wide range of activities. Moreover, since the Bank may not lend from its own resources more than 50 per cent of the fixed asset cost of a project, frequent opportunities are thus available for co-financing. This means that EIB funds are utilised not only in conjunction with the resources of the borrower and of other credits available in the country concerned but also with other international sources of credit available for the co-financing of development projects.

21 THE CANADIAN INTERNATIONAL DEVELOPMENT AGENCY AND THE ARAB WORLD

A.F. Odeh

The upheaval in the world's oil markets in the early 1970s marked the first time that a group of developing countries, the Organisation of Petroleum Exporting Countries (OPEC), made up largely of Arab states, had joined together to assert their national and commercial interests. The quantum leap in prices as the cost of oil was brought more in line with reality catapulted the oil exporting nations into the forefront of international affairs and brought new resources into their respective national treasures.

These oil exporting countries immediately began channelling their increasing revenues into their own much-needed development. Their populations were largely poor, some even destitute, severely lacking in the skills which modernisation required. There was a universal need for improved infrastructure — roads, transportation, communications — and large-scale education and training programmes. Oil revenues gave the exporting countries the luxury of attacking many of these problems simultaneously. Almost overnight countries began to move from a stage of extreme underdevelopment to the modern era.

Although the first priority for financial resources was their own economies, the Arab nations used their power to help the Third World with which, despite their sudden wealth, they remain identified. Surplus oil revenues were channelled, in increasing amounts, into development projects.

Arab aid programmes, however, were not a new phenomenon. Kuwait was the pioneer, establishing its development assistance fund in 1961, followed by the Arab Fund for Economic and Social Development in 1968 and the Abu Dhabi Fund for Arab Economic Development in 1971. The rapidity of the Arab intervention in international development after 1973 and the volume of resources they have been able to mobilise have greatly dramatised their actions. To date, Arab donors have directed approximately $16.5 billion into their bilateral programmes of international co-operation.

Co-financing of Development Projects with Arab Donors

The Global Picture

While the Arab nations have a high level of financial resources available to help Third World nations, they are faced, by the state of their own development, with a shortage of the technical and managerial expertise required for the mounting of large-scale development projects. As a result, they channel the largest part of their development assistance into support of multi-lateral organisations or into bi-lateral projects co-financed by several donors or institutions, each of which contributes something (in cash or kind, i.e., technology, know-how, marketing or other services) to provide the inputs required to implement a project. The Arab agencies often rely on international financial institutions (IFIs) for project identification and feasibility analysis, as well as for overall project administration. Parallel financing — in which each participant finances a distinct part of the project and decides independently on the procurement of goods and services — is the normal approach to project funding.

Co-financed projects, for a variety of reasons, then, are becoming increasingly attractive to both Arab and non-Arab donor countries. Co-financing enables donors to combine their resources to tackle difficult development problems of great magnitude, thereby increasing the development impact of their contributions, while also spreading their resources over a number of countries and sectors.

The member countries of OPEC, the Organisation for Economic Co-operation and Development (OECD), and the multi-lateral institutions have co-financed some 349 projects in 85 developing countries — 188 in Africa, 102 in Asia, 46 in the Americas and the rest in Oceania and Europe. The amount allocated to these projects totals US$22.5 billion. OPEC countries and institutions contributed 34.6 per cent of the funds involved, IFIs 44 per cent, and the Development Assistance Committee (DAC) countries of the OECD 18.1 per cent. The largest portion of the committed funds (60 per cent) was directed to infrastructure, while industry and mining received 22 per cent, and agriculture 6 per cent.

Canada's Relations with Arab Aid Agencies

Like most other Western industrialised countries, Canada is

interested in co-operating closely with the Arab aid agencies with a view to co-financing development projects throughout the Third World. During the past several years, Canada has attempted to establish working relationships with these agencies through a variety of means, including contacts at the policy and operational level and support of proposals in multi-lateral fora.

CIDA's efforts have met with not inconsiderable success. Of 14 DAC members, Canada ranks third after West Germany and France in the number of projects (35) co-financed with Arab donors. The projects, spread throughout countries in Asia, Africa and the Americas, amount to more than US$7 billion which involves an input of approximately US$905 million in Canadian development assistance.

The geographic breakdown of the projects is as indicated in Table 21.1.

Table 21.1: Geographic Breakdown of the Projects

	Countries	Projects
Francophone Africa	14	15
Anglophone Africa	11	10
Asia	4	9
The Americas	1	1

The projects are mainly in energy (hydro-electricity) and transportation, sectors of special interest to Arab donors. In most cases, the projects involve parallel financing of components of very large projects developed by the World Bank and regional development banks.

The major objectives of a closer relationship with the Arab donors include the marshalling of the necessary financing for large projects beyond the capacity of any one donor and the seeking of Arab co-financing of those projects requested by the less-developed countries (LDCs) in high priority economic sectors where Canada has a recognised capability (e.g., transportation, telecommunications, hydro-electric generation and transmission), where Canadian firms are internationally competitive in terms of quality and price, and where Canadian and Arab geographic priorities in development coincide.

The Arab donors have clearly expressed an interest in exploring further the possibility of developing closer ties with Canada and with

CIDA. Efforts to promote such ties are now under way through discussion and meetings between officials of CIDA and the Arab Funds. During the past year, CIDA has arranged a number of important and far-reaching bi-lateral meetings with Arab donors. Visits were made to the Saudi Development Fund, the Islamic Development Bank (Jeddah), the Kuwait Fund, the Arab Fund (Kuwait), the Abu Dhahi Fund, the Arab Bank for Development in Africa (Khartoum) and the OPEC Fund (Vienna). The President and senior management of CIDA also met with the heads of the leading Arab aid agencies during the World Bank meeting in Toronto in September 1982 to discuss future co-operation between CIDA and the Arab donors. The meeting served to demonstrate Canadian interest in establishing and maintaining a strong relationship with the Arab donors. It was also an occasion to renew the range of experiences CIDA has shared with the Arab donors since 1974 and to focus on some mutually-promising areas of concern.

The meeting, the first between CIDA senior management and the heads of Arab financial institutions, ushered in a new phase in CIDA's relationship with the Arab world. Based on the relationship and co-operation of the last several years, it is expected that we will move on to identify opportunities for closer co-operation in particular countries and specific sectors. While the relationship continues to be of an informal nature, it will involve more frequent contacts at the operational level.

A clearly-identified responsibility centre has now been established within CIDA to promote and monitor the co-financing of projects and to report to the senior management of CIDA on a regular basis. A senior officer who has experience working on the staff of the Kuwait Fund, and who speaks Arabic, has been appointed to the position of Senior Adviser and Co-ordinator of Arab/OPEC Liaison.

Perspectives on Arab Aid Institutions

The Philosophy and Concept of Arab Aid

The basic tenet of the aid philosophy of the Arab world, which underlies its institutions, emanates from the teachings of Islam itself: 'To spend in the way of God and to share with other people.' Arab countries accordingly feel a sense of duty to come to the assistance of the less fortunate. This is reflected in the level of their commitment to development assistance. OPEC members are the most generous of donors, greatly outstripping the industrialized powers. In 1980, DAC members committed an average of 0.37 per cent of Gross National Product (GNP) to development assistance while OPEC committed an average of 1.48 per cent of GNP. The average for the Arab nations was even higher — 2.03 per cent. Such a high level of contributions assumes greater significance when it is remembered that Arab donors do not 'tie' their aid — i.e., require aid recipients to use a portion of the funds to buy Arab goods and services.

As a consequence of their humanitarian philosophy, Arab aid agencies give preference to the poorer among 98 recipient countries. In the early years Arab aid was directed toward the Arab Middle East. It has since spread throughout a large part of the world — from West Africa to Bangladesh, Indonesia and, more recently, Central America. In 1973, for example, fellow Arab nations received 97 per cent of the aid from oil exporting countries. In 1981, that percentage had fallen to around 50 per cent. Africa remains the growth area for Arab lending, its relative poverty acting as a magnet to the oil-exporting donors. In 1973, the Arab aid agencies established the Arab Bank for Economic Development in Africa (BADEA), which lends only to non-Arab countries, the first time an Arab aid institution has been designed to serve a non-Arab region.

Although Arab aid is based on a humanitarian philosophy, it is not without pragmatic considerations. For unlike industrialised countries, Arab aid is based not on renewable wealth, but rather on a depletable resource with a short life-span. Contributions to assistance programs come directly out of capital resources. Aid funds are therefore being directed toward the establishment of a new system of international relations in preparation for the post-petroleum period. They are linked to the internal development of countries in the Arab region and to income-generating investments in Third World and industrialised countries.

Major Arab Aid Institutions in the Field of Development Co-operation

- Abu Dhabi Fund for Arab Economic Development (ADFAED)*
- Arab Authority for Agricultural Investment and Development (AAAID)
- Arab Bank for Economic Development in Africa (BADEA)*
- Arab Fund for Economic and Social Development (AFESD)*

Arab Monetary Fund (AMF)
Iraqi Fund for External Development (IFED)*
Islamic Development Bank (IDB)*
Islamic Solidarity Fund (ISF)
Kuwait Fund for Arab Economic Development (KFAED)*
OPEC Fund for International Development (OFID)*
Saudi Fund for Development (SFD)*

*CIDA is currently discussing the co-financing of specific projects with these institutions.

The Arab Co-ordination Group

The emergence of the Arab development institutions as an important factor in the field of development co-operation led to the establishment of a group to co-ordinate the aid efforts and activities of member countries. The first formal co-ordination meeting was held in September 1975, and was attended by representatives of the Kuwait Fund, the Abu Dhabi Fund, the Arab Fund and the Saudi Fund for Development.

Member institutions of the Co-ordination Group (now numbering 10) fall into three categories:

a. *National institutions:* Established and wholely funded by their governments, they are the Abu Dhabi Fund for Arab Economic Development, the Iraqi Fund for External Development, the Kuwait Fund for Arab Economic Development, the Libyan Arab Foreign Bank and the Saudi Fund for Development. The representative of the government of Qatar is also included in this category.
b. *Multi-lateral Arab institutions:* The Arab Fund for Economic and Social Development and the Arab Bank for Economic Development in Africa. There are other Arab multi-lateral financial institutions which are not members of the Co-ordination Group because of their specialised activity, e.g., the Arab Monetary Fund (AMF), the Arab Agricultural Authority (AAAID), and the Inter-Arab Investment Guarantee Corporation.)
c. *Mutli-lateral institutions with mixed Arab and non-Arab participation:* The Islamic Development Bank and the OPEC Fund for International Development. Arab participation in the capital of these two institutions is about 85 per cent and 50 per cent respectively.

Meetings at the Director of Operations level are held twice a year with higher level meetings (Director-General/President level) held as the need arises. The Arab Fund, in Kuwait, has been entrusted with the responsibilities of the Co-ordination Secretariat to service these meetings and act as the channel for the exchange of information and preparation of documents.

The regular meetings of the Co-ordination Group are an important forum for the exchange of technical experience gained by member institutions. Meetings invariably include a review of issues of an operational nature and the discussions are supported by working papers and technical reports prepared in advance of the conference.

These meetings provide an opportunity to exchange information as each fund presents its new projects on a country-by-country basis. They also offer opportunities for vetting loan applications submitted to more than one institution for the same project, for pooling fragmentary and incomplete information available to individual institutions, and for agreeing on financial plans. (The percentage of co-financed projects has increased substantially and co-financing is now the general rule, accounting for some 25 to 60 per cent of the total commitments of Group members.)

The Co-ordination Group has standardised many operational procedures so that member countries are using similar, if not identical, procedures in the area of loan agreements, procurement guidelines and disbursements. This increased uniformity has enhanced the success of joint financing of projects and helped in speeding up loan processing, particularly by the recipient countries, as it has minimised the burden of coping with diverse rules, regulations and documentation.

The Group often delegates to one of its members many if not most of the tasks involved in loan administration of jointly-financed projects. The delegated powers include approval of contracts, checking disbursement applications and, at times, opening letters of credit and actual disbursements on behalf of co-operating sister institutions.

The recommendations of the Group are not binding. Paradoxically, this has led to speedier concensus and greater readiness to accept recommendations.

The Co-ordination Secretariat publishes a quarterly entitled *Summary of Loans and Technical Assistance Granted to Developing Countries by Group Members.*

Review of Arab Development Funds' Activities up to 1983

Since their inception, the seven Arab Development Funds and the OPEC Fund for International Development have disbursed a total of US$16.5 billion on 1,264 projects in 98 countries throughout the world. Overall, 51.3 per cent of Arab funding has gone to Arab states, 26.3 per cent to Asian countries, 20.1 per cent to African countries, 1.9 per cent to American countries, and 0.4 per cent to other countries. In terms of sectors, 56.1 per cent of the funding went to infrastructure-related projects (transportation, power, water), 32.1 per cent to agriculture and industry, and 11.8 per cent to other projects such as foreign trade financing.

Table 21.2: Contributions by Sector

Sector	Amount (US$M)	% of Total
Infrastructure		
Transport and Telecommunications	3,981.57	24.1
Power (Electricity, Oil and Gas)	4,445.97	27.0
Water and Sewerage	835.30	5.0
Sub-total	9,262.84	56.1
Productive		
Agriculture and Livestock	2,459.23	14.9
Industry	2,840.73	17.2
Sub-total	5,299.96	32.1
Others	1,951.79	11.8
Total	16,514.59	100.0

Table 21.3: Contributions by Region

Region	Countries	Number of operations	Amount (US$M)	% of Total
Arab Countries	18	516	8,464.01	51.3
African Countries	39	434	3,328.23	20.1
Asian Countries	21	256	4,337.04	26.3
American Countries	17	49	315.13	1.9
Other Countries	3	9	70.08	0.4
Total	98	1,264	16,514.59	100.0

Source: Arab National and Regional Development Institutions, Statement of Financing Operations, Co-ordination Secretariat, December 1982

Conclusion

The co-financing of development projects by members of the Arab donor community has greatly increased in recent years. Participants in this form of co-operation are able to share their specialised knowledge and benefit from the experience of others and, in so doing, better meet the needs of developing countries. Canada is eager to join with other nations in this form of development co-operation.

Although the collaborative efforts of CIDA and the Arab donors are still at an early stage of development, we have already shared a number of interesting and useful experiences. In the process, each party has acquired a greater knowledge of the aims, procedures and activities of the other which cannot help but strengthen bi-lateral relations. It is now possible to identify a wide range of major projects in several key sectors where we have been working alongside one another. Through collaboration in 35 projects throughout the world, we have found that we share a common approach and a common commitment to development — a concentration of resources on the poorest countries, within which key sectors such as energy and agriculture receive priority. There is, therefore, a natural interest in pooling our resources.

While many of the projects co-financed to date have been identified and developed under the aegis of the World Bank and other regional institutions, it is now CIDA's intention to work together with the Arab Funds in mounting projects from the very first stage of their development. If we are to have a true programme of co-operation with the Arab Funds, it will be extremely important in the future, in carrying out such projects, that we meet and begin negotiations early in the planning stage rather than play the role of what is sometimes called 'gap-fillers' in one another's projects and programmes. Only then will recipient countries receive the full impact of our development assistance.

Table 21.4: Bi-lateral Projects Co-financed by CIDA and Arab Donors (US$Million)*

a.

	Participants			
	Canada	Arab	Others	Total value
Francophone Africa	290.4	878.4	. .	2,712.1
Anglophone Africa	227.8	318.4	584.3	1,089.8
Asia	201.4	430.9	521.3	1,513.3
Americas	35.0	8.5	. .	800.0
Total				
Total in Canadian dollars	905.4	1,963.4	. .	7,338.2

b.

		Participants			
Country	Project	Canada	Arab	Others	Total value
Francophone Africa					
Benin	Cotonou Port	10.0	7.3	. .	59.7
Cameroon	Douala Port	29.0	10.0	. .	148.9
	Douala-Yaoundé Highway	16.0	40.9	. .	238.5
Congo	Railway CFCO	19.4	140.6	. .	343.2
Madagascar	Andekelake Hydroelectric	22.0	58.2	. .	142.2
Mali	Selingue Dam	11.2	60.1	. .	142.0
Mali/Mauritania Senegal	OMVS-Barrage (Senegal River Basin Development)	40.0	380.0	. .	829.0
Mauritania	Road Project	4.5	3.8	3.0	13.7
	Boghe Plain Irrigation	5.3	6.6	9.7	21.6
Niger	Unity Road	32.0	40.0	. .	130.0
Togo	Mono Hydro-electric	12.0	. .	. .	200.0
Togo/Ivory Coast/Ghana	CIMAO Regional Clinker	17.0	10.0	. .	. .
Tunisia	Sidi Saad Dam	55.0	75.0	30.0	150.0
Upper Volta	Kompienga-Poma Dam	16.5	12.0	. .	. .
Zaire	Highway IV	0.5	33.9	. .	143.3
Total Francophone Africa		290.4	878.4	42.7	2,712.1
Total in Canadian dollars		348.5	1,054.1	51.2	3,254.5

c.

Country	Project	Participants: Canada	Arab	Others	Total value
Anglophone Africa					
Botswana	Moruple Power Station	11.0	24.7	238.2	262.9
Egypt	Railways	50.0	64.2	92.3	206.5
Ghana	Kpong Hydro-electric	35.0	90.1	155.0	245.1
Kenya	Kaimbere	41.6	11.6	. .	. .
Malawi/Mozambique	Nacala Railway Link	30.0	50.0	. .	250.0
Tanzania	Mtera Hydro-electric	40.0	. .	. .	. .
Tanzania/Rwanda/ Burundi	Central Corridor Scheme	. .	38.0	. .	. .
Uganda	Reconstruction Credit	2.6	5.0	92.5	100.1
Zambia	Railways	13.0	20.5	. .	. .
Zimbabwe	National Railways	4.6	14.3	6.3	25.2
Total Anglophone Africa		227.8	318.4	584.3	1,089.8
Total in Canadian dollars		273.4	382.1	701.2	1,307.8

d.

Country	Project	Participants: Canada	Arab	Others	Total value
Asia					
Bangladesh	Chittagong Fertiliser	20.0	126.0	325.0	471.0
	Railway Locomotives	38.0	38.0	. .	76.0
Pakistan	Tarbela Dam	8.8	103.4	117.8	230.0
	Tarbela Generating Units	16.0	32.0	30.0	178.0
	Extension of Hydro Power Station	35.0	31.0	38.0	150.0
	Diesel Locomotives	21.0	10.5	10.5	21.0
Sri Lanka	Maduru Oya River Development	40.0	55.0	. .	146.4
Thailand	Rural Electrification Distribution	12.2	7.0	. .	125.0
	Accelerated Rural Electrification	10.4	28.0	. .	115.9
Total Asia		201.4	430.9	521.3	1,513.3
Total in Canadian dollars		241.7	517.1	625.6	1,816.0

e.

		Participants			
Country	Project	Canada	Arab	Others	Total value
Americas					
Honduras	Cajon Transmission Line	35.0	8.5	. .	800.0
Total Americas		35.0	8.5	. .	800.0
Total in Canadian dollars		42.0	10.2	. .	960.0

* or under discussion
. . not available

22 PERSPECTIVES OF BI-AND MULTI-LATERAL CO-FINANCING WITHIN THE ITALIAN POLICY OF CO-OPERATION FOR DEVELOPMENT

Francesco Aloisi

The Department of Co-operation for Development of the Italian Ministry of Foreign Affairs has been in existence for very few years, and it is only since 1980 that the Italian policy of co-operation, a result of political decisions of the government and of parliament, has experienced important qualitative and quantitative changes, with concrete development implications. It is the co-financing of development projects, and of the opportunity to carry out and increase these with the Arab Funds with which this chapter deals.

The turning point of the Italian policy of co-operation took place between 1979 and 1980. Up until then, in fact, economic relations between Italy and the developing countries consisted mainly of export credits, which Italy used to grant with public secured guarantee, in a rather larger volume than the other industrialised countries, both in relative and absolute terms. Up to 1979, the Italian Public Aid to Development, which corresponds with the definitions of aid set down by the OECD, was extremely low; it amounted to the 0.09 per cent of Italian national income, which placed Italy in last position among the seventeen industrialised countries who were members of the Development Aid Committee (DAC) of the OECD and quite removed, both from the average of these countries, which reached 0.36 per cent of their national income, and from the goal which they had set for themselves. This was to increase public aid for development to 0.7 per cent of their own national income.

Since 1979 the situation of Italian development aid has radically changed, and the noticeable progress that has already taken place is certain to continue. It was in that year in fact, when public law no. 38 was passed, that the decision was taken to reorganise the whole field of activity, so as to make possible the preparation and execution of an organic policy of development aid, by bringing together in a single executive organ the responsibilities which up to that time had been divided and managed autonomously by different government agencies. It was to such an end that the Department of Co-operation for Development was created within the Ministry of Foreign Affairs.

It was responsible for the implementation of the Italian policy of co-operation with the Third World, and guidelines were issued at government level by a committee of the ministers accountable for the foreign and economic sectors, known as CIPES.

With regard to allocations, a three-year programme has been set up, which provides for a commitment within the state budget of 1,200 thousand million lire in 1981, 1,500 in 1982 and 2,000 in 1983. This represents a very rapid growth, especially if one compares it with the 273 thousand million allocated in 1979 and the 679 allocated in 1980. Consequently Italian aid for development, measured on the basis of the allocations actually made, has risen from the above-mentioned percentage of 0.07 per cent of national income in 1979, to 0.17 per cent in 1980, 0.19 per cent in 1981, and 0.24 per cent in 1982. The decision-making organs designated by Italian law are now examining programming which foresees a further increase, that within few years will bring public Italian aid to 0.70 per cent of the national income. I apologise for having dwelt on these figures, but I thought that only they could provide the context for the radical change in the situation which has taken place over these years.

Equally important changes of allocations and contributions have shown up in the qualitative aspects and programming of the funds. Without dwelling on minute details, I should like to mention a few of the most important tendencies which have emerged in public Italian aid, while it was gradually increasing.

a. A much quicker growth of the bi-lateral component has taken place (technical co-operation, alimentary aid and aid credits) as compared with the multi-lateral one. The bi-lateral component in fact went from about 20 per cent in 1980 to the present 67 per cent. I mention this percentage figure because it has a specific significance in the area of co-financing. Where in the past technical assistance operations predominated, in the last two years there has been a change toward the financing of productive and social investments, by means of aid credits and donations. The conditions of these have been gradually improving; interest, in fact, have been lowered from 4 per cent to 2.25 per cent, and terms lengthened from 12 to 17 years, with grace periods from 2 to 4 years.
b. The constant feature of Italian co-operation during these years has been that of 'project aid'. The cases of 'programme aid' and 'commodity aid' have been quite rare. The choice carried with

it a greater assumption of responsibilities and a larger work-load for the Co-operation Department.

c. It should be noted that Italian aid has been concentrated in a few top-ranking sectors (agriculture, foodstuffs, energy, transportation and telecommunications), and on a few geographical areas (above all the Mediterranean basin, the Horn of Africa and Southern Africa) for the purpose of avoiding any risk of wasting the resources which, even though they are increasing rapidly, are obviously to be considered extremely limited in view of what can be done.

Within the framework of the rapid increase of allocations and of the qualitative development of the contents of the Italian co-operation, co-financing with international organisations could not fail to have an important role, for a whole series of reasons. From a political point of view, for example, co-financing has supplied the means to keep on giving concrete support to a group of international agencies at a time when allocations for multi-lateral aid were growing, but at a lower rate than the total volume of aid. From another point of view, co-financing has been a very useful formula for the Co-operation Department whose technical and administrative structures had not hitherto had a chance to grow in, at the same accelerated rate of allocations. It also provides technical and economic experience, and the well-known administrative reliability of many international organisations.

At this time, when many international organisations are coping with budget problems, the overtures made by Italy to co-finance the projects of these organisations have often been accepted in a most favourable manner.

In practice, co-financing has taken various aspects, according to whether it was realised by means of donations and with that of the aid credits, or according to the international agency which has become our partner.

In the area of the aid credits, the use of which was mostly tied up with goods and services of Italian origin, the work has taken on the character of 'parallel financing'. This co-operation has grown considerably, especially in conjunction with the World Bank. As a rule, during a continuous exchange of information with that institution, certain projects already set up by the Bank itself are singled out and only partly financed by it. During the triangular negotiations between Italy, the World Bank and the recipient country, two financial covenants are negotiated and signed by the World Bank and Italy, each for its own share of financing with the recipient country. These covenants are, of course, tightly bound together, both because they refer to the same project studied and set up as a unit from a technical and economic point of view, and also because through suitable clauses of 'cross-effectiveness' and 'cross defaults' they will become effective and terminate simultaneously. The only substantial difference consists in the fact that, while the supplies financed through the World Bank are awarded following an international tender, those financed through Italian credit aid are assigned on the basis of a tender reserved for Italian firms.

The first experience of working with the World Bank during 1981 turned out positively, and resulted in the conclusion with the Bank of a Standard Agreement, whereby Italy committed itself to co-finance projects up to the figure of 450 thousand million lire, spread over three years. Pertinent procedures were set down, and this agreement was signed in July 1982. On its basis negotiations relating to co-financings have made considerable headway. The Department has advised the World Bank that it is available in principle to co-finance 12 of it programmes, for a total commitment of $133.5 million in aid credits and donations of technical co-operation, while many other projects of the Bank and of the IDA are under study in view of decisions to be taken shortly. This Agreement represents an outline of conduct which is judged quite positively by the Italian side, and which could also be followed as regards relations with other international financial organisations, for example with the Arab Funds. In this respect it is interesting to note that such an Agreement represents an important precedent for the World Bank itself, as it is the first Agreement of its kind. During the months immediately following it, the Bank signed two more agreements with other donors, affirming the usefulness of the planning adopted by the Italian side.

In parallel with the co-financing with the World Bank, and with other international financial institutions, the Department has developed co-financing with numerous international agencies within the family of the United Nations. In this area we operated predominantly by supplying technical assistance through donations, and many co-financings have been carried out with respect to projects of FAO, WHO, UNICEF, UNIDO, the Fund of Science and on Technology, and several other specialised organisations of the United Nations and regional international agencies, such as, for example, the Organisation of American States.

During 1982, the sum of $42 million has been committed to such donations. Italian co-financing has often been tied to Italian supplies of goods and services, although there have been important exceptions. The use of the 'trust funds' with those agencies that are already practising this form of co-financing has been very profitable, for example, with UNCTAD or UNIDO. With others, including FAO, suitable co-financing agreements have been drawn up.

I hope I have demonstrated the feasibility of a beginning, and substantial development of co-financing between Italy and the Arab Funds. As regards the matter of the respective development policies, I am certain that there is a wide coincidence of respective priorities both geographic and territorial. As far as the Italian co-operation is concerned, consider the importance and priority which is attached by both sides to the alimentary sector, and to that of energy or, at the geographic level, to the Mediterranean countries. Even if on both sides no specific effort has yet been made to favour the development of jointly-financed projects, we find ourselves already doing it, and carry out several co-financings.

As examples I could mention:

a. the Aqaba thermo-electric power-plant in Jordan;
b. the hydro-electric plant at Kiambere in Kenya;
c. the Manantali Dam in Mali.

These are only a few of a list which is much greater and is bound to increase in the near future.

Although I am not in a position to mention specific examples, I am convinced that co-financings with the Italian credit institutions at medium and long-term operate in the sector of export credits. Law 227 of 24 May 1977 allows Italian credit institutions to finance exports of non-consumer goods at fixed rates of interest between 10 and 12.40 per cent, in the case of credits in dollars, and between 13.85 per cent and 15.10 per cent in the case of credits in lire. Extensions of payment are usually contained within commercial terms, from 5 to 8.5 years from exportation, from assemblage or from try-out.

These terms are on the whole not far removed from the ones practised by international agencies, although they are the source of rather modest amounts of financing. During 1981 the Italian government insured export credits for 6.504 billion lire.

In the Italian usage, in addition, and internationally too, it is not uncommon to resort to so called 'mixed credits', i.e., combinations of aid credits and export credits.

The objective to be pursued therefore, is not really to start co-financing between Italy and the Arab Funds, because these are already a concrete and important realisation. What is to be done instead is not to wait for occasions to present themselves by chance, but rather to create them on the basis of an agreed-upon policy. As regards this matter I take the liberty of posing a question, and offering a suggestion. The question, which I am addressing to the Arab Funds, is whether a co-financier such as Italy could find a collective interlocutor within their Co-ordinating Secretariat which, if I am not mistaken, is located in Kuwait. The suggestion is to tackle together the projects to be finalised, from the preparation stage. Italian co-operation is perfectly capable, besides participating in the financing of carrying out projects, of financing, through donations, also the studies and plans which are the indispensable preliminary steps of the projects themselves.

The need for collaboration among countries with different economic structures is to be accepted as permanent, beyond the constant evolution of economics, of interest rates, of prices of raw materials, inflation rates and other economic indicators.

23 THE ITALIAN EXPERIENCE

Nicola Capria

The international economy is still going through a stage of prolonged recession, which provokes and, in its turn determines, serious and wide-spread consequences with respect to those deriving from previous crises, both for industrially advanced countries and for developing ones.

For the industrialised countries, unco-ordinated replies and purely national approaches have caused increasing disorder which comes from almost exclusively competitive management of international relationships. Attempts to make amends at the expense of the weaker countries have prevented them from developing their own autonomous capacity for re-order, and have contributed to the continued and dangerous movement of tensions from one country to another finally causing a general slowing down of development. The explicit and dramatic consequence is represented by the more than 30 million unemployed in the OECD area, and by production capacity destruction.

The developing countries, affected by the drop in price of raw materials and deeply in debt due to previous efforts to finance domestic development plans, bear the burden of international interest taxes which are at record levels, finding that they have to pay more just when their exports are rendering them less.

To a great extent the fall in prices and the increase in interest rates are due to the rigid anti-inflation measures adopted by the industrialised countries. But development mechanisms set up over the last decade by developing countries require stable flows and new forms of financing. The lack of official financing has forced these countries to go to private capital markets whose credit has progressively become concentrated on a limited number of 'large debtors', directing nearly all existing liquidity to where the interest and economic and political involvement of the industrialised countries has been greater.

The double negative effect is in the collapse of the 'large debtor' countries; the lack of resources available for the majority of developing countries; and weak prospects for the availability of private capital to be sent to developing countries. At the end of last year an expert on the international economy from a large American bank maintained that, 'the attraction of granting credit to the Third World no longer exists because the banks can find more favourable opportunities at home'.

This prospect, which I do not hesitate to define as catastrophic for everyone, is confirmed by the fact that today those countries of the so-called Third World which in the past have diversified the use of profits with high investments in foreign industrialised countries, have benefited; whereas the countries which have set up large domestic investment programmes and which today find it necessary to discontinue them or slow down their completion are penalised.

This situation, full of negative consequences, derives from the lack of policy re-alignment in the industrialised countries, and in channels and institutions of international collaboration, to the profound variations in the international division of labour, from the end of the 1960s onwards. The new point of international economic relations is the inclusivity of the economy through the growth of interdependence between the OECD and the Third World, between the OECD and COMECON, and between COMECON and the Third World. This network of interdependence has replaced the previous situation of reciprocal dependence or independence.

In the past, economic trends in the South have had a negligible impact on the international economic picture. Today this is no longer so: the developing countries exercise a considerable influence over industrialised ones and, as this impact is not uniform, it determines new relative disorder, not only economic, even among the advanced countries.

We must be deeply aware of the risks of moving away from a world economic reality which is bound by multiple relationships of interdependence and contrary behaviour, which gives privileges to exclusively national viewpoints and short-term advantage. It is a question of suitable behaviour, rather like the economic climate of the 1930s, when each country defended its own internal interests, both large and small, at the expense of economic development and international commerce.

For this reason, we are not among those who today rejoice in the falling price of raw materials, short-sightedly relying on this for the solution of structural adaptation problems which in fact require much vaster policies of agreement and collaboration.

For this is an attitude which is, in my opinion, not very far-sighted. The fall in income of the countries producing raw materials will increase pressures on the international banking system, it will lead to a fall in exports from industrialised countries and the paralysis of investments and research into alternative raw materials. We must remember that, over the last decade, the developing countries have made a decisive contribution to the growth of international commerce, and that their imports have created approximately one million jobs in Europe.

To this should be added that when the industrialised countries come out of recession, the demand for raw materials will grow, and opportunities to expand supplies will decrease due to the present decline in investment. Prices could undergo a new and abrupt boom.

The experience of the 1970s has shown how order and opportunities for development in economies, both advanced and developing, are threatened with the most serious consequences and unforeseeable repercussions. This is due to the many unforeseen variations in exchange which lead to heavy adjustment costs, not only in terms of financial resources, as the case of Nigeria has recently demonstrated.

Development projects are built up by means of agreements which can offer the time and space necessary for structural changes which are indispensable to both parties, thereby gaining greater fairness of exchange with the conditions of certainty and stability necessary for programming agreements and long-term investments. And it is in this framework that we have made a move as regards a contract for supplying methane gas to Italy from Algeria.

The reality of interdependence is based on collaboration. Market economies can have no short and medium-term development prospects if new markets are not opened. And the new markets are represented by the developing countries and by their efforts to quickly fill the gaps which are still preventing them from satisfying their needs. So developing countries must create their own production capacity and expand their own domestic market. And this is not so much to facilitate industrialised countries' exports, but to create domestic outlets for their products and so supply the pre-conditions of a development policy.

Today, despite definite improvements, the structure of exports from developing countries as a whole is still broadly dependent on basic products, while the share of hand-made goods is increasing very slowly. The commercial balance of hand-made goods from industrialised countries and developing countries is more and more positive. The concrete behaviour of both parties is not consistent with the clear identification of the reciprocal interests of industrialised and developing countries in a collaboration becoming more and more intense.

In the industrialised countries we can see a reborn tendency towards protectionism: the illusion, both growing and anti-historical, that each nation can avoid those changes which inter-dependence brings with it by closing itself into defence of its own position of strength and privilege.

For the first time in twenty years, we have had zero growth in international commerce for two consecutive years. For the industrialised countries, afflicted by inflation, recession and unemployment, protectionism seems to be the easiest and most immediate solution.

The risk, by no means abstract, is that the 1980s will turn out to be a decade of reflux and reversal in respect of the concept of a world economic system which has allowed unprecedented expansion of international commerce. Countries in which the foreign element is greater have acted decisively in order to re-create conditions for a new period of production and exchange innovation.

From the other point of view, an increasing number of developing countries, in particular the so-called countries involved in 'new industrialisation', are tending more and more towards extremely selective development based on specific advantages: low salaries, high volume of work per capita, high immigration and great fiscal advantage. This is a type of growth which pushes the exploitation process to the limit, having no social and democratic development prospects and great risks of internal tensions.

The growth in the penetration of exports from developing countries must be constant. But at the same time these countries must diversify their exports and increase their efforts to develop the domestic market.

From the economic point of view, collaboration is inevitable. Mere exchange of merchandise does not alone satisfy the development needs which characterise present reality. The variety of resources; the differences in availability of labour; differing degrees of research and development, know-how and technology, all lead to the re-creation of a higher and higher level of usage and exploitation of existing resources.

Giving priority to collaboration means identifying all possible areas of techno-financial assistance and the necessary instruments for the arrangement of foreign commercial policies and techno-economic collaboration policies.

We are dealing with themes which are by no means abstract, and which require discussion in the specific and concrete situation of international negotiation.

Today, Arab Development Funds represent perhaps the most advanced example of the value of collaboration. They are able to mobilise economic and financial relationships into bi-lateral and tri-lateral agreements, by means of long-term investment projects. And in this sphere collaboration in the transfer of technology can be developed; we believe that this is indispensable for co-ordinated development between industrialised and developing countries.

To the objection that this would expose advanced countries to the effects of marked re-dimensioning of complete sectors, we reply with three different arguments. The first, which is of a general character, concerns the conviction that balanced and stable development of the international economy can only come about through developing countries' complete acquisition of production capacity in the sector of industrial possessions: this is for the economic reasons which I have already mentioned.

The second concerns the negative value which we give to protectionism, explicit and concealed, as a means of opposing the new international division of labour. A country like Italy, with an extremely high level of exchanges, highly dependent on foreign raw materials and sources of energy, has to remain very open-minded in order to avoid reprisals and the closing of markets which would have extremely serious consequences.

The third argument concerns the true effects of competition on the developing countries. The main studies carried out into the effect of competition on these countries' products on the industrialised countries' markets, tend to demonstrate how the advantages of the latter are greater than the losses. But, while these advantages tend to be spread throughout the production apparatus, the difficulties are concentrated in certain areas and sub-sectors, causing strong reactions.

Research carried out by ICEI in 1980 showed that, given our production structure, an intensification of exchange would be very advantageous to Italy, while risks of marked competition would be contained, due to the infra-sectorial or 'horizontal' nature of our exchange with the developing countries.

I would like to conclude by confirming that our choice is for an open economy working towards the re-balance of collaboration and development. Within the limits of this, both multi-lateral and bi-lateral actions are equally important: multi-lateral actions to be taken in international institutions, renewing their role and order, and bi-lateral ones in which our country has recently taken on new and more suitable responsibility. In this framework, we give priority to greater Euro-Arabic understanding, beside which individual problems, however difficult they may seem, must give first reference to a common interest in collaboration and development.

Agreements which have so far been concluded and experiences we have already had, show the necessity for research into negotiation of a solution to the problems outlined, with a desire to identify areas of reciprocal interest.

24 INTERNATIONAL ECONOMIC CO-OPERATION AND ARAB DEVELOPMENT FUNDS

Piero Bassetti

The disorder of the international economic system, which became dramatically more marked with the end of the era of low cost energy in 1973, has brought the question of problems in North-South relationships to the fore, always keeping in mind the importance of South-South co-operation.

The central problem can be identified in the research into possible correlations between institutional opportunities, both economic/financial and, more correctly, political/diplomatic, and the structure of the world economy or economy-world, as some economists like to call it. More precisely, it would seem necessary to reflect on the character of the growing relationships between political organisations at both the national and super-national levels. Within this framework, the role of the Arab Funds is linked to Europe as a whole and not to individual nations, due to the size of the problems it provokes.

It is, however, necessary to keep sight of the phenomena which are the subject of the analysis: compared with the debt built up by the developing countries, recently estimated at approximately $626 thousand million, aid supplied by the OPEC countries in 1981 was approximately $7.8 thousand million, in other words, 1.46 per cent of the Gross National Product (GNP).

Even though we are dealing with a comparison between stock and flow, it still demonstrates the amount of the OPEC contribution in respect to the dramatic size of the problem to be solved. In fact, public opinion often maintains that the oil dimension has moved mythical financial masses. In reality, these are only a part, admittedly considerable, which, when added to others, can improve the financial framework of the developing countries. The needs of these countries are so pressing that international assistance, such as the Monetary Fund and the World Bank, become inadequate. The gravity of the problem is such that all those who are able to make contributions must firstly feel themselves equally responsible.

The participation of commercial banks, through the World Bank, is of considerable importance for the solution of this problem. Their recent growing debts, not in themselves a negative factor, certainly do not favour programmed and rational management of all the problems relating to international economic co-operation and to overcoming the economic/financial imbalance between the North and South. From this point of view the crux of the matter is still calling in various power centres to collaborate on a financial rationality plan.

From another angle, it is also interesting and opportune to consider, beyond the purely quantitative aspects, the problem of the need for a qualitative approach to the imbalance question. For example, it should be pointed out how, in the new industrialised countries, a considerable, concentrated, financial and entrepreneurial approach has triggered off an extremely interesting development process. Concrete results have been achieved where financial, entrepreneurial and commercial intervention has been started up convergently.

A further element on which to reflect is the role of the multinationals: over the last few years, import/export movement prompted by these has been four times the American exports prompted by other forces. This is a decisive factor in, for example, the development of the new industrialised countries and therefore calls for great involvement of entrepreneurial resources in co-operation problems.

As regards Italy, since it has used its economic potential in sectors close to the early stages of the development process, it is to be hoped that the developing countries will regard it with greater interest for a deeper and more fruitful collaboration. From certain points of view, this could be the same as the experience gained in the south of Italy where, after many years on the wrong road, a fruitful development process was finally adopted, triggered by local factors and by the 'transplanting' of carefully-considered industrial material. Working from this, Italy's role in promoting development could be extremely interesting, keeping in mind that, Japan, not by chance, has been the major propagator of development.

Sectors which are open to the problems of co-operation and development have, for some time, been aware of the need for concrete work towards closer integration between the European financial and political institutions and those of the Arab world. For some years, many European states have engaged in a policy of co-operation towards the Third World, using both their own funds and having recourse to super-national institutions.

Some of these, with greater knowledge of the economical/political divisions of the Middle East and Africa, have set up a relationship of fruitful collaboration with the Arab Funds, and the European Community has also established an excellent relationship with them.

Italy was slow in confronting this problem, both in terms of political strategy and suitable financial commitment. However for some years it has been making up for lost time and this new attitude has been highly appreciated both in the countries concerned and in the organisations which are closely involved in the financial aspects of the problem. This new strategy becomes even more positive if we consider that it is concurrent with a tendency for the countries which had until recently taken on a leading role to reduce their commitment to co-operation.

The system of co-financing between Arab institutions, such as the Funds, and European institutions, principally means a common strategic choice in view of common interests. The specific contributions of each country are evaluated, to resolve the dramatic problems of underdevelopment. It should not be forgotten that without a consistent recovery of the European economy, the consolidation conditions of the present stage of Arab aid will be reduced and repercussions from the crisis will be accentuated in developing countries.

In short, the first assistance to developing countries could come from a European recovery which is closely integrated with the Arab world; in this case the Arab Funds would certainly have an extremely significant role.

NOTES ON CONTRIBUTORS

Michele Achilli is a qualified architect and is currently President of the Institute for International Economic Cooperation, Milan.

Mohamed Khaldi is head of the Department in Cooperation and Development at the Institute for International Economic Cooperation, Milan and is responsible for the service of economic and commercial studies in the Chamber of Commerce for African countries associated with the CEE.

Awni S. Al-Ani is Assistant Director-General (Technical and Economic Services) of the OPEC Fund for International Development in Vienna.

Dr Mahmoud El-Helw is Deputy Director of Operations of the Arab Fund for Economic and Social Development in Kuwait.

Bader Al-Humaidi is Deputy Director-General (Operations and Finance) of the Kuwait Fund for Arab Economic Development in Kuwait.

Dr Saleh H. Humaidan is Director-General (Technical Department) of the Saudi Fund for Development in Riyadh.

Suleiman Al-Salem is Senior Operations Officer of the Islamic Development Bank in Jeddah.

Hamid Chabar is a researcher in Arab-African co-operation at the Centre d'Etude et de Recherche sur le Monde Arabe Contemporain (CERMAC) in Louvain-la-Neuve, Belgium.

Professor Abel Kader Sid Ahmed is Associate Professor at the Institute for Social and Economic Development Studies of the Université Paris-Dauphine.

Georges Hoyos is Secretary General of the Société Internationale de Publications et d'Etudes Multimedia in Brussels.

Dr Bichara Khader is Director of CERMAC.

Yousef Abdelmula is Director of Planning of the Libyan Arab Foreign Investment Company.

Abdul Razek Hassan is Deputy Director of Economic Affairs of the League of Arab States in Tunis.

Abdallah Adam is Counsellor to the General Secretary of the League of Arab States and Executive Secretary of the Arab Fund.

Hussein Elsayed Osman is Director of Operations of the Arab Bank for Economic Development in Africa in Khartoum.

Bernard Petit is Head of Specialised Service Financing at the EEC Commission in Brussels.

Mohammad Tayyarah is Senior Programme Funding Officer at UNICEF in New York.

J. M. Bartsch is Head of the non-DAC unit at the Organisation for Economic Co-operation and Development in Paris.

Ruth Stock is Adminstrator of the non-DAC unit at the OECD in Paris.

Rainer B. Steckhan is Director of the European Office of the World Bank in Paris.

Christopher Lethbridge is Head of the Mediterranean Department of the European Investment Bank, Luxembourg.

A. F. Odeh is Senior Advisor and Co-ordinator of Arab/OPEC affairs at the Canadian Interantional Development Agency (CIDA) in Quebec.

Francesco Aloisi is Head of the Office for Financial Co-operation of the Department for Co-operation for Development at The Ministry for Foreign Affairs in the Italian Government.

Nicola Capria is the Italian Minister for Foreign Commerce.

Piero Bassetti is President of the Chamber of Commerce, Industry, Handicraft and Agriculture in Milan as is President of the Italian Union of the Chambers of Commerce (Unioncamere).

INDEX